ERRATA

A small number of colour illustrations have appeared in black and white in this book. We apologise for this error. Please refer to the correct illustrations below in the following exercises:

Unit 12 Exercise 3 Page 52 (Picture A on Page 106)

Unit 20 Exercise 1 Page 83

In addition, please note the following errors:

Page 19: the word 'dress' should be supplied in the first exercise.

Page 68: the Turkish text should be 'Seni seviyorum'.

Language in use

BEGINNER

Teacher's Book

ADRIAN DOFF & CHRISTOPHER JONES

CAMBRIDGE
UNIVERSITY PRESS

PUBLISHED BY THE PRESS SYNDICATE OF THE UNIVERSITY OF CAMBRIDGE
The Pitt Building, Trumpington Street, Cambridge CB2 1RP, United Kingdom

CAMBRIDGE UNIVERSITY PRESS
The Edinburgh Building, Cambridge CB2 2RU, United Kingdom
40 West 20th Street, New York, NY 10011–4211, USA
10 Stamford Road, Oakleigh, Melbourne 3166, Australia

© Cambridge University Press 1999

First published 1999

Printed in the United Kingdom at the University Press, Cambridge

ISBN 0 521 62704 4   Teacher's Book
ISBN 0 521 62707 9   Classroom Book
ISBN 0 521 62706 0   Self-study Workbook
ISBN 0 521 62705 2   Self-study Workbook with Answer Key
ISBN 0 521 62703 6   Class Cassette Set
ISBN 0 521 62702 8   Self-study Cassette

Contents

Introduction

How the course is organised

Who the course is for

Language in Use Beginner is the first of the four levels in the *Language in Use* series. It assumes no previous knowledge of English and is mainly intended for use by true beginners. However, it can also be used successfully with false beginners (see page 3c).

The components of the course

The course contains 24 units, each designed to last for about three classroom hours, plus regular Study Pages spreads. The students' materials are divided into two major components: a Classroom Book and a Self-study Workbook. Both are accompanied by cassettes.

The syllabus

The course has a dual syllabus: a grammatical syllabus, which deals with the basic structures of English, and a topic syllabus, which deals with vocabulary. These two strands are reflected in Grammar units and Vocabulary units, which alternate through the course. For example:

Unit 7	Things people do	*Grammar unit*
Unit 8	Food and drink	*Vocabulary unit*
Unit 9	Do you ...?	*Grammar unit*
Unit 10	Things people buy	*Vocabulary unit*

This alternation of Grammar and Vocabulary units allows systematic coverage of the two major content areas of English. It also allows a natural recycling of language through the course: structures are recycled in Vocabulary units and vocabulary is recycled in Grammar units.

The Classroom Book

The Classroom Book contains the main presentation and practice material of the course, as well as activities in speaking, writing, reading and listening.

Grammar

The Grammar units cover grammatical areas that are essential for beginners; these include basic verb forms and tenses, mass and unit, comparison and some modal verbs.

Our aim is to help students use grammar actively in communication, so the main activities in the unit provide opportunities for role-play, problem-solving and exchange of information.

Each Grammar unit ends with a section called *Focus on Form*, which provides a summary of the main structures of the unit, together with more controlled practice. It also contains a pronunciation exercise focusing on rhythm and stress.

A typical Grammar unit is shown on page 3d.

Vocabulary

The Vocabulary units deal with key topic areas (e.g. families, clothes, shops and shopping, leisure activities, jobs and work, food and drink, describing people and places). As in the Grammar units, the activities in Vocabulary units provide opportunities for communicative uses of language.

Each Vocabulary unit ends with an integrated reading and listening activity, designed to develop receptive skills.

A typical Vocabulary unit is shown on page 3e.

Study Pages

After every two units, there is a double spread of Study Pages, which contains:

- a *Focus* exercise, presenting a small, self-contained area of language (e.g. possessive pronouns, telling the time), which is then recycled in later units
- a *Sounds* exercise, dealing with pronunciation
- a *Phrasebook* exercise, presenting functional language used in everyday conversation (e.g. asking for things, apologising)
- *Consolidation* exercises, which bring together material from previous units
- *Review* exercises.

A typical Study Pages spread is shown on page 3f.

Other features

After Unit 24, there is a *Final Review* section.

There is also an illustrated *Reference Section*, which includes a full summary of each unit, and *Tapescripts* of the Classroom Book recordings.

The Self-study Workbook

The Self-study Workbook provides back-up for work done in class and opportunities for further self-study. Like the Classroom Book, it has units and Study Pages.

Each unit contains:

- a range of homework exercises
- a listening activity
- a *Words* section, focusing on useful new vocabulary.

Each Study Pages spread contains:

- an informal progress test
- a *Phrasebook* exercise
- a *Writing* exercise, which guides students towards writing sentences and simple paragraphs.

There is also a *Final Review*, in the form of a written test.

Skills development

Speaking skills

Because *Language in Use* is concerned with active use of grammar and vocabulary, oral fluency is developed through many of the exercises in the Classroom Book.

Writing skills

Writing is developed through both the Classroom Book and the Self-study Workbook.

In the Classroom Book, writing is often an integrated part of classroom activities, and takes the form of sentence-writing and note-making.

In addition, the *Writing* exercises in the Self-study Workbook guide students towards writing simple paragraphs; these exercises form part of an independent *Writing skills* syllabus which runs through the course.

Listening and reading skills

In the Classroom Book, listening and reading are used in each unit as a basis for presentation or as a stimulus for a speaking or writing activity.

Each Vocabulary unit also contains an extended activity which integrates reading and listening. This is designed to develop receptive skills.

In the Self-study Workbook, each unit contains a short listening task designed to develop particular listening strategies.

Pronunciation

There are two separate strands of pronunciation exercises running through the course:

– *How to say it* exercises (in Grammar units). These focus on rhythm, stress and weak forms, and are linked to the structures taught in the unit.

– *Sounds* exercises (in Study Pages*)*. These focus on particular vowel and consonant sounds in English.

Functions

The *Phrasebook* exercises in the Study Pages deal with a range of everyday interactional functions, such as greetings, apologising, asking for things, making offers and talking on the phone.

Interactional functions are also practised in many of the activities in the Grammar and Vocabulary units.

Other more general functions (such as describing, giving personal information and narrating) are widely practised throughout the course.

Underlying principles

Flexibility

Language in Use takes account of the fact that, even at Beginner level, no two language classes are alike: students vary in ability, age and interests, and may have different cultural and learning backgrounds; classes vary in size, physical layout and formality; teachers have different teaching styles; and learners may have widely differing ideas about what and how they need to learn. The course caters for some of these variations by:

– providing open-ended activities, so that classes can find their own level, and so that both weaker and stronger students have something to contribute

– encouraging students to contribute their own ideas, and draw on their own knowledge and experience

– providing activities that can be adapted to a variety of different teaching styles and types of class.

Clarity

In any language course, it is important that students understand clearly what they are doing and why they are doing it, and have a clear idea of what they have learnt. In writing *Language in Use*, clarity has been a major consideration, both in the material designed for the student and in the teaching notes.

Recycling

At Beginner level, it is very important for learners to encounter the same language over and over again, and recycling of language is a major feature of *Language in Use Beginner*. This is done in several ways:

● Within each unit, language introduced in one exercise is picked up and given further practice in later exercises.

● The main structures in Grammar units are summarised and recycled in the *Focus on Form* exercises.

● Language which is taught in one unit is reintroduced and integrated into activities in later units.

● The key structures and vocabulary from each unit are consolidated in the Workbook exercises.

● The *Consolidation* and *Review* exercises in the Study Pages (every two units) recycle language from earlier units.

● The *Final Review* sections in both Classroom Book and Workbook review language from the whole course.

In the teaching notes, there is a 'language box' at the beginning of each exercise, which indicates what new language is introduced and what language is recycled.

Learning and acquisition

We believe that both 'learning' and 'acquisition' are important elements in learning a language. In other words, it is useful to spend time consciously focusing on particular language items, and it is also important to provide opportunities for natural language acquisition through fluency activities.

Both these elements are therefore incorporated in *Language in Use*. Some activities involve careful use of language and focus mainly on accuracy; in others, students develop fluency through freer, more creative use of language. Similarly, some reading and listening tasks focus on specific language items, while others are concerned with fluency and skills development.

In addition, the dual syllabus gives opportunity for acquisition of both grammar and vocabulary. In Grammar units, the focus is on learning grammatical structures, and this allows vocabulary to be acquired naturally. In Vocabulary units, the focus is on learning vocabulary, and this allows the natural acquisition of grammatical structures.

Using the course

The teaching notes

The teaching notes are designed to help you to make the most appropriate use of the Classroom activities with your students. They are in two columns.

The main notes for each activity (in the left-hand column) give a simple and straightforward route through the material, and include explanations for students and ideas for blackboard presentations.

In the right-hand column are a variety of options and alternatives which include:

- suggestions for homework both before and after the lesson
- optional phases within the lesson such as extra practice, sentence-writing, comprehension checks, vocabulary work and role-play
- alternative procedures suitable for
  – classes which are better / weaker than average
  – larger / smaller classes
  – monolingual / mixed-nationality classes
  – more formal / less formal teaching situations
- notes giving explanations and examples of further language points arising from the main presentation.

The teaching notes for each unit also contain cross-references to exercises in the Self-study Workbook.

False beginners

Although it is mainly intended for true beginners, *Language in Use* can also be used successfully with 'false beginners' (students who have already learned a little English but now want to start again from the beginning).

If you have a class of false beginners, you will probably be able to move through the first few units fairly quickly, using the exercises to check what students know, what they don't know and where they need more practice.

Even near the beginning of the course, many of the exercises are open-ended, and they can be adapted for false beginners simply by adding more vocabulary or allowing more freedom in the practice stage. Suggestions for ways of doing this are given in the teaching notes.

Using the Focus on Form exercises

The Focus on Form exercises at the end of each Grammar unit provide a summary of the main structures of the unit, plus extra, more controlled practice. They can be used in various ways

- *Basic structure practice*

Main exercise → Focus on Form exercise

  After finishing an exercise, use Focus on Form to focus on the main grammar point and give quick extra practice.

- *Summarising the main points*

Whole unit → Focus on Form exercises

  After finishing a unit, use the Focus on Form page to summarise the main grammar points, and to give extra practice if necessary.

- *Revision*

Series of units → Focus on Form exercises

  Come back to Focus on Form exercises as a way of revising grammar from previous units.

- *Homework*
  Some of the Focus on Form exercises can be set as homework, in addition to or instead of Workbook exercises.

Using the Self-study Workbook

There are various ways of using the exercises in the Self-study Workbook. You will probably want to adopt a mixture of these approaches.

Homework
All the Workbook exercises can be used for homework. In the teaching notes for each classroom activity, there are cross-references to suitable exercises.

Independent self-study
Allow students to work independently, choosing exercises that suit their individual needs. Students can use the Answer Key to check their answers, or give in their books periodically to be marked.

Classwork
Some Workbook exercises are also suitable for use in class. Two possibilities are the Listening and Writing exercises, which are often closely linked to classroom activities.

Short cuts through the course

Language in Use is designed to provide plenty of material, and it is possible to cover the course without doing every single exercise. If you are short of time, or if you wish to move through the units quickly with a good class, there are various short cuts you can take through the book:

- With a good class, leave the Focus on Form exercises for self-study.
- In the combined reading and listening activities, give the reading for homework, and do the listening in class.
- Limit the time you spend in class on material from the Self-study Workbook. If students have the version with Answer Key, they can mark their own work.

Grammar units

Grammar units contain:

– three activities that introduce key structures
– a Focus on Form page. This provides a summary of the main grammar points of the unit,
  together with more controlled practice, and a pronunciation exercise.

Main presentation of the Present continuous tense. Students guess what the people in each room are doing. Then they listen and find out.

Presents question forms. Students hear a short conversation and write down the questions. Then they practise the conversation themselves.

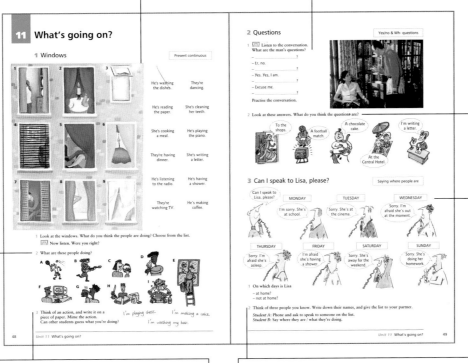

Part 2 – students make up their own questions.

Part 2 – a chance to practise with a range of verbs.

Presents a range of expressions saying where people are, via a series of telephone calls. Also recycles days of the week.

Part 3 – students write a sentence, then mime the action. Other students guess what they're doing.

Part 2 – role-play. Students 'phone' each other, trying to reach people who are not available.

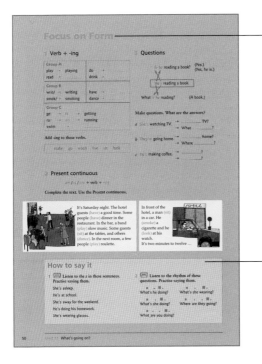

Focus on Form exercises. These summarise the main grammar points of the unit and provide extra controlled practice.

Pronunciation exercise. Focuses on the sound of 's (= is) and on the rhythm of Present continuous questions.

Vocabulary units

Vocabulary units contain:

– three activities introducing a range of vocabulary linked by topic
– an integrated reading and listening activity, for skills development.

Introduces basic clothes vocabulary. Students decide which are women's clothes, which are men's and which can be either.

Part 2 – one student describes what another student is wearing. The others have to say who is being described.

Part 3 – students look at the photos and guess what the people are wearing. At the end, the teacher shows them the 'uncut' photos.

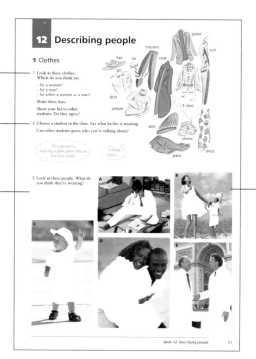

Parts 2 and 3 recycle colours (Unit 4) and the Present continuous tense (Unit 11).

Introduces jobs, plus the expressions *work in* and *work for*. In Part 1, students match job names with simple job descriptions.

Integrated reading and listening activity.

Part 1 – reading. Students read about '60s rock singer Reg Presley, and put the paragraphs in the right order.

Part 2 – students decide who wears what to work, then listen and check.

In Part 3, students talk about their own families.

Students use the adjectives in the box to describe the people in the picture.

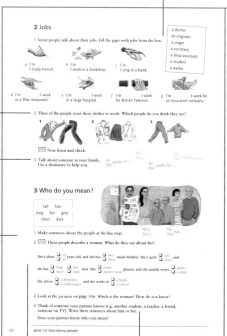

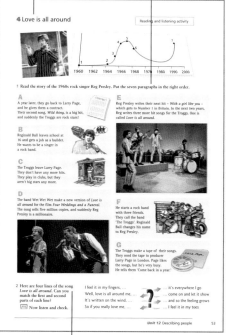

Parts 2 and 3 – students hear a description of a woman, then choose from three pictures in the back of the book.

Part 4 – students describe a familiar person. Other students guess who it is.

Part 2 – listening. Students unscramble some lines from Presley's hit song *Love is all around*. Then they listen and check their answer.

Study pages

Study pages contain:

– a *Focus* exercise, presenting a self-contained area of language
– a *Sounds* exercise, dealing with pronunciation
– a *Phrasebook* exercise, presenting functional language
– *Consolidation* exercises, bringing together language from previous units
– *Review* exercises.

Focus exercise introduces imperative forms. Students tell each other to do things.

Sounds exercise focuses on the sounds /ɒ/ and /ʌ/.

Consolidation exercises:
– *have* used as an action verb
– location expressions using *at*

Parts 2 and 3 introduce negative imperative forms.

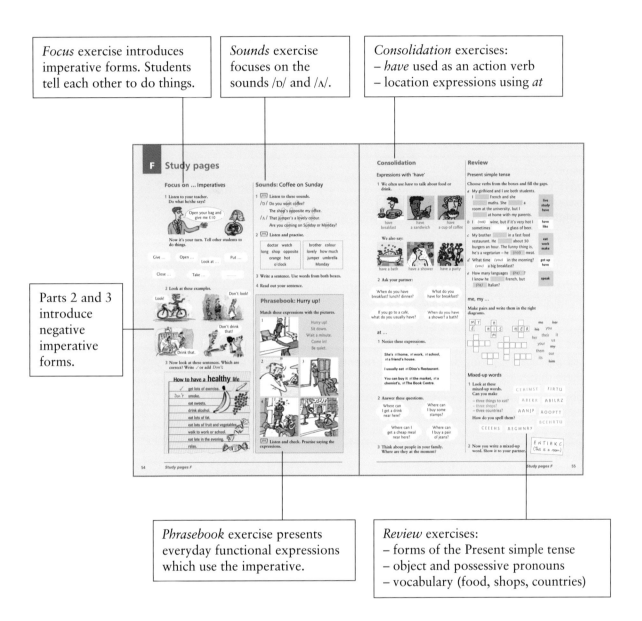

Phrasebook exercise presents everyday functional expressions which use the imperative.

Review exercises:
– forms of the Present simple tense
– object and possessive pronouns
– vocabulary (food, shops, countries)

Guide to units

	Classroom Book	Self-study Workbook
1 **People and places**	Greetings; introductions; saying where you're from **Grammar:** pronouns; Present tense of *to be*; short forms; *This is ...*	Grammar exercises Listening: *Photos*
2 **In the family**	Talking about your family; saying how old people are **Vocabulary:** people; family relationships; singular and plural nouns; numbers 1–20	Vocabulary exercises Listening: *Parents and children*
Study pages A	Focus on ... The alphabet Sounds: /ɪ/, /e/ and /æ/ Phrasebook: Greetings Consolidation: Pronouns; *have/has*; *my, your, his, her* Review	Check your progress Phrasebook Writing: *My friend Maria*
3 **To be or not to be?**	Correcting people; asking questions **Grammar:** negative of verb *to be*; *yes/no* questions; questions with *Who, What* and *Where*	Grammar exercises Listening: *Spell the words*
4 **Things around you**	Describing objects; giving and receiving presents; saying where things are **Vocabulary:** colours; parts of a room; everyday objects; place prepositions	Vocabulary exercises Listening: *Birthday presents*
Study pages B	Focus on ... Numbers 21–100 Sounds: /s/ and /θ/, /z/ and /ð/ Phrasebook: Excuse me Consolidation: *a* and *an*; *this, that, these, those* Review	Check your progress Phrasebook Writing: *Pictures of people*
5 **There's ...**	Describing and asking about places; finding differences **Grammar:** *There is/are*; *some* and *any*; questions with *How many...?*	Grammar exercises Listening: *Language school*
6 **Where you live**	Talking about flats and houses **Vocabulary:** rooms; furniture; things in the home; addresses and telephone numbers	Vocabulary exercises Listening: *Who are you?*
Study pages C	Focus on ... Possessives Sounds: /ɪ/ and /iː/ Phrasebook: Can I have ...? Consolidation: Singular/plural; *a* and *the*; ordinals Review	Check your progress Phrasebook Writing: *Describing places*

	Classroom Book	Self-study Workbook
7 **Things people do**	Saying what people do and don't do **Grammar:** Present simple tense; 3rd person singular; positive and negative forms	Grammar exercises Listening: *I like …*
8 **Food and drink**	Saying what you eat and drink; describing dishes; asking for things in restaurants **Vocabulary:** food and drink; things on the table at mealtimes	Vocabulary exercises Listening: *In a restaurant*
Study pages D	**Focus on …** Telling the time **Sounds:** /e/, /eɪ/ and /aɪ/ **Phrasebook:** On the phone **Consolidation:** Object pronouns; frequency adverbs **Review**	Check your progress Phrasebook Writing: *Breakfast*
9 **Do you …?**	Asking people about what they do; talking about daily routine **Grammar:** Present simple; *yes/no* questions; *Wh-* questions	Grammar exercises Listening: *When are they together?*
10 **Things people buy**	Shopping at a market; talking about shops; saying where shops are **Vocabulary:** buying and selling; shops; things you can buy in shops; place prepositions	Vocabulary exercises Listening: *Shopping*
Study pages E	**Focus on …** Days of the week **Sounds:** /h/ **Phrasebook:** What does it mean? **Consolidation:** Weights and measures; *I like* and *I'd like* **Review**	Check your progress Phrasebook Writing: *My top three places*
11 **What's going on?**	Saying what people are doing and where they are; asking what people are doing **Grammar:** Present continuous tense; *yes/no* and *Wh-* questions; place expressions	Grammar exercises Listening: *On the phone*
12 **Describing people**	Saying what people are wearing and what they look like; talking about jobs **Vocabulary:** clothes; jobs and places of work; adjectives for describing people	Vocabulary exercises Listening: *Where are the Browns?*
Study pages F	**Focus on …** Imperatives **Sounds:** /ɒ/ and /ʌ/ **Phrasebook:** Hurry up! **Consolidation:** Expressions with *have*; *at* + place **Review**	Check your progress Phrasebook Writing: *People doing things*

Classroom Book		Self-study Workbook
Unit 19 You mustn't do that!	Explaining rules; asking for and giving permission; saying what you have to and don't have to do **Grammar:** *must* and *mustn't*; *can* and *can't*; *have to* and *don't have to*	Grammar exercises Listening: *House rules*
Unit 20 The body	Describing bodies and actions; describing physical appearance; describing actions **Vocabulary:** parts of the body; adjectives describing physical appearance; action verbs	Vocabulary exercises Listening: *Exercises*
Study pages J	**Focus on ...** Adverbs **Sounds:** /r/ **Phrasebook:** Could you ...? **Consolidation:** Verbs with *to*, *at* and *about* **Review**	Check your progress Phrasebook Writing: *Animals*
Unit 21 Good, better, best	Making comparisons; describing outstanding features **Grammar:** comparative adjectives; *than*; superlative adjectives	Grammar exercises Listening: *Buying things*
Unit 22 Free time	Talking about leisure activities and sport; talking about likes and dislikes **Vocabulary:** leisure activities and sports; leisure facilities; *like/enjoy + -ing*	Vocabulary exercises Listening: *At the weekend*
Study pages K	**Focus on ...** Verb + *to* + infinitive **Sounds:** /ɑː/, /ɔː/, /ɜː/ and /ə/ **Phrasebook:** What did you say? **Consolidation:** Expressions with *go* **Review**	Check your progress Phrasebook Writing: *and, but, also*
Unit 23 Future plans	Talking and asking questions about future plans; talking about future arrangements **Grammar:** *going to*; questions with *going to*; Present continuous tense with future meaning	Grammar exercises Listening: *At the airport*
Unit 24 Feelings	Describing feelings; expressing opinions about films and TV programmes **Vocabulary:** physical feelings; emotions; adjectives describing quality	Vocabulary exercises Listening: *Three stories*
Final review		

1 People and places

1 Hello Goodbye

Greetings • I'm • this is

1 Imagine you are at this party. What do you reply?

2 🔲 Sam meets some people at the party. Listen and fill the gaps.

A
Hello. I'm Sam.

Oh, hello. .... Anna.

Where ...., Anna?

.... from Berlin.

B
Hello.

Oh, hi. .... Paul.
.... a student here.

Oh, really? .... Sam.

C
Oh, hi, Lisa. How............?

.... fine. ....?

Oh, ... OK.

D
Hello. .... Sam.

Hi. .... John.
.... a teacher here.

Oh, really? ....?

.... London.

3 Meet some other students in the class.

4 Can you remember the names?

This is Emma ...

... and this is Leo ...

... and this is Camilla ...

... and this is, um ...

This unit introduces some of the 'basics' of English:
– introducing yourself: saying who you are and where you're from
– the verb *to be*, with *I, you, he, she, it* and *they*
– the expression *This is …*
– some basic nouns and adjectives (e.g. *student, teacher, car, small, old*)
– names of a few well-known countries
– numbers 1–4
– a few useful set phrases (e.g. *Hello, Goodbye, I'm fine*)
– the questions *Where are you from?*, *What's your name?* and *How are you?*

1 Hello Goodbye

➤ Focus on Form: Exercises 1 & 3
➤ Workbook: Exercise A

In this exercise students learn to introduce themselves and other people, say hello and goodbye, and say where they are from. The exercise introduces a range of very common expressions, which can be learned at this stage as set phrases. The main grammar focus is on the forms I'm … *and* This is …

> *Key structures:* I'm (Sam), I'm from (Spain), This is (Maria).
> *Words and phrases:* Hello, Goodbye, I'm fine, See you soon; student, teacher.
> *Questions:* What's your name? Where are you from? How are you?

False beginners
Use this exercise to find out what students know, don't know and 'half-know'. Move through the stages more quickly, and let students add other information about themselves (e.g. *I'm 18, I'm a student*).

1 Presentation of key expressions

● Look at the picture and use it to teach the words *party* and *people*. Look at each bubble in turn and read it out. Ask students to imagine they are at the party, and to give a reply. The idea of this is to find out if students already know a few basic words in English (e.g. *hello*, the name of their country); if they don't, it's an opportunity to teach them. Possible answers:

Hello. I'm Sam.	Hello. I'm (Paolo).
Hi! How are you?	I'm fine. (How are you?)
What's your name?	(Paolo).
Goodbye. See you soon.	Goodbye.
Where are you from?	I'm from (Spain).

Mixed nationality classes
If you can't talk to the students in their own language, introduce these expressions directly. Introduce yourself (*Hello. I'm …*). Ask students directly *What's your name? How are you? Where are you from?* Pretend to leave the class and say *Goodbye. See you soon.* Elicit responses from the students.

● Write on the board: **I'm = I am**

Ask the class to repeat after you *I'm a student, I'm fine, I'm from (…)*.

Note
Students could give other responses to *How are you?*, e.g. *I'm OK, thanks* or *Not too bad*.

● Practise the remarks and replies with the class, getting students to answer and then to ask the questions.

2 Listening

● ▭ Play the recording, pausing after each conversation. Ask students to complete the gaps. Introduce *teacher* and *Oh, really?*, and make sure students know where Berlin is. Answers:

A I'm, are you from, I'm   B I'm, I'm, I'm   C are you, I'm, How are you? I'm
D I'm, I'm, I'm, Where are you from, I'm from

▭ The tapescript is on page T10.

Alternative: False beginners
Ask students to guess what goes in the gaps. Then play the recording to check.

3 Activation: pairwork dialogues

● Ask students to turn to the person next to them and have a short conversation like the ones they listened to. They can then repeat the conversation with the person on the other side and with people behind or in front of them, until they have 'met' a few people.

Alternatives
1 Students move freely round the class as if at a party, introducing themselves to each other.
2 Put students in groups of four or five to do this activity.

4 Presentation of 'This is …'; practice

● To introduce *This is …*, choose a student and point to him/her. Say *This is (Lisa)*. Get the class to say *Hello* to him/her.

● Ask a few students to introduce the people they spoke to in Part 3 to the rest of the class.

2 Photos

This exercise gives practice in simple description. It picks up the expression This is *from Exercise 1 and adds* he's, she's, it's *and some basic vocabulary.*

> *Key structures:* this is; he's, she's, it's.
> *Other new words:* my, flat, car, friend, small, old, Italy, very; numbers 1–4.

➤ Focus on Form: Exercise 1
➤ Workbook: Exercise B, Listening

1 Matching task; presentation of vocabulary

- Read the sentences in the bubbles, and ask students to match them with the pictures. Use this to present *my, flat, friend, car*. Answers:

  1 This is my car.   2 This is my flat.   3 This is my friend Nina.   4 This is my friend George.

- Ask students to add the continuations. Present *small, old,* and *Italy*. Answers:

  1 It's a Citroën. It's very old.   2 It's very small.   3 She's from Italy.
  4 He's from London. He's a student.

> *Note*
> The pictures introduce the numbers 1–4, but only receptively. If you like, practise them at this stage. Numbers 1–20 are introduced in Unit 2.

2 Listening to check; presentation of 'he's / she's / it's'

- 🔲 Play the recording to check.

- Write these structures on the board:
  Point to students and objects in the class to show the meaning of *he, she* and *it*.

  > he's = he is
  > she's = she is
  > it's = it is

> 🔲 The tapescript is on page T10.

3 Activation: making sentences

- Look at the photos on page 104. Ask the class what they could say about each of them, using the prompts. Expected answers:

  A 1 This is my room. It's very small.   2 This is my bike. It's new.
    3 This is my friend (Laura). She's from London.   4 This is my friend …

  B 1 This is my house. It's very big.   2 This is my car. It's a Porsche.
    3 This is my friend (Leonardo). He's a film star.   4 This is my friend …

- Pairwork. Students take it in turns to show their 'photos' to their partner.

> *Vocabulary option: false beginners*
> The fourth picture is open-ended. This is an opportunity to teach a few other simple words, e.g. *rich, beautiful, poor, nice; boyfriend, girlfriend*.

> *Homework option*
> Ask students to find pictures of their flat, car and friends to show in the next lesson.

3 Where are they from?

This exercise introduces names of countries, and He's/She's/They're from …

> *Key structures:* he's, she's, they're.   *Countries:* Australia, Brazil, Britain, France, Germany, Italy, Japan, Russia, Spain, the USA.   *Phrases:* I think, I don't know.

➤ Focus on Form: Exercise 2
➤ Workbook: Exercise C

1 Presentation of countries; matching task

- Look at the countries in the box. Make sure that students recognise them, and practise saying them. Focus especially on the /ə/ sound and the stress in /ɒˈstreɪlɪə/, /brəˈzɪl/, /ˈbrɪtən/, /ˈdʒɜːmənɪ/, /ˈɪtəlɪ/, /dʒəˈpæn/ and /ˈrʌʃə/.

- Write these structures on the board:

- Look at the people in the photos and ask students to say where they're from. Answers:

  > he's = he is   they're = they are
  > she's = she is

  A She's from Spain.   B He's from the USA.   C She's from Italy.
  D They're from France.   E They're from Japan.   F They're from Brazil.

> *False beginners*
> Ask students to cover the box on the right and see if they can identify the countries from the pictures.

2 Vocabulary expansion: countries

- Ask students to suggest a few other important countries (e.g. countries in their region). Say what they are in English, and write them on the board.

3 Game: famous people

- Look at the examples. Then give time for students to think of a famous person from one of the countries in the list and write down the name.

- Students read out the names. Other students say where the people are from.

> *Idea*
> Bring in pictures of famous people from different countries that your students know (e.g. politicians, pop stars, film stars, TV personalities). Use them for a quiz: see if students know who they are and where they are from.

2 Photos

this is • he's, she's, it's

1 Match the sentences with the photos.

This is my flat.

This is my friend Nina.

This is my friend George.

This is my car.

1 one

2 two

3 three

4 four

Now add other sentences.

He's from London. He's a student.

It's very small.

It's a Citroën. It's very old.

She's from Italy.

2 Listen and check.

3 Turn to page 104. These are your photos! Make sentences about them.

3 Where are they from?

he's, she's, they're

1 Where are these people from?

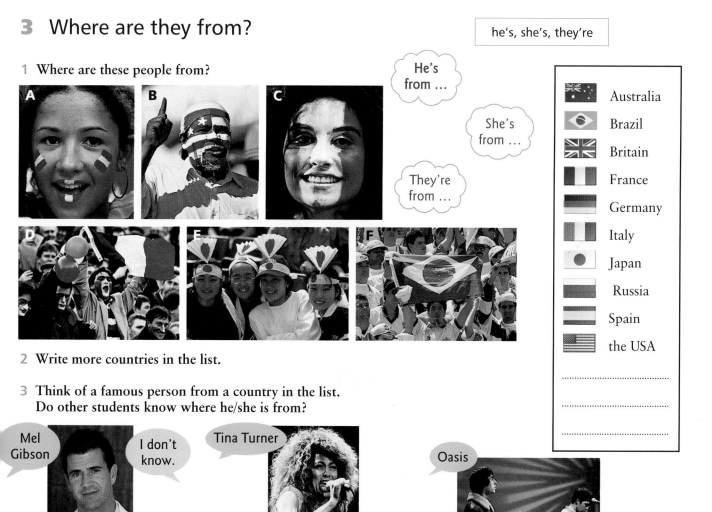

He's from …

She's from …

They're from …

A   B   C

D   E   F

Australia
Brazil
Britain
France
Germany
Italy
Japan
Russia
Spain
the USA

2 Write more countries in the list.

3 Think of a famous person from a country in the list.
Do other students know where he/she is from?

Mel Gibson   I don't know.

Tina Turner

Oasis

I think he's from Australia.

She's from the USA.

They're from Britain.

Focus on Form

1 I, you, he, she ...

Practise saying the words.

2 I am → I'm

I am	→	I ~~a~~m	→	I'm
You are	→	You ~~a~~re	→	You're
He is	→	He ~~i~~s	→	....
She is	→			....
It is	→			....
We are	→			....
They are	→			....

Fill the gaps.

a Hi. .... Michael. What's your name?

b This is Juan and this is Anna. .... from Spain.

c This is Lola. .... a student.

d This is my car. .... very old.

e This is my boyfriend. .... from Brazil.

3 Questions

Learn these questions.

What's your name?

Where are you from?

How are you?

How to say it

1 [cassette] **Listen to these words.**

we	you	they
we're	you're	they're
where	how	

Listen to the sentences. Fill the gaps with words from the box.

a .... are .... ?

b I think .... students.

c .... are .... from?

d .... from the USA.

2 [cassette] **Notice the stress in these words.**

■ ·   ■ ·   ■·
London   teacher   student

■ ·   · ■ ·   ■··
Britain   Australia   Italy

Now listen and say these sentences.

· · ■ ·
I'm from London

· · · ■ ·
This is my teacher.

· · ■ ·
She's a student.

Focus on Form

1 I, you, he, she …

- Use the pictures (and your own gestures) to show the meaning of the words.
- Students practise saying the words.

2 I am → I'm

- Elicit the forms and build them up on the board:

I'm	I'm
You're	You're
He's	He's
She's	She's
It's	It's
We're	We're
They're	They're

Show how the apostrophe (') shows where a letter is missing. Focus on pronunciation of *you're*, *we're*, *they're*.

- Students fill the gaps, working alone or in pairs. Then go through the answers:

  a I'm   *b* They're   *c* She's   *d* It's   *e* He's

3 Questions

- To practise these, ask the questions and get students to give appropriate answers. Then give answers and get students to give the questions.

  Repeat this in one or two later lessons.

How to say it

1 Pronunciation of 'we're', 'they're', etc.

- Read the words, and ask students to repeat them. Focus especially on the pronunciation of *we're*, *where*, *they're*, *you're*.

- 🔊 Play the recording. Pause after each sentence so that students can write the missing words. Then practise saying the sentences. Answers:

a How are you?	*c* Where are you from?
b I think they're students.	*d* We're from the USA.

2 Word and sentence stress

- 🔊 Play the words and the sentences. Pause after each item and get students to repeat them. Focus on the stress pattern.

🔊 Tapescript for Exercise 1: *Hello Goodbye*

A Hello. I'm Sam.
B Oh, hello. I'm Anna.
A Where are you from, Anna?
B I'm from Berlin.

A Hello.
B Oh, hi. I'm Paul. I'm a student here.
A Oh, really? My name's Sam.

A Oh, hi, Lisa. How are you?
B I'm fine. How are you?
A Oh, I'm OK.

A Hello. My name's Sam.
B Hi. I'm John. I'm a teacher here.
A Oh, really? Where are you from?
B I'm from London.

🔊 Tapescript for Exercise 2: *Photos*

This is my car. It's a Citroën, it's very old. This is my flat. It's very small. And this is my friend Nina. She's from Italy. Oh, and this is my friend George. He's from London and he's a student.

2

This unit introduces basic language for talking about yourself and your family. It focuses on:
– words for people (e.g. *boy*, *girl*, *baby*)
– singular and plural nouns
– the verb *have*
– family members (e.g. *mother*, *daughter*, *brother*)
– numbers 1–20, used for talking about age.
The Reading and Listening activity is a logic puzzle about four people.

1 Families

This exercise introduces basic vocabulary for talking about families. It also introduces plural forms, we have as a set expression, and the numbers 5–10.

➤ Workbook: Exercise A

> *People:* boy, girl, baby, child/children.
> *Other new words:* dog, cat, bird; have; big, family; numbers 5–10.
> *Recycled language:* numbers 1–4; I, we.

1 Reading & matching task; presentation of key vocabulary

- Look at the pictures and use them to introduce the key words *boy*, *girl*, *baby*, *dog*, *cat* and *bird*. Then use them to teach *child/children* (say: *Look at picture 1. This is a boy and this is a girl. They're children.*).
- Read the sentences and ask students to identify the pictures. As you go through, show the meaning of the verb *have* (say: *Look, this is my book. I have a book.*). As you read through, make sure students understand *no children*, *big* and *family*. Answers:

  a 6 *b* 8 *c* 2 *d* 4 *e* 9

> *Presentation option*
> Teach *man* and *woman* at this point, although they are not needed for the exercise.

2 Reading task; presentation of plurals

- To introduce the idea of the plural, hold up one book, then several books, or draw a boy on the board, then two or three boys.
- Give time for students to read the texts again silently, and complete the table with plural forms. Then build them up on the board. Point out that:

  – to make most plurals, we add *-s*.
  – *baby* ends in *-y*, so the *-y* changes to *-ies*.
  – *child/children* is irregular.

> *Note*
> The pictures introduce the new numbers 5–10, although students only have to read them from the page. If you like, go through them, getting students to practise saying them aloud. Numbers 1–20 are focused on in the next exercise.

3 Practice: making sentences

- Look at the other pictures and get students to make sentences. If necessary prompt them by starting the sentences for them (e.g. *We have two …*, *And we have a …*).

4 Pairwork game: guessing the picture

- To demonstrate the activity, make a sentence yourself and ask the class to say which family it is.
- Pairwork. Students take it in turns to say a sentence. They should make simple sentences as in the example, *not* give a complete description of the picture they choose.

> *Whole class option*
> Working alone, students choose a picture and write a sentence. In turn, students read out their sentences. The others guess which family it is.

> *Optional extension*
> Tell the class about your family (e.g. *I have one child. He's a boy.*). Then students do the same round the class. Adult classes can say *I have …* or *We have…*, teenagers can say *My parents have …*

🖭 Tapescript for Exercise 2: *How old are they?*

1 My name's André. I'm nine years old, and I'm from Germany.

2 My name's Olga. I'm 16, and I'm from Russia.

3 Hello. My name's Greg. I'm 18 years old, and I'm from the United States.

4 This is Kumiko. She's one year old, and she's from Japan.

5 My name's Caterina. I'm 20, and I'm from Italy.

1 Families

1 one

2 two

3 three

4 four

5 five

6 six

7 seven

8 eight

9 nine

10 ten

a We have one child.
She's a girl.

b We have three children –
two boys and a girl.

c We have no children, but I
have two cats.

d We have a boy and two girls.
The girls are just babies.

e We're a big family. We have four children – two boys and
two girls. And we have two dogs, a cat and three birds!

1 Five people talk about their families. Read what they say.
Which pictures do they go with?

2 Find words in the texts and complete the table.

3 Look at the other families. Make sentences about them.

4 Work in pairs.

Student A: Choose a family, and make a sentence.
Student B: Which family is it?

🧍	🧍🧍+
a boy	*boys*
a girl	....
a dog	....
a cat	....
a bird	....
a baby	....
a child	....

They have
two babies.

That's
picture four.

2 How old are they?

1 Look at these birthday cards. What are the numbers?

one
two
three
four
five
six
seven
eight
nine
ten
eleven
twelve
thirteen
fourteen
fifteen
sixteen
seventeen
eighteen
nineteen
twenty

2 Practise the numbers 1–20.

3 Look at the people on page 105. How old do you think they are?

> I think André's nine.

> I think he's ten.

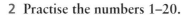 Now listen. How old are they – and where are they from?

3 Parents and children

1 Here are two families. Fill the gaps with words from the box.

mother	father
daughter	son
sister	brother
wife	husband

This is Paul. 1 This is his ....

4 This is her ....

2 This is his .... 3 This is his ....

5 This is her ....

This is Isabelle. 6 This is her ....

2 Paul and Isabelle talk about their families. Who says these things? Write *I* or *P*.

a [P] I'm married.
b [ ] I'm 19.
c [ ] My daughter is eight.
d [ ] We have two children.
e [ ] My mother's a teacher.
f [ ] I have one brother. His name's Alan.
g [ ] My son is three.
h [ ] My wife is a doctor.
i [ ] I'm a student at university.
j [ ] My father's a taxi driver.

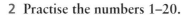 Now listen and check.

3 Write one or two sentences about your family. Read out your sentences.

2 How old are they?

In this exercise students practise numbers 1–20, and talk about people's ages.

➤ Workbook: Exercise B

> Numbers 11–20 *Other new words:* today, birthday, old.
> *Recycled language:* Numbers 1–10; countries; I think; you're, he's, she's; from.

1 Introduction; presentation of numbers

- Look at the birthday cards and ask students to read them aloud (e.g. *You're six today*), using the box to help them.

2 Presentation of numbers; practice

- Get students to read the numbers in the box aloud, and focus on pronunciation. Then get them to try saying them without looking at the box. If you like, write numbers on the board and ask students to say them.

> *Homework option*
> Ask students to learn numbers 1–20 by heart.

3 Activation: interpreting pictures; listening to check

- Turn to page 105 and look at the first picture (André). Ask students to guess his age (ask: *How old is he?*). Get them to reply with *I think (he's 11)*. Ask about the other pictures in the same way. Try to get several different guesses for each one. If you like, build up a list on the board.

> *Pairwork option*
> Students look at the pictures in pairs. Then discuss the answers together.

> The tapescript is on page T11.

- Play the recording. Pause after each item, and establish the person's age and country (ask: *How old is he/she? Where is he/she from?*). Answers:

  1 André is 9. He's from Germany.
  2 Olga is 16. She's from Russia.
  3 Greg is 18. He's from the United States.
  4 Kumiko is 1. She's from Japan.
  5 Caterina is 20. She's from Italy.

> *Optional extension: teenage classes*
> Students ask each other *How old are you?* and say their age.

3 Parents and children

This exercise teaches family relationships and some common jobs.

➤ Workbook: Exercise C, Listening

> *Family:* mother, father, daughter, son, sister, brother, wife, husband.
> *Jobs:* doctor, taxi driver, teacher. *Recycled language:* my, children, have; ages.

1 Presentation of vocabulary; gap-filling task

- Look at the photos and establish who the people are, e.g.: *Who's the boy? It's her brother.* As you do this, present the words in the table and get students to say them aloud. Focus especially on the pronunciation of /ˈmʌðə/, /ˈfɑːðə/, /ˈbrʌðə/, and also /ˈdɔːtə/. Answers:

  1 wife   2 son   3 daughter   4 brother   5 mother   6 father

> *Practice option*
> Use the words to ask a few questions round the class, e.g.
> Who has a brother?
> How old is he?
> Who has two brothers?
> Your mother – what's her name?

2 Matching task; listening to check

- Read the sentences, and present the words *married, doctor, university* and *taxi driver*. Ask students to match the sentences with the people.

- Play the recording, and check the answers. Answers:

  b I   c P   d P   e I   f I   g P   h P   i I   j I

> *Pairwork option*
> Students do this part of the activity in pairs. Then discuss the answers together.

3 Activation: writing sentences

- To introduce the activity, tell the class one or two things about your own family, or write sentences on the board.
- Give time for students to write sentences about their own family. If students want to include names of jobs, help them or let them use a dictionary.
- Students read out their sentences in turn.

> *Game option*
> Students write some true sentences and some that are not true. Other students guess which ones are true. As a preparation, do this yourself on the board.

> Tapescript for Exercise 3: *Parents and children*
>
> 1 My name's Paul. I'm married and my wife is a doctor. We have two children. My daughter is eight and my son is just three.
>
> 2 My name's Isabelle. I'm 19 years old and I'm a student at university. I have one brother – his name's Alan. My mother's a teacher and my father's a taxi driver.

4 Who's who?

This combined Reading and Listening activity is in the form of a logic puzzle, in which students have to find information about four people. It recycles language from Units 1 and 2, and introduces new words for colours and countries. It also introduces the 3rd person form has.

Reading skills: *careful reading of sentences.*
Listening skills: *listening to check.*

Colours: red, blue, grey, green, white, black. *Countries:* England, Scotland, Wales, Ireland. *Other new words:* man/men, woman/women, person/people; singer, police officer, hair, eyes; has.

Note
There is no need to spend too much time on this, as these items are for comprehension only in this activity. Colours are practised further in Study Pages A and in Unit 4.1.

Language note
These are the four countries that make up the *British Isles*. England, Scotland, Wales and Northern Ireland together make up *Britain* (or the United Kingdom). The Republic of Ireland (in the south) is a separate country.

1 Presentation of vocabulary; reading task: completing a table

- Look at the list and read through the items. Check that students understand them and that they know how to say them. Explain that England, Scotland, Wales and Ireland are four countries which are part of the British Isles.

- Draw the table on the board, and tell students the aim of the activity: to find out all the information about all four people.

- Start filling in the table on the board by writing in the four names. Then let students read the information and complete the rest of the table. They could do this either working alone and then comparing answers with their partner afterwards, or working together in pairs.

2 Listening to check

- 🔲 When most students have finished, play the recording, pausing from time to time. Students listen and check their answers.

- Go through the answers together, and get students to help you complete the table on the board. Answers:

Name	Job	How old?	From?	Colour of car?
Donna	police officer	20	Scotland	grey
James	student	17	Ireland	red
Alice	singer	19	Wales	white
Bob	waiter	18	England	green

🔲 Tapescript for Exercise 4: *Who's who?*

A is Donna. She's a police officer, she's 20, she's from Scotland and she has a grey car.

B is James. He's a student, he's 17, he's from Ireland and he has a red car.

C is Alice. She's a singer, she's 19, she's from Wales and she has a white car.

And D is Bob. He's a waiter, he's 18 years old, he's from England and he has a geen car.

4 Who's who?

A **B** **C** **D**

1 Look at these four people.

Now read about them. Can you complete the table?

The two women are Alice and Donna.
The two men are James and Bob.

Donna has black hair.
James has blue eyes.

Bob is a waiter.
One man is a student.
The singer has blue eyes.
One person is a police officer.

The police officer is twenty years old.
The waiter is eighteen years old.
One woman is nineteen years old.
One person is seventeen years old.

Alice is from Wales.
The student is from Ireland.
One man is from England.
One person is from Scotland.

The waiter has a green car.
The person from Scotland has a grey car.
One woman has a white car.
One person has a red car.

hair   eyes

red   white   black

grey   green   blue

a singer   a student

a waiter   a police officer

Ireland   Scotland   Wales   England

	Name	Job	How old?	From?	Colour of car?

2 Someone does the puzzle. Listen and check your answers.

Focus on ... The alphabet

1 🔊 Listen to these colours.

green red grey blue

2 🔊 Listen to the English alphabet.

A B C D E F G H J

K L M N O P Q R S

T U V W X Z

How do you say

– the green letters?
– the red letters?
– the grey letters?
– the blue letters?
– the   letters?

What about the black letters?

3 Ask the teacher to spell the words.

> What's number three?

1 .... 2 .... 3 ....

4 .... 5 .... 6 ....

7 .... 8 .... 9 ....

4 Now test your partner.

> Spell 'book'.   B-O-O-K.

Sounds: Ten big cats

1 🔊 Listen to these sounds.

/ɪ/ This is my sister.
/e/ Look at the red letters.
/æ/ He has a black cat.

2 🔊 Listen and practise.

children	sister	is	big	picture
	friend	ten	seven	
cats	family	have	has	married	Japan

3 Write a sentence. Use words from the box.

4 Read out your sentence.

Phrasebook: Good morning

Look at the bubbles. Which mean *Hello*?
Which mean *Goodbye*?

Good morning.

Good afternoon.

Good evening.

Good night.

🔊 Listen and practise the conversations.

Study pages A

Focus on ... *The alphabet*

This exercise teaches the letters of the English alphabet, and gives practice in spelling words. It also pre-teaches some basic vocabulary needed in Unit 4 and later units.

> *Key language:* letters of the alphabet; What's ...?
> *New words:* tree, door, book, chair, table, sun, fish, lamp, window. *Recycled language:* colours.

1 🖭 Play the first part of the recording. Practise saying the colours.

2 🖭 Play the second part of the recording. Point out that letters of the same colour have the same sound: green = /iː/ red = /e/ grey = /eɪ/ blue = /uː/ white = /aɪ/. The black letters have different sounds.
Practise saying the letters group by group.

3 Say the question *What's number 1?* and get the class to repeat it. Then get students to ask you about the pictures. Spell the words and ask students to write them on a piece of paper, e.g.
S: What's number 1?
T: It's a tree: T-R-E-E.
The other items are:
2 door 3 table 4 chair 5 book 6 fish
7 sun 8 lamp 9 window

4 To show what to do, choose one of the words (e.g. *book*) and ask students to spell it. In pairs, they then choose words themselves and ask their partner to spell them.

> *Other ideas for practice*
> 1 Go through the alphabet. Stop at a letter (e.g. *J*) and ask students to say the next one (*K*).
> 2 At the beginning of lessons from now on, write a few words on the board and ask students to spell them.

Sounds: *Ten big cats*

> The short vowels /ɪ/, /e/ and /æ/.

1, 2 🖭 If students have problems, focus on these features:
  – All the sounds are short.
  – /ɪ/ is like e.g. French or Spanish *i*, but with lips less spread and mouth more loosely open.
  – For /e/ the tongue is a little lower and further back, the mouth more open (like e.g. French *é*, Spanish *e*, but with lips less spread and mouth more loosely open; like French *è* but short).
  – /æ/ is between /e/ and the /ɑ/ sound in French, German, Spanish, etc.

3 Students write a sentence using words from the box and including any other words they like, e.g.
  – My sister has seven children.
  – This is a picture of Japan.

4 Students read out their sentences in turn. Focus on the pronunciation of /ɪ/, /e/ and /æ/.

Alternative: Dictation. Students dictate their sentence to the person next to them. As a check, ask students to read out the sentence they wrote down.

Phrasebook: *Good morning*

This exercise teaches basic greetings and responses.

> *Key language:* good morning, good afternoon, good evening, good night.
> *Recycled language:* hello, goodbye.

● Use the pictures to teach *morning, afternoon, evening,* and *night*.
● Establish that *Good morning, Good afternoon* and *Good evening* are all ways of saying 'Hello'. *Good night* is a way of saying 'Goodbye' before you go to bed. Write two lists on the board, one of 'hello' words and one of 'goodbye' words:

Hello	Goodbye
Good morning	Good night
Good afternoon	
Good evening	

● 🖭 Play the dialogues. Pause after each one and check what the speakers said.
● Practise the dialogues with the class.

🖭 Tapescript for Phrasebook: *Good morning*

1 A Good morning.
  B Good morning. How are you?
  A Fine, thanks.
2 A Good afternoon.
  B Good afternoon.

3 A Good evening, sir.
  B Good evening. Room 315, please.
4 A Good night.
  B Good night. See you tomorrow.

Consolidation

the woman = she

This exercise focuses on is *and* are *after nouns and pronouns. It consolidates language introduced in Units 1 and 2.*

1 Write these examples on the board:

| The girl | is 6 | The girls | are 6 |
| She | | They | |

Students complete the table. Answers:

the girl	= she	the girls		= they
Maria	= she	Maria and Anna	= they
John	= he	John and Maria	= they
my car	= it	the cars		= they
London	= it	London and Paris	= they

2 Students fill the gaps. Answers:

a is *b* are *c* are *d* is *e* is *f* are

have and has

This exercise focuses on forms of the verb have. *It consolidates language introduced in Exercises 2.1, 2.3 and 2.4.*

1 Ask students to look back at Unit 2 and find examples of *have* and *has* to fill the gaps. Answers:

We have three children. (2.1)
I have one brother. (2.3)
James has blue eyes. (2.4)
Donna has black hair. (2.4)

2 Ask students to complete the table, and write forms of the verb *have* on the board:

I have	We have
You have	You have
He/She has	They have

3 Students write sentences. As a round-up, ask some students to read out their sentences.

This is my …

This exercise focuses on possessives: my, your, his *and* her. *It consolidates language introduced in Exercises 1.1, 1.2 and 2.3.*

Ask students to fill the gaps. Answers:

a My car is a BMW.
b What's your name?
c His car is very old.
d Her name is Louisa.

If you like, write these forms on the board:

I	→	my
you	→	your
he	→	his
she	→	her

Review

Questions

Review of language from Exercises 1.1 and 2.2.

Establish what the questions are. Answers:

How are you?
What's your name?
Where are you from?
How old are you?

Countries

Review of language from Exercise 1.3.

1 Students complete the sentences. Answers:

a Brazil *b* Britain (or England) *c* Japan *d* France
e Australia *f* Germany *g* the USA

2 • Students write a simple sentence like those in the exercise, with the country missing. (This could be about a place, a person or a product.)

• Students give their sentence to the person next to them, who tries to complete it.

• As a round-up, ask students to read out their sentences to the class.

Numbers

Review of language from Exercise 2.2.

1 Ask students to say the numbers, and write them on the board. Answers:

seven, fifteen, four, eleven,
thirteen, nine, twelve, eight, twenty

2 Students continue the sequences. Answers:

a six, seven, …
b sixteen, fifteen, …
c twenty …

3 In turn, students write a number between 1 and 20 on a piece of paper. Their partner says what number it is.

Other ideas for practice

1 Start spelling a number, letter by letter. Students listen and see how quickly they can guess it, e.g. F-I-F-T… = 15).

2 One student thinks of a number between 1 and 20, without saying what it is. Other students try to guess it.

Consolidation

the woman = she

1 Fill the gaps with *he*, *she*, *it* and *they*.

the girl = she   the girls = they

Maria = ...   Maria and Anna = ...

John = ...   John and Maria = ...

my car = ...   the cars = ...

London = ...   London and Paris = ...

2 Fill the gaps with *is* and *are*.

a My brother .... sixteen.

b Leo and Angela .... married.

c My friends .... at the party.

d My flat .... very small.

e Carla .... from Russia.

f New York and Los Angeles .... in the USA.

have and has

1 All these sentences are in Unit 2. Fill the gaps.

a We .... three children.

b I .... one brother.

c James .... blue eyes.

d Donna .... black hair.

2 When do we use *have* and *has*?

I ....   We ....

You ....   You ....

He ....   They ....

She ....

3 Write true sentences about yourself or other people.

My brother has two children.

I have a red car.

My sister has a new bike.

This is my …

| her | your | my | his |

Fill the gaps with the right words.

a I have a BMW. ↔ .... car is a BMW.

b Who are you? ↔ What's .... name?

c He has a very ↔ .... car is very old.
   old car.

d She's Louisa. ↔ .... name is Louisa.

Review

Questions

Here are some answers. What are the questions?

a – Hi. ....?
  – I'm fine, thanks.

b – I'm Bill. ....?
  – Oh, I'm Philippa.

c – ....?
  – I'm from Madrid.

d – ....?
  – I'm thirteen.

Countries

1 Complete these sentences with the name of a country. All the answers are in Unit 1.

a Rio de Janeiro is in ....

b Buckingham Palace is in ....

c Mitsubishi cars are from ....

d Paris is in ....

e The country in the picture is ....

f Berlin and Frankfurt are in ....

g Hollywood is in ....

2 Write a sentence yourself.
Can your partner complete it?

Numbers

1 How do you say these numbers?

7   15   4   11

13   9   12   8   20

2 Look at these numbers. What comes next?

a three, four, five, ...

b nineteen, eighteen, seventeen, ...

c five, ten, fifteen, ...

3 Now test your partner.

3 To be or not to be?

1 Sorry

I'm not, He isn't …

1 Look at the picture. Can you find
   – a baby?   – a waiter?   – a car?
   – a cup of coffee? – a customer?   – a taxi?

2 🔲 Listen to the conversations and complete the sentences.

Conversation A
She isn't ....
She's ....

Conversation B
He isn't ....
He's ....

Conversation C
It isn't ....
It's ....

Conversation D
He isn't ....
He's ....

Conversation E
They aren't ....
They're ....

3 Imagine you're in the pictures. What do you say?

> Hello, Chris. How are you?
> I'm not Chris, actually. I'm …

> Where are you from in England? London?
> Actually, …

> Happy birthday!
> Thanks. Actually, …

Have the conversations.

This unit is concerned with correcting people, making enquiries and identifying people. It introduces these forms of the verb *to be*:
– negatives
– *yes/no* questions
– *Wh-* questions with *Who?*, *What?* and *Where?*

1 Sorry

This exercise introduces negative forms of the verb to be, *used for correcting people.*

➤ Focus on Form: Exercise 1
➤ Workbook: Exercise A

Structures: He isn't, She isn't, It isn't, They aren't, I'm not.
New words: cup of coffee, waiter, customer, English, American.

1 Introduction: presentation of vocabulary

● Look at the picture and use it to focus on the vocabulary in the box. Either do this by asking *What's this? Who's this?*, or by saying *Find a car, Can you see a baby?*

2 Listening; presentation of key structures

● 🔲 Play the dialogues. Pause after each one and ask students to complete the sentences. Answers:

A She isn't Jane. She's Cathy.   B He isn't a waiter. He's a customer.
C It isn't a car. It's a taxi.   D He isn't a girl. He's a boy.   E They aren't American. They're English.

● Show how these structures are formed:

He/She is + not = He/She isn't
They are + not = They aren't

3 Activation: dialogues

● Look at the three situations and ask students how the replies might continue. Possible answers:

I'm not Chris, actually. I'm (Michael).
Actually, I'm not from England. I'm from (Russia).
Thanks. Actually, I'm not seventeen. I'm eighteen. (*or* It isn't my birthday.)

● Use this to present *I'm not*:

I am + not = I'm not

● Pairwork. Students practise the conversations. Get them to give their real names, ages and countries.

Language note
As well as *He isn't, You aren't, They aren't*, we can also say *He's not, You're not, They're not*. With a good class, you could present both forms. In the first person, there is only one form: *I'm not*.

Language note
Actually means the same as *in fact*, and is often used when saying 'no' politely.

🔲 Tapescript for Exercise 1: *Sorry*

A A Jane – hello. How are you?
  B I'm not Jane, I'm Cathy.
  A Oh – yes, sorry. Cathy, hello. How are you?

B A Excuse me. Two coffees, please.
  B Actually, I'm not a waiter. I'm a customer.
  A Oh, I'm sorry.

C A Oh, good. A taxi.
    Hello. The Hilton Hotel, please.
  B Sorry. This isn't a taxi. It's my car!
  A Oh, I'm so sorry.

D A Oh, is that your baby? Isn't she lovely? What's her name?
  B He isn't a girl, actually. He's a boy.
  A Oh, of course. Isn't he lovely?

E A So where are you from? New York?
  B No, we aren't American. We're English.
  A Oh, you're English.
  C Yeah, that's right – we're from London.

2 Is this seat free?

This exercise introduces yes/no questions with the verb to be. *Students fill gaps in a dialogue, then make up questions from prompts.*

> **Structures**: Is this …? Are you …? Is it …? *New words:* umbrella, seat, free.

➤ Focus on Form: Exercise 2
➤ Workbook: Exercise B

1 Listening; presentation of yes/no questions

- Look at the picture and establish the situation: *What can you see? A man, a woman, a table, an umbrella, a cup of coffee. Where are they? Maybe at a café.*

- [cassette] Play the dialogue once through, then see if students can say what the questions were. If necessary, play the dialogue again, pausing after each question. The questions are:

  Is this your umbrella?   Are you a student here?   Is this seat free?

[cassette] The tapescript is on page T18.

2 Practice

- Show how we make questions by changing the word order:

  1 2
  This is my umbrella

  2 1
  Is this your umbrella?

  1 2
  He's a teacher

  2 1
  Is he a teacher?

- Demonstrate the conversation with one or two students. Then divide the class into pairs to practise it.

False beginners
Ask students to suggest other things you might leave in a café (e.g. a book, a coat, a bag) and write them on the board. Students then improvise conversations, adding details of their own.

3 Activation: making questions

- Look at the bubbles and establish what the questions might be. Expected answers:

  Is this your book?   Are you from Ireland?   Is she a teacher?   Is this a taxi?
  Is this seat free?

3 What's this?

This exercise is an informal quiz, in which students identify people, places and things. It focuses on questions with Who?, Where? *and* What?

> **Key language:** Verb *to be:* Wh- questions with *Who?, Where?* and *What?*; *this* and *these*.

➤ Focus on Form: Exercise 4
➤ Workbook: Exercise C

1 Presentation of 'this/these' & Wh- questions

- To show the difference between *this* and *these*, hold up a book and ask *What's this? (It's a book).* Then hold up two or three books and ask *What are these? (They're books).*

- Look at the pictures and ask the questions. Expected answers (left – right):

  It's King Kong. He's in New York (on the Empire State Building).   It's Tina Turner. She's from the USA.   They're Prince Charles and his sons, Prince William and Prince Harry.   It's a boomerang.   It's the Kremlin. It's in Russia.   They're bananas.

Language note
This, these, that and *those* are taught in Study Pages B.

Notes
King Kong is a gorilla in an early horror film; Tina Turner is a pop singer; Prince Charles is the son of Queen Elizabeth II of Britain.

2 Activation: asking & answering questions

- Turn to page 104. Look at the pictures and establish the questions. Expected answers (left – right):

  What's this? Where is it?   Who's this? Where is he from?   Who are these people? Where are they from?   What are these? Where are they?   What's this? Where is it? What are these? Where are they from?

- Pairwork. Student A asks the questions. Student B answers, using the text.

- Discuss the answers together. Answers (left – right):

  It's the Eiffel Tower. It's in Paris.   It's/He's Ronaldo. He's from Brazil. They're Bill and Hillary Clinton. They're from the USA. They're the Pyramids. They're in Egypt.   It's a taxi. It's in London. They're kangaroos. They're from Australia.

Optional extension
Find pictures of famous people and places from your own country or region, and use them for further practice. You could also organise a quiz, with the class divided into two teams and asking each other questions.

2 Is this seat free?

Yes/no questions

1 ▦ Listen to the dialogue. What are the questions?
- Excuse me. ....?
- Oh. Yes, it is. Thanks. ....?
- Yes. Yes, I am. My name's Mark.
- Hi. I'm Sonia.
- Hi, Sonia. Um, ...?
- Yes, of course ...

2 Practise the conversation.

3 Look at the bubbles. What are the questions?

3 What's this?

Wh- questions

1 Can you answer these questions?

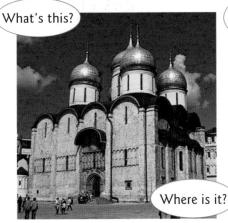

2 Look at the pictures on page 104. Ask your partner questions with *Who*, *What* and *Where*.

Focus on Form

1 I'm not ...

I am not	→	I ~~a~~m not	→	I'm not
You are not	→	You are n~~o~~t	→	You aren't
She is not	→	She is n~~o~~t	→	She isn't
He is not	→			....
It is not	→			....
We are not	→			....
They are not	→			....

Are these sentences true or false?

a Paris is in Spain.

False. Paris isn't in Spain. It's in France.

b We're in Italy.

c Moscow and St Petersburg are in Russia.

d Toyko and Osaka are in China.

e Bill Clinton is from Brazil.

f This exercise is on page 18.

g This sentence is in German.

Now write a sentence of your own.

2 Yes/no questions

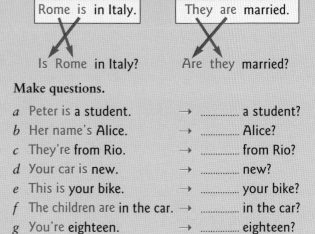

Rome is in Italy.

Is Rome in Italy?

They are married.

Are they married?

Make questions.

a Peter is a student.	→	.... a student?
b Her name's Alice.	→	.... Alice?
c They're from Rio.	→	.... from Rio?
d Your car is new.	→	.... new?
e This is your bike.	→	.... your bike?
f The children are in the car.	→	.... in the car?
g You're eighteen.	→	.... eighteen?

3 Wh- questions

Make questions.

a Are you *sixteen*?	→	How old are you?
b Is he *in London*?	→	Where is he?
c Is that *Prince Charles*?	→	Who is that?
d Is your father *45*?	→	How old ....?
e Are they *in the car*?	→	Where ....?
f Are those people *your parents*?	→	Who ....?
g Is her name *Anne*?	→	What ....?
h Are they *in the café*?	→	.............?
i Is this *your daughter*?	→	.............?

How to say it

1 ▭ **Listen to these phrases and practise saying them.**

■ · ■ · ■
brothers and sisters

■ · ■
cats and dogs

■ · ■ · ■
London and Paris

■ · ■ · ■ ·
two girls and a boy

2 ▭ **Listen to *isn't* and *aren't*. Practise saying the sentences.**

· ■ · · ■ ·
He isn't a student.

· ■ · ■ ·
They aren't in London.

■ ■ · · ■ ·
It isn't my birthday.

· ■ · ■ ·
They aren't married.

Focus on Form

1 I'm not …

- Elicit the forms and build them up on the board:

> *I'm not*
> *You aren't*
> *She isn't*
> *He isn't*
> *It isn't*
> *We aren't*
> *They aren't*

- Give time for students to look at the exercise, then go through it together. Expected answers:

  b (False: We aren't in Italy. We're in …)
  c True.
  d False: They aren't in China. They're in Japan.
  e False: He isn't from Brazil. He's from the USA.
  f True.
  g False: It isn't in German. It's in English.

- Ask students to write a simple sentence – it can either be true or false.
- Students read out their sentences in turn. Other students say if they are true or false, and correct them if necessary.

2 Yes/no questions

- Go through the examples. Then either do the exercise round the class or let students do it in pairs and go through the answers together. Answers:

  a Is Peter a student?
  b Is her name Alice?
  c Are they from Rio?
  d Is your car new?
  e Is this your bike?
  f Are the children in the car?
  g Are you eighteen?

3 Wh- questions

- Go through the exercise together. Answers:

  d How old is your father?
  e Where are they?
  f Who are those people?
  g What is (What's) her name?
  h Where are they?
  i Who is this?

How to say it

1 Phrases with 'and'

- ▣ Play the recording, pausing and getting students to repeat the phrases. Pay attention to:
  - the way the words run together (especially the way *and* links to the word before it)
  - the reduced vowel and lack of stress in *and*: /ˈbrʌðəz ən ˈsɪstəz/.

2 'Isn't' and 'aren't' in sentences

- ▣ Play the sentences. Pause after each one and get students to try saying it. Focus on the pronunciation of /ɪznt/ and /ɑːnt/, and the rhythm of the sentences.

▣ Tapescript for Exercise 2: *Is this seat free?*

A Excuse me. Is this your umbrella?
B Oh. Yes, it is. Thanks. Are you a student here?
A Yes. Yes, I am. My name's Mark.
B Hi. I'm Sonia.
A Hi, Sonia. Um, is this seat free?
B Yes, of course.

4

This unit is about everyday objects and things around us, and focuses on four areas of vocabulary:
– colours
– common objects (e.g. *watch, book, camera*)
– things in rooms and outside (e.g. *window, table, lamp; tree, mountain*)
– place prepositions (e.g. *in, under, behind*).
The Reading and Listening activity is about precious stones.

1 Painting by numbers

This exercise introduces a number of basic nouns and more colour adjectives.

> ➤ Workbook: Exercises A & B

> *New colours:* yellow, brown, pink, orange.　*Nouns:* door, window, floor, wall, table, chair; sky, mountain, tree; dress, shoes; face, hair.
> *Recycled language:* colours; numbers 1–6; verb *to be*.

1 Presentation of nouns & colour adjectives

- Use the picture to introduce the nouns. Say each word and check that students can say it.
- Look at the colours. Say the words and get students to repeat them. Then use the colours to ask about the picture, e.g. *What's blue in the picture? What colour are the shoes?*

Practice option
Give more practice, using the classroom. Say words (e.g. *a window, a face, the sky*) and ask students to point to them if they can see them.

Practice option
Point to things around the classroom and ask *What colour is that?* or *Where is something black?*

2 Practice: making true/false sentences

- To introduce this stage, say a few sentences yourself and ask students if they are true or false.
- Pairwork. Students take it in turns to make sentences about the painting.

3 Activation: guessing colours in paintings

- Look at the three paintings (on page 105) and read the example. Show the meaning of *I think* (mime 'thinking'; = 'maybe'). Use the example to show what to do – say: *I think 2 is blue. I think it's blue.* Ask students what they think.
- Pairwork. Students look at the pictures and choose colours for each number.
- Discuss the answers together and build up a list on the board.
- Show the paintings (on page 128 of the Teacher's Book) and check the answers:
  1 = blue　2 = green　3 = white　4 = pink　5 = brown　6 = yellow

Vocabulary extension: better classes
Before the activity, ask students what they can see in the paintings (e.g. a woman in a dress, in a big chair). Build up other useful vocabulary, e.g. *field, clouds, building, water, swimming pool.*

Whole class option
Simply ask students to suggest colours round the class. Get different opinions by asking *What do you think?*

🔲 Tapescript for Exercise 2: *Birthday presents*

1　A Here's a present for you.
　　B Hmm, what is it? … It's a football … Oh, thank you!

2　A Here you are. Happy birthday.
　　B Oh, thanks … Ooh, a CD. Flamenco music. That's nice. Thank you.

3　A A present for you.
　　B Ooh … It's a jumper! Lovely, thank you!

4　A A present for you. Happy birthday.
　　B An umbrella! Thanks.

5　A A present for you. Happy birthday.
　　B Mmm … A watch! Wow! Thank you!

6　A Here you are. Happy birthday.
　　B Oh, thanks. Ooh, a lamp! It's lovely! Thank you.

4 Things around you

1 Painting by numbers

1 Which colours are in the painting?

red   yellow   black   grey   green

pink   orange   white   brown   blue

2 Work with a partner. Make sentences about the painting. Are they true?

The door's blue.   Yes. That's true.   The shoes are white.   No. They aren't white. They're brown.

3 Now look at these paintings. (They're also on page 105.) What colour is each number?

I think 3 is white.   I think it's blue.

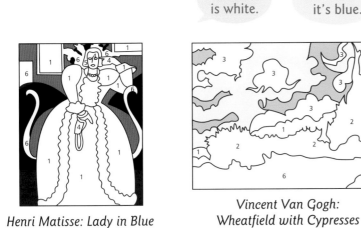

Henri Matisse: Lady in Blue

Vincent Van Gogh:
Wheatfield with Cypresses

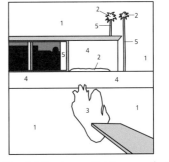

David Hockney: A bigger splash

2 Birthday presents

1 Here is a photo of some birthday presents. What do you think they are?

a ring   a watch

an umbrella

a CD   a pen   a lamp   a football

a camera   an address book   a jumper

2 🔲 Now listen. What are the presents?

3 Write down a 'birthday present'. Give it to your partner.

3 Where's my ...?

Where's my watch?

Where are my glasses?

1 Answer the man's questions. Choose expressions from the box.

2 Ask and answer questions about these things.

– umbrella
– shoes
– jumper

3 Work in pairs.

Student A: Turn to page 106.
Student B: Turn to page 108.

Ask and answer questions.

It's ...   They're ...

... on the floor.
... on the desk.
... by the window.
... by the computer.
... in the bag.
... under the table.
... behind the chair.

2 Birthday presents

This exercise teaches the names of common objects, and introduces a and an.

> *Objects:* a pen, a football, a CD, a lamp, an address book, an umbrella, a camera, a jumper, a watch. *Phrases:* Happy birthday! Thank you. Here you are. It's lovely. *Recycled language:* colours; it's.

1 Presentation of vocabulary; matching task

- Read out the new words and get students to repeat them. Focus on pronunciation of *a* (/ə rɪŋ/) and *an* (/ən ʌmˈbrelə/, /ən əˈdres bʊk/).
- Pairwork. Students decide what the presents are. Then discuss this together.

2 Listening to check

- 📼 Play the recording and establish what the presents are. Then show the photo of the unwrapped parcels on page 129 of the Teacher's Book. (Answers: see page T129.)

Write these expressions on the board:

Happy birthday	Thank you	It's lovely
Here you are	Thanks	

3 Game: giving presents

- To demonstrate the activity, give one student a 'present'. Say *Here you are. Happy birthday!* and get him or her to say *Thank you.*
- Give time for students to write the name of a present on a piece of paper. They could either choose something they know already or use a dictionary.
- Students fold their piece of paper and give their 'present' to another student.

▶ Workbook: Exercise B, Listening

> *Language note*
> We use *an* instead of *a* before words starting with a vowel (*a, e, i, o, u*). Mention this in passing here: it is focused on in Study Pages B Consolidation.

> *Presentation option*
> Teach the phrases *the red one, the blue one*, etc. to talk about the presents. It is also a good chance for students to use *I think* again.

> 📼 The tapescript is on page T19.

> *Alternatives*
> 1 Students 'give' each other real things that they have with them (e.g. a dictionary, a pen, a watch).
> 2 Ask students beforehand to bring a 'present' with them to the lesson.

3 Where's my …?

This exercise recycles vocabulary and introduces place prepositions.

> *New words:* bag, computer, desk, glasses. *Structures:* Where's …? Where are …? *Prepositions:* on, in, by, behind, under. *Recycled language:* chair, table, window, floor; jumper, watch, shoes, umbrella, camera, ball, pen.

1 Presentation of 'Where?' questions & prepositions

- Use the classroom and students to teach *bag, glasses* and *desk.*
- Look at the picture and play the part of the man. Ask *Where's my watch? (It's by the window, It's behind the chair).* Then ask *Where are my glasses? (They're on the desk, They're by the computer).*
- Show these question forms on the board:

Where's my	watch? jumper?	Where are my	glasses? shoes?

2 Practice

- Get students to ask and answer the other questions round the class:
  Where's my umbrella? It's in the bag, on the floor.
  Where are my shoes? They're on the floor, under the table.
  Where's my jumper? It's on the floor, by the window, behind the chair.

3 Pairwork game: finding objects in a picture

- Divide the class into pairs, and give each student a letter, A or B. Make sure that students only look at their own page at the back of the book.
- Students find out where their objects are by asking questions.
- Go through the questions and answers together:
  A: Where are my shoes? They're on the floor, under/by the window.
     Where's my ball? It's in the bag, under the table.
     Where are my glasses? They're on the desk, by the computer.
  B: Where's my umbrella? It's on the desk, behind the computer.
     Where are my pens? They're on the floor, under the table by the window.
     Where's my camera? It's on the chair, by the door.

▶ Workbook: Exercise C

> *Presentation option*
> Teach place prepositions before doing the exercise. Take a bag and a watch. Put the watch in the bag, by the bag, under the bag, on the table, etc.

> *Pairwork option*
> Students repeat the activity in pairs.

> *Optional preparation*
> Write all the objects students are looking for on the board, and establish what questions they should ask.

> *Optional extension*
> Students think of other objects, and 'hide' them in the picture. Other students guess where the object is by asking questions, e.g. *Is it under the desk?*

4 Precious stones

This combined Reading and Listening activity is about the appearance of precious stones and where they come from.

Note: the aim of this and later Reading and Listening activities is to expose students to authentic language slightly above their own active language level. Encourage them to try to grasp the main meaning of the reading texts without necessarily understanding every word (although afterwards you may wish to go through the texts in more detail).

Reading skills: *reading for key facts.*
Listening skills: *listening to confirm predictions.*

Key words: colours (including the new word *purple*).
Precious stones: amethyst, diamond, aquamarine, sapphire, ruby, emerald.
For comprehension: stone, sea, most, best, south, especially, hard, precious, almost, sometimes, many, country, the same, are called, east, gold, sword, necklace, brooch, bottle.

---

1 Introduction: presentation of vocabulary

● Look at the pictures. Ask students if they know what the stones are in their own language. (If the names are similar, this will be easy. If not, tell them, or let them look the words up in a dictionary.)

2 Reading & gap-filling

● Give time for students to read the texts and identify the stones. They should be able to do this without understanding every word of the texts, but if you like, let them use dictionaries to help them.

● Go through the answers together, and write the plural forms of the words on the board:

A aquamarines   B emeralds   C diamonds   D rubies, sapphires   E amethysts

● Ask a few questions round the class to check comprehension, e.g.

– What colour are emeralds?
– Where are the best emeralds?
– Which stones are from Australia?

3 Discussion: identifying stones; listening to check

● Look at the objects. Use gestures or show examples to present the words *sword, brooch, necklace* and *bottle*. Ask students to try to identify the stones in them, using the pictures at the top to help them.

● 🔲 Play the recording, pausing after each description, and check the answers:

1 diamonds and emeralds   2 diamonds   3 rubies and diamonds
4 rubies and emeralds

Note
Don't worry if students don't know all the stones. The texts will tell them about them!

Pairwork option
Students do the task in pairs. Then discuss the answers together.

Language note
The plural of *ruby* is *rubies* – like *baby–babies* and *family–families*.

Intensive reading option (single language classes)
Go through the texts, asking students to guess what the new words mean, and explaining them as you go.

🔲 Tapescript for Exercise 4: *Precious stones*

This is a gold sword, and it's from Istanbul in Turkey. And as you can see, it has lots of diamonds on it, and three very big emeralds.

Now this is a very beautiful brooch. It's from the USA. It has about a hundred very small diamonds in it.

And this necklace has rubies and diamonds in it. It's very old and it's from France.

And this is a very beautiful green bottle. It's from India, and it has red and green stones on it. The red stones are rubies and the green stones are emeralds.

---

4 Precious stones

1 Look at these precious stones. What are they called in your language?
Use a dictionary to help you.

amethyst   aquamarine   diamond

sapphire   emerald   ruby

2 Read the descriptions. Fill the blanks.

A _____ are a light blue-green colour (the name means 'sea-water'). Most _____ come from Brazil.

B The best _____ come from South America, especially Colombia. They are green in colour, and very hard.

C _____ are very hard, and also very precious. _____ have almost no colour, but they are sometimes very light yellow, blue or pink. They come from many countries, but especially Australia and South Africa.

D _____ and _____ are actually the same stone. If they are red, they are called _____ , and if they are blue they are called _____ . Most of them come from India and South-East Asia.

E _____ are a light purple colour. Most of them come from Russia, South America and India.

3 Someone talks about these four things.
Where are they from? What stones do they have in them?

1 a sword   2 a brooch   3 a necklace   4 a bottle

Study pages

Focus on ... Numbers 21–99

1 Can you guess the missing numbers?

12 twelve	20 twenty
13 thirteen	30 thirty
14 fourteen	40 forty
15 fifteen	50 fifty
16 sixteen	60 ....
17 seventeen	70 ....
18 eighteen	80 ....
19 nineteen	90 ....

2 Look at these. What comes next?

41	42	43	44	45
forty- one	forty- two	forty- three	....	....

3 Say these numbers.

21 **33** 47 56 **62** 78 94

4 Play *Bingo*.

Write ten different numbers (between 1 and 99) in the white squares.

The teacher will read out numbers.

When you hear one of your numbers, cross it out.

Sounds: I think they're sisters

1 [cassette] Listen to these sounds.

/s/   My sister is a student in France.
/θ/   – You're thirteen. Happy birthday!
        – Thank you.
/z/   He's my husband. He's from Brazil.
/ð/   This is my father, and this is my mother.

2 [cassette] Listen and practise.

Spain	think		is	mother
office	birthday		has	brother
student	three		boys	they

3 Write a sentence. Use words from both boxes.

4 Read out your sentence.

Phrasebook: Excuse me

1 Look at these people. Where are they?

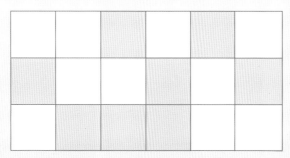

2 [cassette] Listen to the conversations. Match them with the pictures.

3 Choose one of the pictures. Practise the conversation.

Study pages B

Focus on ... *Numbers 21–99*

This exercise revises numbers 1–20 (from Unit 2 Exercise 2), and introduces numbers up to 99.

> *Key language:* numbers 21–99.
> *Recycled language:* numbers 1–20.

1 • Start by checking that students know the numbers 1 to 20.
   • Look at the numbers in Section 1, and ask students to complete the column. Answers:

   sixty, seventy, eighty, ninety

   • Point out that:
     – we add -*teen* to make numbers 13–19.
     – we add -*ty* to make *sixty, seventy*, etc.
     Point out the irregular forms: *twenty, thirty*, and the spelling of *forty* and *fifty*.

2 Look at the numbers and ask students to continue the series:

   forty-four, forty-five, forty-six, forty-seven, etc.

   If you like, give other series for students to continue, e.g.
   – twenty-one, twenty-two, ...
   – sixty-five, sixty-six, ...

3 Ask students to say the numbers:

   twenty-one, thirty-three, forty-seven, fifty-six, sixty-two, seventy-eight, ninety-four.

   If you like, ask them to write the numbers down, or tell you how to spell them on the board.

4 • Students write ten different numbers on the 'bingo card' in their book.
   • Say numbers at random. As you say the numbers, keep a check by crossing them out in the box below. When students hear one of their numbers, they cross it out in their book.
   • The first person to cross out all his/her numbers calls *Bingo!* and wins the game.

1	2	3	4	5	6	7	8	9	10
11	12	13	14	15	16	17	18	19	20
21	22	23	24	25	26	27	28	29	30
31	32	33	34	35	36	37	38	39	40
41	42	43	44	45	46	47	48	49	50
51	52	53	54	55	56	57	58	59	60
61	62	63	64	65	66	67	68	69	70
71	72	73	74	75	76	77	78	79	80
81	82	83	84	85	86	87	88	89	90
91	92	93	94	95	96	97	98	99	

Sounds: *I think they're sisters*

> The sounds /s/, /z/, /θ/ and /ð/.

1, 2 🔲 Use /s/ and /z/ to help students pronounce /θ/ and /ð/. To help them pronounce /θ/, get them to say /s/ but with their tongue between their teeth. Similarly, to produce /ð/, students could try saying /z/ with their tongue between their teeth.

3 Students write a sentence using one or more words from each box, and including any other words they like, e.g.
   – My mother is in Spain.
   – I think they are brothers.

4 Students read out their sentences in turn. Focus on the pronunciation of /s/, /z/, /θ/ and /ð/.

   Alternative: Dictation. Students dictate their sentence to the person next to them. As a check, ask students to read out the sentence they wrote down.

Phrasebook: *Excuse me*

This exercise teaches the use of Sorry *to apologise and* Excuse me *to attract attention.*

> *Key language:* Sorry, Excuse me.

1 Look at the pictures and establish where the people are:
   A in an office   B in a house or flat   C in the street
   D in a café

2 🔲 Play the recording, pausing after each conversation. Ask students which picture it is. Answers:

   1 C   2 A   3 D   4 B

   Establish when we say *Sorry* and when we say *Excuse me*:
   – *Sorry* = you've done something bad.
   – *Excuse me* = you want to attract attention.

   If possible, explain this in the students' own language. Otherwise, do it through mime (e.g. pretend to spill coffee on someone, or tread on their toe, and say *Sorry*; tap someone on the shoulder and say *Excuse me*).

3 Give students a chance to quickly practise the situations. You could do this by choosing a situation and asking two students to come to the front of the class to act it out.

🔲 Tapescript for Phrasebook: *Excuse me*

1 A Ooh, sorry!
  B Oh, that's all right.
  A No, no, I'm sorry, really.
  B It's OK.

2 A Excuse me.
  B Yes?
  A Mr Brown's on the phone.
  B Oh, OK. Excuse me just a moment.

3 A Excuse me!
  B Yes, sir?
  A A glass of water, please.
  B Certainly, sir.

4 A Excuse me ... Excuse me!
  B Oh, sorry.
  A Thank you.

Consolidation

a or an?

This exercise focuses on the use of a *and* an. *It consolidates language from the first four units, but especially from Exercise 4.2.*

Look at the examples, and establish that:
– we use *a* before most words.
– we use *an* instead of *a* if the word begins with a vowel (*a, e, i, o* or *u*).

this, that, these and those

This exercise focuses on the use of this, that, these *and* those. *This, that and these were introduced in Units 1–4; those is a new item.*

1 Look at the pictures. Establish that:
   – we use *this* and *these* for things near to us ('here'); we use *that* and *those* for things further away ('there').
   – *these* is the plural form of *this, those* is the plural form of *that*.

   Give examples by pointing to things in the classroom (e.g. *This is a book. These are books. That's a door. Those are windows.*)

2 Look at the sentences. Ask students to fill the gaps. Answers:

   a Is that your car?
   b Look, those are nice jumpers.
   c Are these your glasses?
   d Is this seat free?
   e Look! What's that?
   f Hey! Those are my cigarettes!

Review

Vowels

Review of language from Study Pages A (Focus on the alphabet).

1 Practise saying the letters.
2 In pairs, students work out the missing letters. Then go through the answer. Make sure students say the letters correctly. The sentence should read:

   Your watch is on the table behind the computer.

Male and female

Review of language from Exercises 2.1, 2.3 and 2.4.

Students write the words. Go through the answers, and write them on the board:

man	woman
boy	*girl*
father	*mother*
son	daughter
brother	*sister*
husband	wife

The verb 'to be'

Review of language from Units 1 and 3.

Remind students of the forms of the verb *to be*:

I am (I'm)	*we are (we're)*
you are (you're)	*they are (they're)*
he is (he's)	
she is (she's)	

Students fill the gaps. Then go through the answers together. Answers:

a is
b Are; aren't; are *or* 're
c is *or* 's
d isn't; is *or* 's
e are; are *or* 're
f 'm not; am *or* 'm

Consolidation

a or an?

a book

a house

an apple

a watch

a cat

a taxi

an ice-cream

a ring

an orange

an egg

an umbrella

a jumper

When do we use *a*? When do we use *an*?

this, that, these and those

This is my brother.

That's my father.

These are my children.

Those are my dogs.

1 When do we use *this* and *these*?
When do we use *that* and *those*?

2 Fill the gaps with *this*, *that*, *these* or *those*.

a Is .... your car?

b Look, ... are nice jumpers.

c Are .... your glasses?

d Is .... seat free?

e Look! What's ....?

f Hey! .... are my cigarettes!

Review

Vowels

1 How do you say these letters?

a   e   i   o   u

2 Can you read this sentence? What letters are missing?

Y••r w•tch •s •n th•
t•bl• b•h•nd th• c•mp•t•r.

Male and female

Write the missing words in the table.

....	woman
boy	....
father	....
....	daughter
brother	....
....	wife

The verb 'to be'

Fill the gaps with words from the box.

am	'm	'm not
are	're	aren't
is	's	isn't

a Excuse me, ... this your umbrella?

b – .... they from China?
– No, they .... from China. They ....
from Japan.

c – What .... your name?
– George Smith.

d Madrid .... in France. It .... in Spain.

e – Where .... my glasses?
– They .... on the table.

f – A cup of coffee, please.
– Sorry. I .... a waiter. I .... a
customer!

5 | There's …

1 Favourite places

there is/are

I Penang, Malaysia

2 Glenelg, Scotland

3 Ouro Preto, Brazil

1 Three people talk about their favourite places. Here are some of the things they say.
Can you match the sentences with the places?

a [1] 'There's a very big airport.'

b [ ] 'There are four or five hotels.'

c [ ] 'There are lots of hotels.'

d [ ] 'It's a very old town.'

e [ ] 'There's just one small shop.'

f [ ] 'There are lots of tourists.'

g [ ] 'There are lots of restaurants.'

h [ ] 'There are mountains all round.'

i [ ] 'There's a church.'

j [ ] 'There are some beautiful old churches.'

k [ ] 'It's a very small village.'

l [ ] 'There are some beautiful beaches.'

▭ Now listen and write *1, 2* or *3*.

2 Look at the sentences again. What follows *There's …* ? What follows *There are …* ?

3 What is your favourite place?
Write two or three sentences about it.

> My favourite place is …

This unit deals with basic ways of describing things in English. It introduces:
– *there is, there are, there isn't, there aren't*
– *some* and *any*
– questions with *Is there …?, Are there …?* and *How many …?*

5

1 Favourite places

In this exercise, students hear three people talk about their favourite places. Before they listen, they read sentences and predict which will be about which place. The sentences introduce structures with there is *and* there are.

➤ Focus on Form: Exercise 1
➤ Workbook: Exercise A

> *Quantity expressions:* there is/are, some, lots of.
> *Places:* town, village, building, house, shop, restaurant, hotel, church, airport.
> *Other new words:* favourite, hot, tourist.

1 Presentation of vocabulary; matching task; listening to check

● As a lead-in, teach the words *town, village* and revise *big* and *small*. Look at the pictures, and ask *Is it a big place? Is it a town or a village?*

● Read through the sentences, and present new vocabulary (some words, e.g. *tourist, shop*, may already be known). Establish the basic meaning of *there is/are* (if possible, use the students' own language).

● Discuss which place or places each sentence could describe. Note: various suggestions are possibe, e.g. *k* is probably about Glenelg, but *h* could be about all three places.

● 🔲 Play the recording and check the answers. As they listen, students mark the boxes *1, 2* or *3*. Then go through the answers together.

   1 *Penang:* a, c, f, g, l   2 *Glenelg:* e, h, i, k   3 *Ouro Preto:* b, d, j

2 Presentation of 'There is/are'

● Use the sentences to present *there is* and *there are*:

There's	a hotel an airport	There are	five hotels lots of tourists

● Ask students to make a few sentences about the place where you are now, and write them on the board. Prompt them if necessary (e.g. *What about cafés? Yes, there are lots of cafés.*).

3 Activation: writing sentences

● Working alone, students choose a place and write two or three sentences about it. The idea of this is just to activate the language they have learned, and the sentences do not have to be too ambitious.

● Ask students to read out their sentences to the class.

Language note
Instead of *lots of*, we can also say *a lot of*. We do not usually use *many* in spoken English (although we do say *not many* and *How many?* – see Exercise 3).

Alternative
Present *there is* and *there are* at the beginning, before you do the matching and listening.

Practice option
Give simple phrases that students know, and ask them to add *there is* or *there are*:
a man → there's a man
some shoes → there are some shoes

Game option
Students read out their sentences, without saying the name of the place. Other students try to guess where it is.

🔲 Tapescript for Exercise 1: *Favourite places*

1 My favourite place is Penang, in Malaysia. It's very hot, and there are some beautiful beaches. There's a big airport, there are lots of hotels, there are lots of restaurants, and there are lots and lots of tourists.

2 My favourite place is Glenelg in Scotland. It's a very small village – there's just one small shop, there's a church, and

that's all. But it's a very beautiful place. It's on the sea, and there are mountains all around.

3 My favourite place is a town called Ouro Preto in Brazil. It's not very big – there are four or five hotels, maybe. But it's a very old town, and there are lots of beautiful old buildings and some beautiful old churches.

2 Find the differences

In this exercise, students find the differences between two pictures. It introduces there isn't *and* there aren't, *and also the use of* some *and* any.

> Key language: there isn't, there aren't; a, some, any.
> Recycled language: there's, there are; vocabulary from Units 1–4.

1 Presentation of 'there isn't/aren't' & 'some/any'; practice

- Look at the pictures and read the sentences. Point out that:
  – before singular nouns, we say *There's a* or *There isn't a*.
  – before plural nouns, we say *There are some* but *There aren't any*.
- Students make sentences about the other items. Answers:
  In picture A: There are some birds. There's a book. There isn't an umbrella. There aren't any mountains.
  In picture B: There aren't any birds. There isn't a book. There's an umbrella. There are some mountains.

2 Activation: finding differences between the pictures

- In pairs, students look for other differences. Then go through the answers together, getting students to make sentences. Answers:
  In picture A: There's a tree. There's a football. There's a car. There isn't a bag. There aren't any cats.

  In picture B: There isn't a tree. There isn't a football. There's a bag. There's a taxi. There are some cats.

3 Buildings

This exercise is about about buildings and what there is in them. It introduces questions with Is there …?, Are there …? *and* How many …?, *and vocabulary for talking about buildings.*

> Key language: Is there …? Are there …? How many …?
> Parts of buildings: floor, stairs, lift, car park, library, toilet, swimming pool.
> Recycled language: restaurant, room, shop, café, teacher, computer; numbers.

1 Presentation of questions; reading & guessing task

- Look at the questions and present these question forms on the board:

Is there a	restaurant?	**Are there any**	stairs?
	swimming pool?		shops?

  Then show how we make questions with *How many …?*:

How many	stairs	**are there?**
	shops	

- Ask the questions, and get students to guess the answers. If you like, write 'class guesses' on the board.

2 Reading to check

- Read the text on page 107 and check the answers. Answers:
  There are 5 restaurants. There are nearly 2,000 stairs. There are 102 floors. There are 73 lifts. There are about 10 shops. There isn't a swimming pool. There are 7–12 rooms on each floor.

3 Presentation of vocabulary; activation: asking & answering questions

- Look at the pictures, and establish what the questions will be, e.g.
  How many teachers are there? Are there any videos? How many toilets are there? Are there any computers? Is there a café? Is there a lift? Is there a library? Is there a swimming pool? Is there a car park?
- Pairwork. Students ask each other their questions.
- As a round-up, see if students knew the answers to the questions.

➤ Focus on Form: Exercise 1
➤ Workbook: Exercise B

> **Note**
> If students find this difficult, do not insist on the correct use of *some* and *any* at this stage. It is also practised in Focus on Form Exercise 3, and it is introduced again in Unit 13.

> **Option**
> Ask students to say where the things are, e.g.
> There's a football by the tree. There's a bag under the table.
> This recycles place prepositions from Unit 4 Ex. 3.

➤ Focus on Form: Exercises 2 & 3
➤ Workbook: Exercise C, Listening

> **Reading options**
> Either read the text aloud yourself, or give time for students to read it silently.

> **Note**
> The answers include the words *hundred* and *thousand*. If you like, teach *a hundred, two hundred …* and *a thousand, two thousand …* at this point.

> **Option**
> Students make up other questions of their own, e.g.
> How many rooms are there? How many students are there?

2 Find the differences

there isn't/aren't • some & any

1 Look at the two pictures.

In picture A there's a dog.
In picture B there isn't a dog.

In picture B there are some flowers.
In picture A there aren't any flowers.

Find other differences.
Make sentences with
these words:

– birds
– book
– umbrella
– mountains

2 Can you find any
other differences?

3 Buildings

Questions • How many …?

1 These people are in the
Empire State Building
in New York.
Can you guess the
answers to their questions?

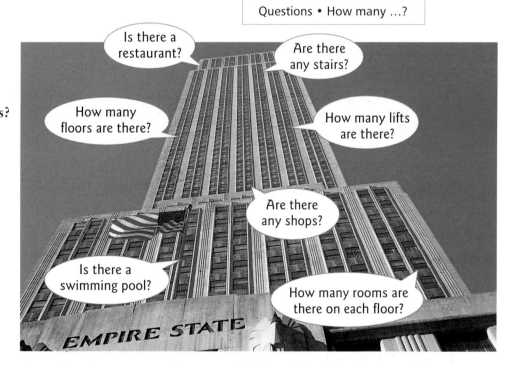

Is there a
restaurant?

Are there
any stairs?

How many
floors are there?

How many lifts
are there?

Are there
any shops?

Is there a
swimming pool?

How many rooms are
there on each floor?

EMPIRE STATE

2 Read the text on page 107, and check.

3 Think about the building where you are now.
Ask questions about these things. Do you know the answers?

Is there a … ?   Are there any … ?

How many … are there?

Focus on Form

1 there is & there are

Look at this room.

There's a phone.   There are some flowers.
There isn't a computer.   There aren't any books.

Complete these sentences.

a .... pictures.   c .... chair.
b .... lamp.   d .... boxes.

2 Yes/no questions

Make questions. What are the answers?

Is there	a computer	
	a lamp	in the room?
Are there	any flowers	
	any pictures	

Look at the pictures on page 107.

Student A: Choose one of the pictures.
Student B: Ask questions. Which picture is it?

3 How many ... are there?

Student A: Look at the street, and ask questions with *How many ...?*

Student B: Look at the street. Then close your book, and answer B's questions.

How many cars are there?   Three.

cars
people
children
buildings
buses
trees
birds

How to say it

1 [cassette] Listen to the the rhythm of these sentences.

There's a shop in the village.

There are lots of restaurants.

There isn't an airport.

How many shops are there?

2 [cassette] Listen to *there* in these phrases.

There's a ...
There are some ...
There isn't a ...
Is there a ...?

[cassette] Now listen to the sentences, and practise saying them.

There's a phone on the desk.
There are some beautiful beaches.
There isn't a lift.
Is there a toilet here?

Focus on Form

1 *there is & there are*

- Students complete the sentences. Answers:

  a There aren't any pictures.
  b There's a lamp.
  c There isn't a chair.
  d There are some boxes.

2 *Yes/no questions*

- Ask students to make questions from the table and answer them. Questions and answers:

  a Is there a computer in the room? (No)
  b Is there a lamp in the room? (Yes)
  c Are there any flowers in the room? (Yes)
  d Are there any pictures in the room? (No)

- Look at the pictures on page 107. To demonstrate the activity, choose a picture yourself and get students to guess which one it is by asking questions with *Is there / Are there?*

- Students do the exercise in pairs, taking it in turn to choose a picture.

3 *How many … are there?*

- Look at the picture and quickly check that students know what all the items are. Do *not* ask how many there are at this stage!

- Give students a short time (e.g. half a minute) to look at the picture and notice what there is in it.

- Pairwork. One student asks questions with *How many …?* The other student tries to answer them from memory, without looking at the picture. If you like, stop the activity half-way through, and ask students to change roles. Possible questions and answers:

  How many cars are there? Three.
  How many people are there? Nine.
  How many children are there? Four.
  How many buildings are there? Seven.
  How many buses are there? Two.
  How many trees are there? Four.
  How many birds are there? Five.

How to say it

1 *Stress and rhythm*

- ⌸ Play the recording, pausing and getting students to repeat the sentences. Focus on these features:
  - the stressed and unstressed parts of the sentence
  - the way the /z/ and /r/ sounds are linked to the next word in /ðeəz‿ə/ and /ðeər‿ə/
  - the reduced /ə/ sound in *a*, *an* and *of*.

2 *Pronunciation of* 'there's', 'there are', *etc. in sentences*

- ⌸ Play the phrases. Pause after each one and get students to try saying it. Focus on the links between the sounds, and the reduced /ə/ sounds.

- ⌸ Play the complete sentences. Get students to practise saying them.

2 There's one in the hall ...

1 What do you think these people are talking about?

a 'Well, there's one in the bathroom, of course, and one in the hall. And there's a big one in the living room. And there's one in the bedroom, on the door of the cupboard.'

b 'There are three. There's one on the wall just by the front door. And there's one on the table in the living room. And there's one in the bedroom, just by the bed.'

c 'There are five in the living room, and three in the kitchen, on a shelf by the window. And there's a big one on the floor in the bathroom, and five or six out on the balcony.'

plants

pictures

mirrors

phones

clocks

lamps

radios

2 Think about your own house or flat. Choose one of the objects, and make some notes.

– How many are there?
– Which rooms are they in?
– Where are they in the room?

on the floor?   on the wall?   on a shelf?

by the window?   in the corner?   .... ?

3 Talk to other students. Can they guess which object you're talking about?

3 What's your address?

1 Here's part of an address book. Find examples of these things.

country	street	last name
phone number	first name	city
post code		

2 📼 Listen to the three conversations.

There are four mistakes in the address book. Can you find them?

3 Role-play.

Student A: Tell B your address and phone number. (You can use your real one or you can make one up.)

Student B: Write down A's address and phone number. Show them to A. Are there any mistakes?

✉ Alison DALEY
Flat 2, 52 New Brighton Road,
Ealing, London W5 9QT
☎ 0181 746 9032
✉ Mario DIMAMBRO
247 Via Napoli, Genova,
Italy
☎ 656631
✉ Philip DENVER
1058 Lincoln Drive,
BOSTON 342354 USA
☎ (001) 617 584 3921

D
E
F
G
H
I
J

Focus on Form

1 there is & there are

- Students complete the sentences. Answers:

    a There aren't any pictures.
    b There's a lamp.
    c There isn't a chair.
    d There are some boxes.

2 Yes/no questions

- Ask students to make questions from the table and answer them. Questions and answers:

    a Is there a computer in the room? (No)
    b Is there a lamp in the room? (Yes)
    c Are there any flowers in the room? (Yes)
    d Are there any pictures in the room? (No)

- Look at the pictures on page 107. To demonstrate the activity, choose a picture yourself and get students to guess which one it is by asking questions with *Is there / Are there?*

- Students do the exercise in pairs, taking it in turn to choose a picture.

3 How many … are there?

- Look at the picture and quickly check that students know what all the items are. Do *not* ask how many there are at this stage!

- Give students a short time (e.g. half a minute) to look at the picture and notice what there is in it.

- Pairwork. One student asks questions with *How many …?* The other student tries to answer them from memory, without looking at the picture. If you like, stop the activity half-way through, and ask students to change roles. Possible questions and answers:

    How many cars are there? Three.
    How many people are there? Nine.
    How many children are there? Four.
    How many buildings are there? Seven.
    How many buses are there? Two.
    How many trees are there? Four.
    How many birds are there? Five.

How to say it

1 Stress and rhythm

- ▭ Play the recording, pausing and getting students to repeat the sentences. Focus on these features:

    – the stressed and unstressed parts of the sentence
    – the way the /z/ and /r/ sounds are linked to the next word in /ðeəz_ə/ and /ðeər_ə/
    – the reduced /ə/ sound in *a*, *an* and *of*.

2 Pronunciation of 'there's', 'there are', etc. in sentences

- ▭ Play the phrases. Pause after each one and get students to try saying it. Focus on the links between the sounds, and the reduced /ə/ sounds.

- ▭ Play the complete sentences. Get students to practise saying them.

6

This unit teaches students how to talk about their own and other people's homes and the things in them. It focuses on:
– rooms and furniture
– other common items in the home (e.g. clocks, pictures)
– addresses and telephone numbers.
The Reading and Listening activity is about the homes of billionaires.

1 From room to room

This exercise introduces rooms and furniture. Students listen to identify rooms and fittings in a flat, and then talk about their own home.

➤ Workbook: Exercise A

> *Rooms:* hall, living room, bedroom, bathroom, kitchen, balcony.
> *Furniture:* sofa, bed, cupboard, TV, carpet, cooker, fridge, bath, shower, toilet.

1 Introduction: presentation of rooms

- Look at the photos and the plan, and establish which rooms are shown in the pictures. Answers:

  A bedroom   B kitchen   C bathroom   D bedroom   E living room (balcony)

- Look at the advertisement. Make sure students understand *to let* (= it's empty, they want someone to live there) and *ground floor*.

2 Presentation of furniture; matching task

- Look at the photos, and ask students to match them with the words. Focus on pronunciation, especially /ˈkʌbəd/, /ˈdʌbl/ and /frɪdʒ/. Answers:

  A cupboard   B sofa   C single bed   D carpet   E bath   F cooker
  G double bed   H shower   I fridge

- Discuss which rooms they could go in. Expected answers:

  A hall or bedroom   B living room   C small bedroom   D living room or bedroom
  E bathroom   F kitchen   G big bedroom   H bathroom   I kitchen

3 Listening & sequencing task

- 🔲 Play the recording. Pause after each room, and establish where the people are and what there is in the room. Answers:

  1 hall: cupboards   2 living room: TV, sofa, table, carpet   3 balcony: table and chairs   4 bedroom: bed, cupboard   5 bedroom: bed, cupboards, TV
  6 bathroom: bath, shower, toilet   7 kitchen: cooker, fridge, cupboards

4 Activation: describing a house or flat

- To introduce this, draw a simple plan of part of your own house or flat. Then say briefly what the rooms are and what there is in them.
- Give time for students to draw a simple plan of their house or flat. Emphasise that their plan doesn't have to be very detailed or accurate.
- Pairwork. Students use their plan to tell their partner about their house/flat.

> *False beginners*
> Elicit other vocabulary for each room, e.g. *armchair, (book)shelf, desk, (wash)basin, sink, washing machine, curtains.*

> *Optional lead-in (single language classes)*
> To prepare students for the listening, talk in their own language about the situation. Discuss why the man is coming to see the flat, what he might want to know, etc.

> *Homework option*
> Students draw their plan at home and prepare to talk about it. They then show their plans in the next lesson.

🔲 Tapescript for Exercise 1: *From room to room*

A Well, this is the hall – there are two cupboards here, for coats (B: Oh yes) … And here's the living room.
B Oh good – there's a TV.
A Yes, there's a nice sofa too, and a table. And this is a new carpet.
B And that's the balcony?
A Yes, through there. It's a big balcony, again with a table and chairs.
B Mm. Nice place to eat.
A Yes … Now if we go back through here … This is the small bedroom – just a bed and a small cupboard here … And this is the big bedroom through here.
B Oh yes, a nice big bed.
A And there are cupboards here for clothes, and a small TV.
B Great. That's lovely.
A Yeah, it's a nice room. OK, so … This is the bathroom. Quite small, but there's a bath and a shower, as you can see.
B And the toilet's here.
A Yes, that's right … OK … And this is the kitchen. Again, quite small. There's a cooker here, and a fridge, and cupboards of course … And that's it.

6 Where you live

1 From room to room

TO LET
GROUND FLOOR FLAT Two bedrooms, balcony, parking. £950 a month.
Tel: 042 938048.

1 Here are two photos of a flat, and a plan of the rooms.
  Which windows can you see in the photos?

2 What are the things in the pictures? Match them with the words in the box.

bath	fridge	cupboard
carpet	sofa	single bed
cooker	shower	double bed

Which rooms do you think they're in?

3 🔲 A man comes to see the flat. What rooms does he go into?

  What is there in each room?

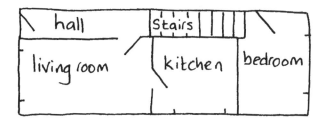

1. hall — two cupboards
2.

4 Draw a very quick plan of part of your house or flat.

  Show it to another student.
  Say what there is in the rooms.

2 There's one in the hall ...

1 What do you think these people are talking about?

   a 'Well, there's one in the bathroom, of course, and one in the hall. And there's a big one in the living room. And there's one in the bedroom, on the door of the cupboard.'

   b 'There are three. There's one on the wall just by the front door. And there's one on the table in the living room. And there's one in the bedroom, just by the bed.'

   c 'There are five in the living room, and three in the kitchen, on a shelf by the window. And there's a big one on the floor in the bathroom, and five or six out on the balcony.'

plants

pictures

mirrors

phones

clocks

lamps

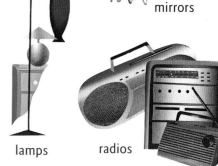

radios

2 Think about your own house or flat. Choose one of the objects, and make some notes.

   – How many are there?
   – Which rooms are they in?
   – Where are they in the room?

   on the floor?   on the wall?   on a shelf?

   by the window?   in the corner?   ....?

3 Talk to other students. Can they guess which object you're talking about?

3 What's your address?

1 Here's part of an address book. Find examples of these things.

country	street	last name
phone number	first name	city
post code		

2 🔲 Listen to the three conversations.

There are four mistakes in the address book. Can you find them?

3 Role-play.

Student A: Tell B your address and phone number. (You can use your real one or you can make one up.)

Student B: Write down A's address and phone number. Show them to A. Are there any mistakes?

✉ Alison DALEY
Flat 2, 52 New Brighton Road,
Ealing, London W5 9QT
☎ 0181 746 9032

✉ Mario DIMAMBRO
247 Via Napoli, Genova,
Italy
☎ 656631

✉ Philip DENVER
1058 Lincoln Drive,
BOSTON 342354 USA
☎ (001) 617 584 3921

D
E
F
G
H
I
J

2 There's one in the hall ...

This exercise is about common objects in the home. Students talk about objects in their own home and which rooms they are in.

➤ Workbook: Exercise B

> *Objects:* mirror, lamp, clock, phone, picture, radio, plant; shelf, corner.
> *Recycled language:* names of rooms; there is/are; place prepositions; numbers.

1 *Presentation of vocabulary; reading & matching task*

- Look at the objects, and make sure students can say them correctly. Focus especially on the pronunciation of *picture* and *mirror*.

- Read the text. Ask students what object they think each person is talking about. Expected answers:

  a mirrors *b* phones *c* plants

  Show how we can use *one* instead of a noun:

  | There's | a phone
one | in the hall. |

2 *Presentation of phrases; writing notes*

- To introduce the activity, choose one of the objects yourself. Tell the class how many there are in your home, what rooms they are in and where they are. See if students can guess what object you are talking about.

- Show the meaning of the phrases *in the corner*, *on the wall* and *on a shelf*, using the classroom or drawings on the board.

- Give time for students to think about an object and make brief notes.

3 *Guessing game: describing things in the home*

- Ask students in turn to talk about the object they chose. The rest of the class try to guess what object it is.

> *Pairwork option*
> Students do the activity in pairs. As a round-up, ask a few students what they found out from their partner.

> *Homework option*
> Students write a paragraph for homework, like the one in the example.

3 What's your address?

This exercise teaches students to understand addresses and telephone numbers in English, and to give their own.

➤ Workbook: Exercise C, Listening

> *Key vocabulary:* first name, last name, address, street, city, country, phone number, post code. *Recycled language:* numbers, letters of the alphabet.

1 *Presentation of vocabulary*

- Ask students to find examples of each of the words in the box, and use this to establish what they mean. Possible answers:

  Country: Italy, USA
  Phone number: 0181 746 9032, 656631, 001 617 584 3921
  Post code: W5 9QT, 342354
  Street: New Brighton Road, Via Napoli, Lincoln Drive
  First name: Alison, Mario, Philip
  Last name: Daley, Dimambro, Denver
  City: London, Genova, Boston

> *Presentation option*
> To check that students understand the words, ask a few questions round the class, e.g.
> What city are we in?
> What street are we in?
> What's your last name?
> What's my first name?

> *Language note*
> All the larger numbers in this exercise are expressed in individual digits, e.g.
> 9032 = nine O three two
> 1058 = one O five eight
> 584 3921 = five eight four three nine two one

2 *Listening & correcting mistakes*

- ▭ Play the recording, pausing after each exchange. Ask students to spot the mistakes. Answers:

  1 Bailey, not Daley; Brighton Road, not New Brighton Road
  2 Via Roma, not Via Napoli   3 1049, not 1058

> ▭ The tapescript is on page T29.

3 *Role-play: dictating addresses & phone numbers*

- To demonstrate the pairwork, tell the class your name, address and phone number and get them to write it down. Then ask them to dictate it back to you and write it on the board.

- In pairs, students tell each other their name, address and phone number.

4 Billionaires

This combined Reading and Listening activity is about the houses of two of the richest men in the world: Bill Gates (owner of the American software company Microsoft) and the Sultan of Brunei (ruler of the oil-rich state of Brunei in Southeast Asia). Students read short descriptions, some of which are about Bill Gates's house and some of which are about the Sultan of Brunei's palace, and decide which are which. They listen to the descriptions to check.

Reading skills: *Reading for main idea; guessing meaning from context.*
Listening skills: *Listening to a connected description; listening to check predictions.*

> *New words (reading):* billionaire, richest, world, palace, dining room, dinner party, nearly, throne, covered in, notebook, video, screen, just, show, next, can, underground, garage, lake.
> *New words (listening):* go, boat, beautiful, cost, million, interesting, everywhere, even, nice; huge, thousand, hundred, want, park, himself.

1 Introduction: presentation of vocabulary; reading & matching task

- To lead in to the activity, ask students if they know anything about the Sultan of Brunei or Bill Gates. Use this stage to introduce the key expressions *millionaire*, *billionaire*, *richest man in the world*. Then look at the pictures of where they live, and introduce the word *palace*.

- Read through the descriptions one by one. Present key language as you go (e.g. *dining room*, *throne*), but avoid dealing with every single new word. When each description is understood, ask students whether they think it is about Bill Gates's house or the Sultan's palace.

> *Paired reading option*
> Students read through the texts in pairs, using a dictionary to look up words they don't know. Then go through the texts together.

2 Listening to check

- Play the recording, pausing to give time for students to check their answers.
Answers:
Bill Gates's house: A, E, F, H, I
The Sultan's Palace: B, C, D, G

3 Extension

- Ask students which place they'd choose to spend a weekend in, and why. If you like, get a class vote on which place they'd choose.

🔲 Tapescript for Exercise 3: *What's your address?*

1 OK, my name's Alison Bailey, that's B-A-I-L-E-Y, OK? And the address is Flat 2, 52 Brighton Road – yes, B-R-I-G-H-T-O-N, Brighton Road, Ealing – E-A-L-I-N-G, and that's London W5 9QT – that's the post code. The phone number is 0181 746 9032.

2 Right. It's Mario Dimambro, D-I-M-A-M-B-R-O, Dimambro. 247 Via Roma – R-O-M-A, Genova – G-E-N-O-V-A, Italy. And the phone number: 656631. That's it.

3 Yes, Philip Denver. Philip – that's P-H-I-L-I-P, one L, and Denver, D-E-N-V-E-R. And it's a thousand and forty nine, 1-0-4-9 Lincoln Drive – L-I-N-C-O-L-N Drive, Boston, 342354, USA. Oh, the telephone? It's 001 – that's for the USA, then 617 584 3921.

🔲 Tapescript for Exercise 4: *Billionaires*

1 Bill Gates's house is on a lake, so you can go there by car or by boat. It's quite big – it has six bedrooms and about 20 other rooms. There's a big dining room, which has seats for about 100 people, and there's also a beautiful library, with lots of old books. The library also has a notebook with writing by Leonardo da Vinci, and that cost more than $30 million. And what's interesting is that there are video screens everywhere – on the walls in all the rooms, even the bathrooms – and these just show pictures – so one day you can have a Picasso, and the next day you can have a Van Gogh, and so on. So it's a nice place, and the rooms have big windows, so you can see the lake and the mountains.

2 The Sultan's Palace is huge – it has nearly 1,800 rooms, 18 lifts, and about 250 toilets. It's huge – very, very big – and some of the rooms are also very big. The dining room, for example, has seats for 4,000 people – that's a big dinner party. And there's also a throne room for the Sultan, and the walls of the throne room are covered in gold, 22-carat gold. And if you want to park your car, there's an underground garage with places for about 700 cars – the Sultan himself has 150 cars, and they're all down under the palace, in the garage.

4 Billionaires

The Sultan of Brunei

These are the two richest people in the world …

Bill Gates

… and these are the places where they live.

The Istana Nurul Iman, the Sultan of Brunei's Palace

Bill Gates's house near Seattle, USA

1 Read these descriptions. Which do you think are about the Sultan's Palace? And which do you think are about Bill Gates's house?

A There's a big dining room, which has seats for about 100 people.

B It has nearly 1,800 rooms, 18 lifts and about 250 toilets.

C The dining room has seats for 4,000 people – that's a big dinner party!

D In the throne room, the walls are covered in 22-carat gold.

E There are video screens on the walls in all the rooms. These just show pictures – so one day you can have a Picasso, and the next day you can have a Van Gogh.

F There's a library with lots of old books. It also has a notebook by Leonardo da Vinci, which cost more than $30 million.

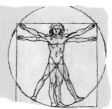

G If you want to park your car, there's an underground garage with places for about 700 cars.

H The rooms have big windows, so you can see the lake and the mountains.

I It's quite big – it has six bedrooms and about 20 other rooms.

2 🔊 Listen and check your answers.

3 Imagine you can spend the weekend at *one* of these places. Which do you choose?

Focus on ... Possessives

1 Read the captions, and complete the table.

I	........my.......
you	......your......
he	....
she	....
we	....
they	....
Peter	....
my uncle	....

My uncle's car!

This is our flat.

My aunt and uncle, and their baby. Her name is Susie.

My brother Peter on his new bike.

Peter's old bike.

2 Now write captions for this photo.

Sounds: This and these

1 Listen to these sounds.

/ɪ/ The fridge is in the kitchen.

/iː/ Three ice-creams, please.

Listen to the two sounds together.

– Excuse me. Is this seat free?

– His sister's a teacher.

2 Listen and practise.

this	is	in	six	pictures	kitchen	fridge

these three CD

please evening excuse me

3 Write a sentence. Use words from the box.

4 Read out your sentence.

Phrasebook: Can I have ...?

1 Fill the gaps. Use the words in the bubbles.

Here you are

Thank you

please

– Can I have a glass of water, ...?

– Yes, of course. ....

– ....

2 Listen to the conversation.

3 Practise the conversation. You are at a friend's flat. You want:

a cup of coffee / a glass of water / an apple / a banana / a glass of orange juice

Study pages C

Focus on ... *Possessives*

This exercise builds on the possessive forms that students already know, and introduces our, their *and noun + 's.*

> *Key language:* our, their, noun + 's.
> *Other new words:* aunt, uncle, bike.
> *Recycled language:* my, your, his, her.

1 ● Look at the picture and read the captions. Ask students to find the missing words for the table, and build it up on the board:

I	*my*
you	*your*
he	*his*
she	*her*
we	*our*
they	*their*
Peter	*Peter's*
my uncle	*my uncle's*

● Focus on the new forms, *our* and *their*. If necessary, give other examples to show how they are used (e.g. <u>We</u> have a dog – it's <u>our</u> dog. <u>They</u> have a dog – it's <u>their</u> dog).

● Show how we form possessives from nouns by adding 's. Give other examples of your own, and write them on the board, e.g.

Anna	→	*Anna's room*
my mother	→	*my mother's friends*
the teacher	→	*the teacher's book*

2 ● Look at the picture together and establish what there is in it: *a garden, an old man in a chair, a dog, a young woman, a young man, a motorbike.*

● Ask students to imagine that this is 'their' photo – either they are one of the people in it, or it shows people they know. Give time for them to write captions for it like those in the other picture. They could do this alone or in pairs or groups. Example answers:
  – This is my friend Maria. Maria's friend Matteo. This is Matteo's motorbike. Maria's father and his dog.
  – Our house. My father and his dog. My brother Alex and his girlfriend. This is their motorbike.

● Ask students to read out their captions. Focus on the way they use possessive forms, and improve their sentences if necessary.

Sounds: *This and these*

> Contrast between the vowels /ɪ/ and /iː/.

1, 2 ▭ If students have problems, focus on these features:
  – /iː/ is a long sound, /ɪ/ is a short sound.
  – for /iː/ you spread your lips, for /ɪ/ less so.
  – for /ɪ/ the tongue is little lower and further back than for /iː/.

3 Students write a sentence using words from the box, and including any other words they like, e.g.
  – Excuse me, is this the kitchen?
  – My brother has three CDs.

4 Students read out their sentences in turn. Focus on the pronunciation of /ɪ/ and /iː/.

Alternative: Dictation. Students dictate their sentence to the person next to them. As a check, ask students to read out the sentence they wrote down.

Phrasebook: *Can I have ...?*

This exercise teaches students to ask for things, to give them, and to say please *and* thank you.

> *Key language:* Can I have ...? Here you are.
> *Recycled language:* please, thank you.

1 ● To introduce the expression *Can I have ...?*, ask a few students for things (e.g. *Can I have that book, please? Can I have a pen? Can I have your bag, please?*).

● Look at the picture and establish the situation (the people are at a table, one wants a glass of water).

● Ask students to fill the gaps in the dialogue. (Answer: see tapescript.)

2 ▭ Play the recording to check.

3 ● Look at the other items and practise saying them.

● Students practise having conversations. You could ask one or two students to do this in front of the class first, and then let all the students practise in pairs.

> ▭ Tapescript for Phrasebook: *Can I have ...?*
>
> A Can I have a glass of water, please?
> B Yes, of course. Here you are.
> A Thank you.

Consolidation

Singular and plural

This exercise focuses on plural forms of nouns. It consolidates language introduced in Exercise 2.1 and Exercise 4.3.

- Use the examples to present rules for plurals:
  - To make a noun plural, we usually add *-s* (pronounced /s/ or /z/).
  - After some words (ending in *-x*, *-s*, *-ch* and *-sh*), we add *-es* (pronounced /ɪz/).
  - *-y* changes to *-ies* (pronounced /ɪz/).
- Students write the words in the plural. Then go through the answers, and write them on the board. Answers:

  tables, countries, boys, beaches, universities, books, glasses, watches, airports, students

a and the

Nouns with both a *and* the *have appeared in earlier units:*
– nouns with a: *2.1, 3.2, Unit 5*
– nouns with the: *4.1, 4.3*
– nouns with a *and* the: *6.1, 6.2.*
The purpose of this exercise is to show examples of how we use a *and* the.

- Look at the examples. If students have a similar article system in their own language (e.g. French *un journal*, *le journal*; German *eine Zeitung*, *die Zeitung*), refer to it.

  If students have no article system in their own language, try to let them 'feel' the difference from the examples rather than giving long explanations. But it may be worth pointing out (using the students' own language):
  - *a* roughly means 'one': we use *a* especially when we mention things for the first time.
  - *the* means 'the one we know about': we use *the* to talk about things we can see, or which are well-known.
- Do the exercise in pairs or round the class. Answers:

  a a cat   *b* the door   *c* a student   *d* a bottle, the fridge
  e a clock

First, second, third …

This exercise teaches ordinal numbers referring to floors in a building. It builds on language taught in Exercise 6.1.
Note: These numbers are practised again in Study Pages H.

- Look at the building and remind students of the flat on the ground floor in Exercise 6.1.
- Get students to read out the other floors (*first* to *fifth*), focusing on pronunciation. If you like, write the numbers on the board.
- Ask students to guess the other numbers, and write them on the board:

sixth
seventh
eighth
ninth
tenth
- To activate the language, ask round the class: *Who has a flat on the ground floor? Who has a flat on the first floor?*, etc.

Review

Where …?

Review of Where? *questions and place prepositions from Exercise 4.3.*

- Look at the picture. Get a student to ask a question, and a different student to answer it. Answers:

  Where's the man? He's by the car.
  Where's the woman? She's in the car.
  Where's the cat? It's under the car.
  Where are the children? They're behind the car.
  Where are the birds? They're on the car.
- Students practise asking and answering the questions in pairs.

Vocabulary

Review of jobs (Exercises 1.1, 2.4, 3.1), colours (Exercise 2.4, Study Pages A, Exercise 4.1); family (Exercise 2.3, Study Pages C).

- Working alone or in pairs, students think of words to add to the lists and write them down.
- Go through the answers together, and write the words on the board. If you like, ask students to spell them. Expected answers:

  a teacher, student, waiter, singer
  b green, red, black, white, brown, grey, yellow
  c son, brother, sister, uncle, aunt

Consonants

Review of letters from Study Pages A (The alphabet).

1 Practise saying the letters.
2 In pairs, students work out the missing letters. Then go through the answers. Make sure students say the letters correctly. Answers:

Idea for further practice
Play 'Hangman'. Think of a word that students know, and write a line for each letter (so '*teacher*' would be '_ _ _ _ _ _ _'). Students suggest letters. When they suggest one correctly, write it in its place. The winner is the first person to guess the word. For each false guess, you can also add one line to a gallows, as in the picture.

Consolidation

Singular and plural

Singular		*Plural*	
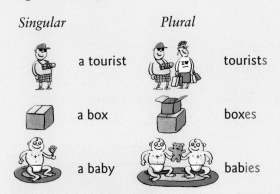 a tourist		tourists	
a box		boxes	
a baby		babies	

Make these words plural.

table	country	boy	beach	university
book	glass	watch	airport	student

a and the

Can I have a paper, please?

Where's the paper?

My father's a teacher.
My mother's a teacher too.

Sh! Here's the teacher.

Is there a library in this town?

Sorry – the library's closed.

Choose a or the.

a I have two dogs and $^a_{the}$ cat.

b – Where's my umbrella? – It's by $^a_{the}$ door.

c My sister's 18. She's $^a_{the}$ student.

d I think there's $^a_{the}$ bottle of water in $^a_{the}$ fridge.

e – Here you are – happy birthday.

 – Oh, it's $^a_{the}$ clock! Thanks!

First, second, third …

Look at this building. Can you label floors 6–10?

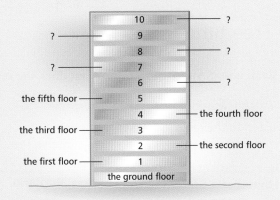

Review

Where …?

Ask and answer questions with *Where* …?

Ask about

– the man
– the woman
– the cat
– the children
– the birds.

Vocabulary

Add words to these lists.

a police officer, taxi driver, ...

b orange, pink, blue, ...

c mother, father, daughter, ...

Consonants

1 How do you say these letters?

b d f j l m n p r t w

2 What are the missing letters?

7 Things people do

1 Free time

Present simple

1 Read about Annabelle Smith. What does she say? Use phrases from the box.

watch television	read a newspaper	have a sandwich	play table tennis
listen to the radio	go to the shops	talk to my friends	look out of the window

Annabelle Smith is from London, England.
She's 22 years old, and she's a computer programmer.

When I'm on a bus ...

... I ___ or ___ .

Sometimes I just ___ .

In my lunchbreak ...

... I go to a café with some friends, and we ___ .

Then we usually ___ or sometimes I ___ .

When I'm ill in bed ...

... I ___ or ___ . And I sleep a lot!

2 Three other people talk about what they do.
What do you think they say? Use the red verbs.

Speaker 1: **When I'm on a bus ...**

a magazine   *a computer game*   *music*

Speaker 2: **In my lunchbreak ...**

a burger   *the park*   *football*

Speaker 3: **When I'm ill in bed ...**

a book   *videos*   *cards*

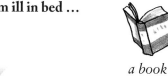 Listen and check your answers.

3 Choose one of the situations. Say what you do.

7

This unit introduces common verbs in the Present simple for talking about habits and about likes and dislikes. It focuses on:
– common verbs for talking about habits
– the verb *like*
– positive forms (1st and 3rd person singular)
– negative forms (1st and 3rd person singular).

1 Free time

This exercise is about things people do in their free time. It introduces a number of common phrases using activity verbs (e.g. play football, read a newspaper, watch television*). In this exercise, these verbs are used in the 1st person singular only, so they can be taught as vocabulary rather than as grammatical structures.*

➤ Workbook: Exercise A

Verbs: go, have, listen, look, play, read, talk, watch.
Other new words: sandwich, newspaper, magazine, table tennis, lunchbreak, music, ill, burger, park, cards; out of; sometimes, usually.

---

1 Presentation of verbs & other vocabulary; reading task

● Look at the text about Annabelle Smith. Establish what phrase goes with each picture. If necessary, use gestures and mime to make the meaning of the verbs clear. Answers:

When I'm on a bus, I *read a newspaper* or *talk to my friends*. Sometimes I just *look out of the window*.
In my lunchbreak … we *have a sandwich*. Then we usually *play table tennis* or sometimes I *go to the shops*.
When I'm ill in bed, I *watch television* or *listen to the radio* …

2 Practice: making sentences

● Look at the pictures and ask students to choose verbs to go with them. Answers:

1 *read* a magazine; *play* a computer game; *listen to* music.
2 *have* a burger; *go to* the park; *play* football.
3 *read* a book; *watch* videos; *play* cards.

● 🔲 Play the recording to check. Focus on the words *usually* and *sometimes*:

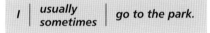

| I | usually / sometimes | go to the park. |

Note
Usually and *sometimes* are practised in Study Pages D Consolidation (page 39).

---

3 Activation: talking about free time

● Choose a situation, and get responses round the class. Either ask a question (*What do you do in your lunchbreak?*) or simply prompt students by giving the situation (*OK, in your lunchbreak … Yes, Juan? … What about you, Anna?*).

🔲 Tapescript for Exercise 1: *Free time*

1 Well, when I'm on a bus, I usually read a magazine, or sometimes I play a computer game, or maybe listen to music.

2 In my lunchbreak? Oh, sometimes I have a burger – maybe go to the park. Sometimes I play football after lunch.

3 Well, when I'm ill in bed, usually I just read a book, maybe, or watch videos, or if a friend's there, I play cards, maybe.

2 Friends

This exercise is based on a poem about two friends and what they like. It introduces like *in the 1st and 3rd person singular, and opposite pairs of adjectives.*

> *Adjectives:* hot, cold; new, old; long, short; weak, strong; high, low; fast, slow.
> *Other new words:* like, wear; friend, daytime, night, hair, tea, heel.

➤ Focus on Form: Exercise 1
➤ Workbook: Exercises B & C

1 Vocabulary task; presentation of adjectives

- Working alone or in pairs or groups, students look up the words in a dictionary and find the opposite pairs.
- Look at the words together and build up a list of opposite adjectives on the board:

high	low	old	new
cold	hot	short	long
slow	fast	strong	weak

  Use gestures, simple examples and (if possible) the students' own language to make the meaning of the words clear.

> *Alternative*
> Simply present the words, building them up on the board to show pairs of opposites.

2 Reading & gap-filling; listening to check

- Introduce *I like* with a simple example, e.g. tell the class: *I like chocolate – it's nice, I like it* (lick your lips).
- Read the poem, presenting new words as you go (use the illustration to help you). Pause at each gap, and ask students what word to put in it.
- 🔲 Play the recording to check. (Answer: see tapescript.)

> 🔲 The tapescript is on page T34.

3 Grammar focus; presentation of -s ending

- Students complete the table. Write it on the board:

I like	He likes
I wear	He wears
I have	He has

4 Activation: writing sentences

- Ask students to think of someone they know and to write sentences about them, using *likes*, *has* or *wears*.
- In turn, students read out their sentences, and say who they are about.

> *Homework option*
> Students write the sentences for homework, and read them out in the next lesson.

3 I don't smoke

This exercise presents positive and negative sentences about habits and abilities. It introduces the Present simple negative, 1st and 3rd person singular.

> *New verbs:* smoke, eat, drink, speak.
> *Other new words:* meat, alcohol, piano, German.

➤ Focus on Form: Exercise 2
➤ Workbook: Exercise D, Listening

1 Presentation of 'I don't' + verb; choosing between true/false sentences

- Use the examples to show how to form the Present simple negative with *I*. Point out that *I don't = I do not*:

  I + don't + verb

I	don't	smoke
		eat meat

- Read through the pairs of sentences, presenting the new words.
- Working alone, students decide which sentences are true of them.
- Pairwork. Students tell each other their answers.

2 Presentation of 'he/she doesn't' + verb; practice: making sentences

- Show how to form the negative with *He/She*. Point out that *He doesn't = He does not*:

  He/She + doesn't + verb

He		
She	doesn't	smoke
		eat meat

- Ask students to say how they are different from their partner.

> *Language note*
> We form the negative with *do/does* + *not* followed by the infinitive (the basic form of the verb). So in *She doesn't smoke*, *do* changes to *does*, but *smoke* doesn't change. If you like, explain this to the class using their own language.

3 Game: guessing facts about a person

- Together, choose a person you know. This could be another teacher, someone else in your school, or someone who is absent from the class. Either let students write their guesses and then discuss them together, or discuss them straight away and build up a list of 'class guesses' on the board.
- During the break, or before the next lesson, find out if the guesses are correct.

> *Alternative*
> Ask students to make guesses about you. In this case you should sit at the back of the class and let students organise the discussion, so that it is realistic for them to use *He/She*.

2 Friends

verb + s

1 Find opposites in the table. Use a dictionary.

high	weak
cold	long
slow	hot
old	low
short	fast
strong	new

2 Fill the gaps in the poem.

🔲 Now listen to the poem.

3 Look at the poem and complete the table.

I like	He ....
I	He wears
I have	He ....

4 Write about a friend or someone in your family.

My sister has long black hair. She wears jeans. She likes pizza.

Friends

John likes black coffee, I like white.
I like daytime, John likes night.
I like .... showers, he likes cold ones.
I wear new clothes, he wears .... ones.

John has .... hair, I have long.
I like weak tea, he likes ....
I wear high heels, he wears .... ones.
He likes .... cars, I like slow ones.

Why are we friends? Because, you see,
I like him, but he likes me.

3 I don't smoke

don't & doesn't

1 Which sentences are true of you? Write ticks (✓) in the boxes.

Tell your partner your answers.

2 How are you different from your partner? Tell other students.

She wears glasses. I don't wear glasses.

I drink alcohol. He doesn't drink alcohol.

1	☐ I smoke.	☐ I don't smoke.
2	☐ I eat meat.	☐ I don't eat meat.
3	☐ I play tennis.	☐ I don't play tennis.
4	☐ I wear glasses.	☐ I don't wear glasses.
5	☐ I drink alcohol.	☐ I don't drink alcohol.
6	☐ I play the piano.	☐ I don't play the piano.
7	☐ I speak German.	☐ I don't speak German.

3 Choose someone you all know. What do you think his/her answers are? Write down your guesses.

Now find out the answers!

1 She doesn't smoke.
2 She eats meat.
3

Focus on Form

1 Verb + s

I You We They + verb	He She It + verb + s

I speak French.	She speaks French.
You like pizza.	He likes pizza.
We play football.	He ....
They drink coffee.	She ....
My parents live in London.	My father ....

> **Note:**
> have → he has   do → she does
> watch → he watches   go → she goes

Talk about these two people.

> I'm Spanish. I live in Valencia. I work in a school. I teach English. At the weekend I play tennis, I read and I watch football.

> I'm Spanish. I live in Valencia. I work in a bank. I have a car, but I walk to work. At the weekend I go out with friends and I play tennis.

He ...   They ...   She ...

2 don't & doesn't

I You We They + don't + verb

don't
I smoke → I ⟨ smoke → I don't smoke

I drink coffee.	→	I ....
We like pizza.	→	We ....

He She It + doesn't + verb

doesn't
He smokes → He ⟨ smokes → He doesn't smoke

She speaks French.	→	She ....
John likes pizza.	→	John ....

Complete the sentences.

a My boyfriend smokes, but I _don't smoke_
b I speak English, but my parents ....
c My father has a car, but my brother ....
d I like football, but my girlfriend ....
e Dogs like water, but cats ....

> **Note:**
> don't = do not   doesn't = does not

How to say it

1 🔊 Listen to the -s ending. Practise saying the sentences.

He lives in London.
She has a good car.
She likes pizza.
He smokes a lot.
She wears glasses.
He speaks English.

2 🔊 Listen to the /nt/ sound in *don't* and *doesn't*. Practise saying the sentences.

We don't go to church.
I don't like dogs.
He doesn't smoke.
He doesn't take sugar in coffee.
I don't speak German.
They don't drink beer.

Focus on Form

1 Verb + -s

- Students complete the table. Answers:
  He plays football.
  She drinks coffee.
  My father lives in London.

- Point out that:
  – we only add -s in the 3rd person singular:
  He *plays* football.
  Alex *plays* football.
  but: They *play* football.
  – *watch*, *do* and *go* add -*es* instead of -*s*.
  – *have* is irregular: it becomes *has*.

- Read through the bubbles, then ask students to talk about the two people. Build up the verbs on the board. Expected answers:

  They are both Spanish. They live in Valencia.

  He works in a school. He teaches English. At the weekend he plays tennis, reads and watches football.

  She works in a bank. She has a car, but she walks to work. At the weekend she goes out with friends and she plays tennis.

2 don't & doesn't

- Look at the examples with *don't*. Show how we add *don't* before the verb.

- Students complete the table. Answers:

  I don't drink coffee.
  We don't like pizza.

- Look at the examples with *doesn't*. Show how we add *doesn't* before the verb, and the verb drops the -*s*.

- Students complete the table. Answers:

  She doesn't speak French.
  John doesn't like pizza.

- Students complete the sentences. Answers:

  b ... my parents don't speak English.
  c ... my brother doesn't have a car.
  d ... my girlfriend doesn't like football.
  e ... cats don't like water.

How to say it

1 Pronunciation of -s endings

- 🔲 Play the recording, pausing and getting students to repeat the sentences. Point out the /z/ (*lives*, *has*) and /s/ (*likes*, *smokes*) sounds, but do not make too much of it, as the difference is slight. Focus more on the way the *s* links with the next sound: /lɪvz‿ɪn/, /hæz‿ə/, and /sməʊks‿ə lɒt/, /spiːks‿ɪŋglɪʃ/.

2 Reduced vowels in unstressed syllables

- 🔲 Play the recording. Pause after each sentence and get students to practise saying it. Focus on the /nt/ sound and the way it links with the following sound (e.g. /dʌznt‿teɪk/.

🔲 Tapescript for Exercise 2: *Friends*

John likes black coffee, I like white.
I like daytime, John likes night.
I like hot showers, he likes cold ones.
I wear new clothes, he wears old ones.

John has short hair, I have long.
I like weak tea, he likes strong.
I wear high heels, he wears low ones.
He likes fast cars, I like slow ones.

Why are we friends? Because, you see,
I like him, but he likes me.

8

This unit covers a range of vocabulary connected with food and drink:
– basic types of food (e.g. *rice, fish, fruit, potatoes*), and the verb *eat*
– names of drinks (e.g. *milk, coffee*) and the verb *drink*
– things on the table (e.g. *plate, knife, glass, salt*)
– asking for things in restaurants or cafés using *Can I have …?* and *I'd like …*
The Reading and Listening activity is about fast food.

1 Food …

This exercise begins with a crossword introducing common types of food. Students then hear people from different countries saying what kind of food they eat, as a preparation for talking about the food they eat themselves.

> ➤ Workbook: Exercise A

> *Food*: fruit, vegetables, salad, rice, bread, meat, fish, eggs, cheese, pasta, oil, beans, potatoes.   *Recycled language:* eat.

1 Presentation of food; completing a crossword

● Use the pictures to establish the meaning of *fruit*, *vegetables* and *salad*. Then either:

 – do the crossword with the class, trying to elicit words from the students and presenting those that they don't know;
 – or let students try to do the crossword alone or in groups, using a dictionary to help them, and then go through the answers together.

 Answers:
 1 cheese   (2 fruit)   (3 vegetables)   4 bread   5 rice   6 fish   7 eggs
 8 *across* pasta   8 *down* potatoes   9 meat   10 beans   (11 salad)   12 oil

2 Identifying food from pictures

● Look at the bags of shopping and ask students what they can see in each one. Use this to activate the words they have just learned.

3 Listening & matching task

● 🔊 Play the recording. Pause after each person and ask students to match them with the pictures. Discuss what country they think they are from. Answers:

 1 B (Thailand)   2 D (Egypt)   3 C (Britain)   4 A (Italy)

4 Activation: writing a list

● Working alone, students think of what they eat a lot of in their own family, and write a list. They can limit themselves to words they know, or use dictionaries to help them.

● Write this structure on the board:

We eat	a lot of …
	quite a lot of …

 Ask different students to tell the others what they eat and drink in their family. Present any new words that students use.

Homework preparation option
Ask students to do the crossword at home before the lesson, using a dictionary to help them. Then go through the answers in class and present the new vocabulary.

Language note
Eggs, *vegetables*, *beans* and *potatoes* are plural nouns. All the other items are non-count nouns used in the singular (e.g. we say *fruit*, not *fruits*). Point this out if there are differences in the students' own language. Count and non-count nouns are taught systematically in Unit 13.

Vocabulary option
It is enough for students to use the words *fruit* and *vegetables*, rather than identify particular types. But if students are interested, you could teach the names of particular fruit and vegetables (e.g. *pepper, carrot, cauliflower, onion; lemon, grape, banana, apple*).

Language note
A lot of has exactly the same meaning as *lots of* (see Unit 5). However, we cannot use *quite* with *lots of*.

🔊 Tapescript for Exercise 1: *Food …*

1 We eat a lot of rice, we eat rice every day. We eat a lot of fish, a lot of vegetables, and we eat a lot of fruit.
2 We eat quite a lot of bread, and also rice and beans. We sometimes eat meat. We eat a lot of vegetables, and we eat a lot of fruit.
3 We eat a lot of bread, eggs, cheese. We eat a lot of meat, a lot of potatoes and other vegetables. And quite a lot of fruit.
4 We eat a lot of pasta, olive oil, quite a lot of salad and vegetables. But we eat also fish and cheese.

🔊 Tapescript for Exercise 3: *Waiter!*

A Can I have a knife and fork, please?
B I'm very sorry. Yes, of course, sir.
C And I'd like some ketchup, please.
B Ketchup, yes, certainly.

8 Food and drink

1 Food …

1 Look at the pictures and complete the crossword.
  Use a dictionary to help you.

2 Look at these bags of shopping. What food can you see?

3 [cassette] Four people say what they eat.
  Listen and match them with the bags of shopping.

  What countries do you think the people are from?

4 What do you eat in your family? Write a list.

  Show the list to your partner.

2 ... and drink

1 Match the drinks with the pictures.

water	milk shake
milk	lemonade
tea	Coca-Cola
coffee	beer
fruit juice	wine

2 Write the drinks in four lists.

> LIST 1 I drink this every day.

> LIST 2 I often drink this, but not every day.

> LIST 3 I sometimes drink this, but not often.

> LIST 4 I never drink this.

Show your lists to your partner.

3 Which are the top three drinks in the class?

3 Waiter!

1 🔲 Listen to the conversation and fill the gaps.

2 Here are three more tables in the restaurant. What do you think the people want?

3 *Role-play.* Work in threes. Have the conversations.

2 ... and drink

This exercise is an informal survey of the most popular drinks in the class. It introduces the names of drinks, and also frequency adverbs.

➤ Workbook: Exercise B

> *Drinks:* water, milk, tea, coffee, fruit juice, milk shake, lemonade, Coca-cola, beer, wine. *Frequency expressions:* often, sometimes, never; every day.

1 *Presentation of drinks; matching task*

- Go through the words in the list, and see how many students can identify in the pictures (many will be known already or easy to guess). Answers (left – right): Coca-Cola, coffee, fruit juice, lemonade, water; wine, milk shake, tea, beer, milk

2 *Presentation of frequency adverbs; writing a list*

- Look at the list headings, and write these structures on the board to present frequency adverbs:
- Working alone, students write drinks in the four lists.

| I | often
sometimes
never | drink Coca-cola. |

I drink Coca-cola every day.

- Pairwork. Students read out their lists to their partner.

3 *Class survey: favourite drinks*

- Ask students round the class which drinks they drink every day. Write these on the board, and keep a 'score' to see which are the most popular drinks.

> *Vocabulary option*
> Ask students what else they drink, and add other names to the list.
> Apart from trade names (e.g. *Fanta*, *7-up*), other words that may be useful are *mineral water* (as opposed to *ordinary* or *tap water*), and particular types of fruit juice, e.g. *apple juice*, *orange juice*.

3 Waiter!

This exercise introduces vocabulary for things on the table (e.g. knife, fork, glass, salt). It also gives practice in asking for things.

➤ Workbook: Exercise C, Listening

> *New words:* knife, fork, spoon, glass, plate; salt, pepper, sugar, ketchup.
> *Expressions:* Can I have ...? I'd like ...

1 *Presentation of vocabulary; listening & gap-filling*

- Look at the small pictures, and get students to say the words. Focus on pronunciation, especially of /sɒlt/ and /'sʊgə/.
- Look at the first picture of the restaurant, and discuss what the people want.
- 🔲 Play the recording, and establish what the people say. Answers:
  Can I have a knife and fork, please?
  And I'd like some ketchup, please.

2 *Activation: interpreting pictures*

- Look at the picture of the three tables. Establish what people want, and what they might say. Possible answers:
  Table 1: Can I have a fork, please? I'd like a spoon, please.
  Table 2: I'd like a plate, please. Can I have some sugar, please?
  Table 3: Can I have some pepper, please? I'd like a glass, please.

3 *Role-play: asking for things in a restaurant*

- Write these structures on the board:

Can I have ... , please?
I'd like ... , please.

- Divide the class into groups of three (two customers and a waiter). Groups act out the conversations.

> *Language note*
> Some of the items are count nouns: so we say *a glass, a knife, a plate.*
> Some are non-count nouns: so we say *some salt, some pepper, some ketchup.*
> Count and non-count nouns are focused on in Unit 13.

> *Language note*
> *I'd like* (= *I would like*) is a polite way of saying *I want*. Students should learn it simply as a set phrase. It is practised further in Study Pages E Consolidation.

> 🔲 The tapescript is on page T35.

> *Role-play idea*
> Divide the class into groups of three or four as if they are in a restaurant, with each group sitting at one table. Choose one or two students to be waiters, with each waiter serving a few tables. The 'customers' call their waiter and ask for things that they need.

4 Fast food

This combined Reading and Listening activity is about fast food restaurants. In the listening, three people order food from the menu.

Reading skills: *Reading for specific information; understanding a menu.*
Listening skills: *Following a conversation.*

> *New words (text):* fast food, kind of, chips, everywhere, around, more than, includes, put, biggest, cook, French fries, probably.
>
> *New words (menu and listening):* bun, hamburger, cheeseburger, chilli, slice, chicken nuggets, pieces, dessert, apple pie, vanilla, strawberry, chocolate.

1 *Reading & answering questions; presentation of vocabulary*

- Look at the questions and give examples to make sure students understand the word *company*.
- Ask students to read the text and find answers to the questions.
- Discuss the answers together. Answers:

  a More than 13 million   *b* McDonalds   *c* In the Middle East
  d Kentucky Fried Chicken

- Read through the text together, making sure that students understand it.

Optional lead-in
Write the words *McDonald's*, *Pizza Hut*, *Kentucky Fried Chicken* and *Burger King* on the board. Ask students what food they sell.

2 *Discussion: fast food restaurants*

- Talk about each company in turn. Ask students if there is a restaurant in the town where you are, and also (if this is different) near the town where the students live.

3 *Reading & presentation of vocabulary*

- Read through the menu, making sure that students understand it (this should be easy as most items are illustrated). Focus on the words *small* and *large*, and the flavours *vanilla*, *strawberry* and *chocolate*.

Language note
French fries is American English, but is also used in Britain in fast food restaurants. *Chips* is the usual British English word (as in *fish and chips*).

4 *Listening*

- 🔲 Play the recording. Students listen and mark the items people order on the menu.
- Play the recording again. Pause after each section and check the answers. Answers:

  1 Two cheeseburgers, one large French fries, a small diet Coke.   £4.80.
  2 One big burger bonanza, a cup of coffee.   £3.20.
  3 Two children's meals: one chicken nuggets and Fanta, one pizza slice and Coke.   £5.20.

5 *Extension: role-play*

- Ask students to imagine they are in the restaurant. Give them time to choose something from the menu, then ask a few students to order something.

Role-play option
Students sit in groups. Each group is in a fast-food restaurant, with one person taking the orders. The others in the group choose what they want, order it, and pretend to pay for it.

🔲 Tapescript for Exercise 4: *Fast food*

1 A Two cheeseburgers, please ...
   B Two cheeseburgers ...
   A ... and one French fries.
   B Is that small or large?
   A Large, please. And a diet Coke – small.
   B OK. Any dessert?
   A No, that's all, thanks.
   B OK, that's four eighty, please.

2 B Yes please?
   C The hot chilli burger – is that very hot?
   B It's quite hot, yes.
   C OK, I'll have the big burger bonanza then, please.

   B A big burger bonanza. OK ... anything else?
   C Just a cup of coffee, please.
   B OK, that's three twenty, please.

3 B Yes please?
   D The children's meals – what do you get?
   B They come with a small French fries and a small drink.
   D OK, so ...
   E Nuggets and Fanta!
   F Pizza slice and Coke!
   D Two children's meals, please. One chicken nuggets and Fanta, and one pizza slice and Coke.
   B Pizza slice, Coke. Anything else?
   D No, that's all, thanks.
   B OK. Five twenty, please.

4 Fast food

Reading and listening activity

1 Read the text and find out:

  a How many people eat at Burger King every day?
  b Which company is the biggest?
  c Where do people eat falafel?
  d Which company has 200 restaurants in China?

2 Do these companies have a restaurant near you?

THERE'S A *FAST FOOD* RESTAURANT NEAR YOU

Every country has its own kind of fast food – fish and chips in Britain, pizza in Italy, falafel in the Middle East. But some kinds of fast food are everywhere these days.

BURGER KING has around 10,000 restaurants in 56 countries. Every day more than 13 million people eat at a Burger King restaurant .

KENTUCKY FRIED CHICKEN has more than 9,000 restaurants around the world. This includes more than 200 restaurants in China.

PIZZA HUT puts 160 million kilos of cheese on its pizzas every year. There are more than 10,000 Pizza Hut restaurants around the world.

McDONALD'S is the biggest of them all. There are 22,000 McDonald's restaurants in 109 countries – that includes 13,000 in the USA and around 1;500 in Japan. McDonald's cook three million kilos of French fries every day.

That's a lot of restaurants – there's probably one near you.

3 Look at this fast food menu. Do you understand it all?

In a bun

Hamburger		1.20
Cheeseburger		1.40
HOT Chilli Burger		1.60
BIG Burger Bonanza		2.25

In a box

Fish Pieces		1.50
Pizza Slice		1.25
Chicken Nuggets		
	6 pieces	1.00
	12 pieces	1.80

French fries

Small	0.75
Large	1.30

Children's meals

Hamburger	2.60
Cheeseburger	2.60
Chicken Nuggets	2.60
Pizza Slice	2.60
Fish Pieces	2.60

Desserts

Apple Pie	0.80
with ice-cream	1.20
Ice-cream *vanilla • strawberry • chocolate*	0.80

Cold drinks

Coke, Diet Coke, Sprite, Fanta	
small	0.70
large	1.10
Milk Shakes *vanilla • strawberry • chocolate*	1.20
Orange Juice	1.20

Hot drinks

Tea	0.60
Hot Chocolate	0.95
Coffee	0.95

4 Three customers order food and drink. What do they order? How much do they pay?

5 Imagine you're in the restaurant. What do you order?

D Study pages

Focus on ... Telling the time

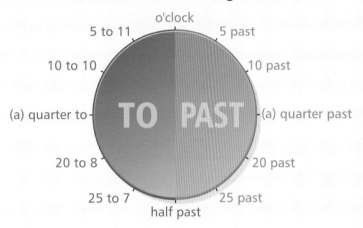

o'clock
5 past
5 to 11
10 past
10 to 10
TO PAST
(a) quarter to
(a) quarter past
20 to 8
20 past
25 to 7
25 past
half past

1 Look at the clocks. What's the time?

It's 8 o'clock.   It's half past 4.   It's (a) quarter to 6.   It's 10 past 7.   It's 25 to 11.

It's ....

2 We can also do this:

It's half past four. It's four thirty.

It's twenty to six. It's five forty.

What time is it on these clocks?

3 Think of a TV programme you watch. Say when it starts and when it finishes.

> I watch Star Trek. It starts at ten past eight and it finishes at nine o'clock.

> I watch the news. It starts at six o'clock and it finishes at quarter past six.

Sounds: Bread, cake and wine

1 🔊 Listen to these sounds.

/e/ They eat eggs, vegetables and bread.
/eɪ/ They play table tennis.
/aɪ/ I like rice.

2 🔊 Listen and practise.

restaurant	bread	vegetables
table	plate	baby	grey
wife	I	my	like	white	wine

3 Write a sentence. Use words from the box.

4 Read out your sentence.

Phrasebook: On the phone

Here are two phone conversations.

Fill the gaps. Use the words in the bubbles.

> Can I speak to George

> Never mind

> Just a moment

> Is Louisa there

1 – Hello. Jane Miller.
   – Hello. .... , please?
   – Yes. ....
   – Hello.
   – Hello, George. It's Mike .

2 – Hello. 26439.
   – Hello. .... , please?
   – No, she isn't. Sorry.
   – OK. ....

🔊 Now listen and check.

'Phone' your partner. Ask to speak to a friend.

Study pages D

Focus on ... *Telling the time*

This exercise introduces clock times, and gives practice in talking about times using at.

> *Key language:* clock times; at, start, finish.
> *Recycled language:* numbers 1–12.

1 ● Use the clock diagram to establish the basic rules for telling the time:

  – If the time is on the hour, we say *o'clock*.
  – Up to the half-hour, we say *past*.
  – After the half-hour, we say *to*.
  – 15 minutes = *(a) quarter*, 30 minutes = *half*.

 ● Ask students to read out the clock times. Focus on pronunciation of /hɑːf/, /ə ˈkwɔːtə/, /əˈklɒk/.

 ● Ask students to give the other clock times. Answers:

  It's (a) quarter past six.
  It's 10 to 12.
  It's half past 9.
  It's 1 o'clock.
  It's 20 past 6.

2 Read the digital clock times, then ask students to say the times shown in two ways. Answers:

  It's seven fifteen. It's (a) quarter past seven.
  It's eleven forty. It's twenty to twelve.
  It's two fifty. It's ten to three.
  It's twelve twenty-five. It's twenty-five past twelve.

3 ● Read the sentences about TV programmes. Present these expressions on the board:

It	starts finishes	at 6 o'clock.

 ● To introduce the activity, tell the class what you watch on TV, and when it starts and finishes.

 ● Give time for students to think about programmes they watch. If they like, they can note down programmes and times.

 ● Ask students to talk about programmes they watch.

> *Ideas for further practice*
> From time to time during the next few lessons, do some of these:
> 1 Write clock faces on the board, and ask students to say what time they show.
> 2 Ask students what the time really is at various points in the lesson.
> 3 Dictate times: say e.g. *a quarter past six*, and students write 6.15. Then ask the class to read the times back to you.

Sounds: *Bread, cake and wine*

> Short vowel /e/ and diphthongs /eɪ/ and /aɪ/.

1, 2 🔊 If students have problems, focus on these features:

  – /eɪ/ is made up of two sounds: /e/ followed by /ɪ/ (not the same as the pure *e* in Spanish, Italian, German, etc.).
  – /aɪ/ is made up of /a/ followed by /ɪ/.

3 Students write a sentence using words from the box, and including any other words they like, e.g.

  I like bread and vegetables.
  Is the white wine on the table?

4 Students read out their sentences in turn. Focus on the pronunciation of /e/, /eɪ/ and /aɪ/.

  Alternative: Dictation. Students dictate their sentence to the person next to them. As a check, ask students to read out the sentence they wrote down.

Phrasebook: *On the phone*

This exercise teaches basic expressions used in phoning people.

> *Key language:* Can I speak to (John)? Is (John) there? Never mind. Just a moment.
> *Recycled language:* hello, please, sorry.

 ● Read through the conversations, and ask students to fill the gaps. As you go through, present key expressions:

  – *Can I speak to (John)?* and *Is (John) there?* (both common ways of asking for people on the phone)
  – *Just a moment.* (= Wait.)
  – *Never mind.* (= It doesn't matter, it isn't important.)

 ● 🔊 Play the recording, so that students can listen to the complete conversations.

 ● To introduce the role-play, 'phone' someone in the class, and ask for someone else e.g. a friend, his/her brother, his/her mother. Then get a student to 'phone' you, and give a suitable reply.

 ● Students have similar conversations privately in pairs, or publicly across the class.

🔊 Tapescript for Phrasebook: *On the phone*

1 A Hello. Jane Miller.
  B Hello. Can I speak to George, please?
  A Yes. Just a moment.
  C Hello.
  B Hello, George. It's Mike.

2 A Hello. 26439.
  B Hello. Is Louisa there, please?
  A No, she isn't. Sorry.
  B OK. Never mind.

Consolidation

Subject and object

This exercise focuses on subject and object pronouns, and shows how they work as a system. This consolidates language from Unit 1 and from Exercise 7.2.

- If necessary, give a few simple examples to show the difference between subject and object, e.g.

  Maria lives in Spain → *She* lives in Spain.
  I like *Maria* → I like *her*.

  If possible, refer to similar forms in the students' own language.

- Read through the examples with the class. Then ask them to complete the table, and write it on the board:

I	*me*
you	*you*
he	*him*
she	*her*
it	*it*
we	*us*
they	*them*

Always, usually, sometimes, never

This exercise focuses on common adverbs of frequency. Always and never are new items; usually and sometimes appeared in Exercise 7.1 and Exercise 8.1.

- Read through the examples, and make sure students understand the meaning of *always, usually, sometimes* and *never*. If possible, use students' own language for this; otherwise, give other examples of your own to make the meaning clear, or show them on a scale:

never	sometimes	usually	always
0%			100%

- Look at the sentences and make true sentences about yourself.
- Ask students to make sentences about themselves. They could either write them or work through them in pairs.
- As a round-up, find out what students said or wrote.

Review

There is/are

Review of language from Unit 5, Exercises 1 and 2.

- If all the students live in the same town, go through the signs and prompt sentences using *There is(n't)* and *There are(n't)*, e.g.:

  What about a river? Yes, there are two rivers.
  What about an airport? ...

- If students come from different places, begin by talking about the town where you are now. Then ask students to write sentences about their own town or village.

Rooms

Review of rooms (Exercise 6.1), furniture (Exercises 6.1, 6.2), colours (Exercise 4.1).

1 Working alone or in pairs, students answer the questions. Then discuss them together. The answers are personal, but likely answers are:

   wash your hands: bathroom, kitchen
   have breakfast: kitchen, dining room, (bedroom)
   watch TV: living room, bedroom, kitchen
   sleep: bedroom
   have a shower: bathroom
   phone your friends: hall, living room, kitchen, bedroom

2 Give time for students to think about a room and make some notes. Then ask students to tell you about their favourite room. Write these structures on the board as a guide:

   My favourite room is ...
   It's ...
   It has ...
   There's a ...
   There are ...

More consonants

Review of letters from Study Pages A (The alphabet).

1 Practise saying the letters.

2 In pairs, students work out the missing letters. Then go through the answers. Make sure students say the letters correctly. Answers:

   knife and fork, sixty, seventy, question, magazine, cheese, pizza, church

Consolidation

Subject and object

I like John.   John likes me.

Subject	Object
I	me
you	....
he	....
she	....
it	....
we	....
they	....

Look at these examples, and complete the table.

a – I think she likes you.
– Yes. But I don't like her.

b I sometimes eat potatoes, but I don't like them.

c – Have some coffee.
– No thanks. I don't drink it.

d He talks a lot, but I never listen to him.

e We go to church on Sunday, and my girlfriend sometimes goes with us.

Always, usually, sometimes, never

Mrs Black always goes to church on Sunday morning. She never watches TV.

Jack Green usually plays football on Sunday morning, but he sometimes stays at home.

Mary Grey never goes out on Sunday morning. She usually watches TV.

What do you do on Sunday morning?
Add *always*, *usually*, *sometimes* or *never* to these sentences.

I work.
   I watch TV.
      I go to church.
         I stay at home.
            I visit friends.
               I play football.
                  I …

Review

There is/are

Talk about the town where you live, using *There is(n't)* and *There are(n't)*. Use these ideas:

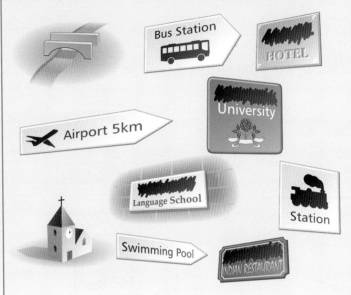

Rooms

1 Think of the rooms in your flat or house. Where do you

– wash your hands?   – sleep?
– have breakfast?   – have a shower?
– watch TV?   – phone your friends?

2 Which is your favourite room? What's in it? What colours are the things in the room?

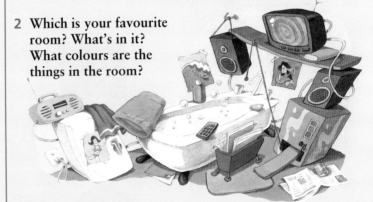

More consonants

1 How do you say these letters?

c g h k q s v x y z

2 What are the missing letters in these words?

•nife and for• •i•t• •e•ent• •ue•tion

ma•a•ine •ee•e pi••a •ur••

9

Do you ...?

1 Men and women

Present simple • Yes/no questions

Here are 10 questions, and answers from 200 people – 100 women and 100 men.
Which do you think are the men's answers, and which are the women's?

Q.1 Do you play computer games?

65 __men__ play computer games.

Only 35 __women__ play computer games.

Q.2 Do you wear earrings?

Only six _____ wear earrings – and five out of the six wear just one earring.

69 _____ wear earrings. Some wear three, four, five and six. One person wears ten.

Q.3 Do you sleep on your back?

54 _____ sleep on their back. Most of the others sleep on their side. One sleeps 'in a chair'.

43 _____ sleep on their back. Most of the others sleep on their side.

Q.4 Do you like Arnold Schwarzenegger?

24 _____ like Arnold Schwarzenegger. The favourite films are *Terminator I* and *II*.

59 _____ like Arnold Schwarzenegger. The favourite films are *Terminator I* and *II*.

Q.5 Do you carry a bag?

95 _____ carry a bag.

69 _____ carry a bag.

Q.6 Do you have a pet?

34 _____ have pets. Dogs are the favourite pets. Two people have parrots. One has four dogs and five cats.

51 _____ have pets. Dogs are the favourites, then cats, then fish.

Q.7 Do you have sugar in coffee?

47 _____ have sugar in coffee. 30 don't. (The other 23 don't drink coffee.)

62 _____ have sugar in coffee. 24 don't. (The other 14 don't drink coffee.)

Q.8 Do you eat at McDonald's?

82 _____ eat at McDonald's. Most of them go 20–30 times a year. One goes every day.

80 _____ eat at McDonald's. Most go 25–50 times a year. One goes every day.

Q.9 Do you keep a diary?

24 _____ keep a diary.

Only 16 _____ keep a diary.

Q.10 Do you like classical music?

50 _____ like classical music. Mozart and Beethoven are the favourites.

65 _____ like classical music. Mozart, Beethoven and Chopin are the favourites.

1 Read the article, and write *men* or *women* in the gaps.

2 Work in pairs. Ask your partner the questions.

3 Think of some questions of your own.

_____ eat _____?   _____ drink _____?   _____ like _____?   _____?

_____ have _____?   _____ wear _____?   _____ play _____?

4 Choose one of the questions, and ask other students. What are the answers?

This unit introduces Present simple question forms, and also practises the use of the Present simple for talking about daily routines. It focuses on:
– Present simple *yes/no* questions
– Present simple *Wh-* questions (*Where? When? What? What time?*)
– ways of talking about daily routine (e.g. *get up, go to work, have dinner*).

1 Men and women

This exercise is about people's habits and introduces Present simple questions with Do you …? *It is based on a questionnaire given to 200 foreign students in Britain. Students read the results and decide which apply to men and which to women; they then use the questions to find out about each other.*

> ➤ Focus on Form: Exercises 1 & 2
> ➤ Workbook: Exercise A

> *New verbs:* sleep, carry, keep. *Other new words:* diary, earring, on your back, pet, classical music. *For comprehension only:* on your side, parrot.

1 Presentation of yes/no questions; reading & gap-filling

- To introduce the activity, establish that this is a survey; a hundred men answered the questions, and a hundred women (they were all foreign students in Britain). If possible, tell students about this in their own language.

- Read through the questions, presenting new words as you go.

- Show how we form Present simple questions with *Do you …?*:

> I **play** computer games.
> **Do** you **play** computer games?

- Read the answers to Question 1 together, then look at Question 2. Ask students which answer is about men, and which about women. (Answer: 6 men, 69 women.)

- Give time for students to read the other answers and decide which are about men and which are about women. They can do this alone or in pairs.

- Discuss the answers together. Answers:

Q1 65 men, 35 women	Q6 34 women, 51 men
Q2 6 men, 69 women	Q7 47 men, 62 women
Q3 54 men, 43 women	Q8 82 men, 80 women
Q4 24 women, 59 men	Q9 24 women, 16 men
Q5 95 women, 69 men	Q10 50 men, 65 women

> *Optional activation*
> Ask one or two students each question as you come to it. But do not get answers from too many students at this stage; everyone will ask and answer the questions in Part 2.

> *Language note*
> In this exercise, students only have to produce questions with *Do you …?* Other forms (*Do they …? Does he …?* etc.) are practised in Focus on Form Exercise 1.

2 Activation: asking & answering questions

- Show on the board how to answer the questions:

> Do you keep a diary? | Yes, I do
> | No, I don't

- Pairwork. Students ask and answer the questions.

- As a round-up, choose some of the questions and find out how many students answered *Yes* and how many answered *No*.

3 Preparation for the survey: writing questions

- Look at the verbs, and ask students to think of other questions. Build ideas up on the board.

4 Class survey: asking & answering questions

- Give each student one of the questions to ask. Students go round the class, asking the question and recording the answers.

- Find out how many *Yes* and *No* answers students got to each question.

> *Organising the survey*
> If you have less than ten students, leave some questions out or assign two questions to some students. If you have more then ten, ask some students to operate as pairs, or have only ten of the students asking the questions but everyone answering. If it is difficult for students to move freely, have only two or three students asking questions at a time, or pass the questions round on pieces of paper.

🔲 Tapescript for Exercise 2: *What do you do?*

A So … what do you do?
B Oh, I'm a student.
A Oh, yes. What do you study?
B Music.
A Really? I'm a music teacher.
B Are you really? Where do you work, then?
A Oh, at a school, in Cambridge.

B Really? Do you live in Cambridge?
A Yes. Yes, I do. Why, where do you live?
B Cambridge. I live in Cambridge, too.
A Really? Where?
B In Bridge Street – I have a flat in Bridge Street.
A No, that's amazing …

2 What do you do?

This exercise introduces common Present simple Wh- questions that might be used when talking to someone you don't know.

> Key language: Wh- questions; They both …

➤ Focus on Form: Exercise 3
➤ Workbook: Exercise B

1 Listening

- Look at the picture, and establish the situation: a man and a woman at a party.

- 🔲 Play the recording. Establish how similar they are. Expected answer:

  She is a music teacher.   He is a music student.   They both live in Cambridge.

🔲 The tapescript is on page T40.

2 Listening; presentation of Wh- questions

- 🔲 Play the recording again, pausing if necessary. Establish what the questions are and write them on the board:

  – What do you do?　　　– Where do you work?
  – What do you study?　　– Where do you live?

- Show the structure of *Wh-* questions:

  | **What** | |
  | **Where** | **do you (+ verb)?** |

Language note
What do you do? is a general question, meaning *What work do you do?* or *What is your occupation?*

3 Role-play: finding similarities

- Turn to page 107. To introduce the activity, choose a 'role' yourself from the sentences (e.g. *I'm a student. I study business at a college in Edinburgh. I live in King Street.*). Get students to ask you questions, and answer them according to your role.

- Working alone, students choose a sentence for themselves and write it down.

- Divide the class into groups. Students ask questions, and answer according to the role they have written down.

- As a round-up, ask students if they found someone who was similar to them.

Option
If possible, let students wander freely round the class, having conversations with two or three other people.

3 From morning till night

This exercise is about a woman's daily routine. It introduces common phrases (e.g. go to work, have dinner) *and practises* Wh- *questions and clock times.*

> Key phrases: have breakfast/lunch/dinner, get up, go to bed, go to work, start/finish work, come home; What time …?
> Recycled language: clock times; always, usually.

➤ Workbook: Exercise C, Listening

1 Presentation of key phrases; sequencing task

- Look at the sentences. Ask students to match them with the pictures and put them in order.

2 Listening & noting times

- 🔲 Play the recording, pausing from time to time. Students note down the times in the boxes.

- Go through the answers together. Focus on both ways of saying the time (*seven fifteen* and *(a) quarter past seven*). Answers:

  1 *g*　7.15 (a quarter past seven)　　6 *i*　5.00 (five o'clock)
  2 *d*　8.00 (eight o'clock)　　　　　　7 *e*　5.30 (half past five)
  3 *f*　8.30 (half past eight)　　　　　8 *h*　7.00 (seven o'clock)
  4 *c*　9.15 (a quarter past nine)　　　9 *b*　11.30 (half past eleven)
  5 *a*　12.30 (half past twelve)

🔲 The tapescript is on page T42.

3 Practice: asking & answering questions

- Look at the pictures, and establish what the other questions should be. Write this structure on the board:

  | **When** | | **get up** |
  | **What time** | **does she** | **have lunch?** |

4 Activation: finding out about daily routine

- Pairwork. Students ask and answer questions.

2 What do you do?

Wh- questions

1 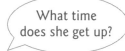 Two people meet at a party. Listen to their conversation. How similar are they?

> The woman is … | The man is … | They both …

2 Complete these questions.

– What ....?
– I'm a student.

– What ....?
– Music.

– Where ....?
– At a school in Cambridge.

– Where ....?
– I live in Cambridge, too.

3 Role-play. Turn to page 107 and choose a role. Write it on a piece of paper.

Imagine you're at the party. Meet two or three other people. Try to find someone who is similar to you!

3 From morning till night

Daily routine • Wh- questions

1 Here are some sentences about a woman's day. Put them in the right order.

a ☐ She has lunch.
b ☐ She goes to bed.
c ☐ She starts work.
d ☐ She has breakfast.
e ☐ She comes home.
f ☐ She goes to work.
g ☐ 1 She gets up.
h ☐ She has dinner.
i ☐ She finishes work.

2 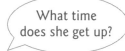 Listen and write the times in the boxes.

3 Work in pairs.
Test your partner.

> What time does she get up? | At a quarter past seven.

4 Now find out about your partner's day.

Focus on Form

1 Yes/no questions

 They speak English but ...
... do they speak French?

 She eats meat but ...
... does she eat fish?

 He drinks coffee but ...
... does he drink beer?

Add questions.

a They have a dog ...   (cat?)
b He has a radio ...   (television?)
c You play the piano ...   (guitar?)
d She works on Saturdays ...   (Sundays?)
e He likes Mozart ...   (Beethoven?)

2 Short answers

Look at these questions and short answers. Which answers are true?

> Do you wear glasses?

> Does your teacher wear glasses?

Yes, I do.

No, I don't.

Yes, he/she does.

No, he/she doesn't.

Now answer these questions.

> Do you like chocolate?

> Does your teacher speak Chinese?

> Does your teacher have long hair?

> Do you wear high heels?

3 Wh- questions

> Do you study French / Maths / Economics ...?
> → What do you study?
>
> Does he work in a bank / in a supermarket ...?
> → Where does he work?
>
> Does she get up at 7.00 / 7.30 / 8.00 ...?
> → When
>   What time does she get up?

Ask Wh- questions.

a Does she live *in Bangkok / in Budapest* ...?
b Do you work *at home / in a restaurant* ...?
c Does the film start at *5.00 / 6.00 / 7.00* ...?
d Do cats eat *meat / vegetables / salad* ...?
e Does he go to bed at *8.00 / 9.00 / 10.00* ...?
f Do they *watch TV / read* in the evenings?

How to say it

1 Listen to *do you, does he, does she.*

▪ ▪ ■ ▪
Do you like him?

■ ▪ ▪ ■
Where do you live?

▪ ▪ ▪ ■ ▪
Does he speak English?

■ ▪ ▪ ■ ■
When does she get up?

2 Listen to the /ə/ sound in these phrases.

listen to the radio   have a pizza

look out of the window   go to school

Now practise saying these sentences.

I get up at a quarter to five.

I'd like some salt and pepper.

Focus on Form

1 Yes/no questions

- Read through the examples. Emphasise that the -s ending is carried by the *does*, not by the main verbs (*speak, eat, drink*).
- Do the exercise round the class, or ask students to write the questions. Answers:

  a Do they have a cat?
  b Does he have a television?
  c Do you play the guitar?
  d Does she work on Sundays?
  e Does he like Beethoven?

2 Short answers

- Point out that to give short answers, we repeat the *do/does*, or make it negative: *don't/doesn't*.
- Ask the example questions round the class, and get students to give true answers.
- Then ask the other questions round the class, or get students to ask and answer in pairs. Possible answers:

  Do you like chocolate?
  – Yes, I do.
  – No, I don't.

  Does your teacher have long hair?
  – Yes, he/she does.
  – No, he/she doesn't.

  Does your teacher speak Chinese?
  – Yes, he/she does.
  – No, he/she doesn't.

  Do you wear high heels?
  – Yes, I do.
  – No, I don't.

3 Wh- questions

- Read through the examples.
- Either do the exercise with the whole class or let students do it in pairs and then go through it together. Answers:

  a Where does she live?
  b Where do you work?
  c When/What time does the film start?
  d What do cats eat?
  e When/What time does he go to bed?
  f What do they do in the evenings?

How to say it

1 Reduced vowels in questions

- [cassette] Play the recording, pausing and getting students to repeat the questions. Focus on:
  – the rhythm of the questions.
  – the reduced vowel in *do* and *does*.
  – the running together of *does* and *she*.

2 Reduced vowels in unstressed syllables and words

- [cassette] Play the phrases. Pause after each one and get students to try saying it. Focus on the stress pattern and the /ə/ sounds.
- [cassette] Play the sentences, and get students to practise them.

[cassette] Tapescript for Exercise 3: *From morning till night*

Well, I usually get up at a quarter past 7, and then I have breakfast around 8. Then I go to work at half past 8. I start work at a quarter past 9, usually, and I work till half past 12, and then I have lunch. Then I work again in the afternoon, and I always finish work at 5 o'clock. So I get home at 5.30. I have a sandwich then, when I come home, and then I usually have dinner quite late, at about 7 o'clock in the evening. And I go to bed, ooh, at around half past 11, usually.

10

This unit covers a range of vocabulary connected with shops, shopping, and places in towns. This includes:
– expressions used in buying and selling (e.g. *How much is …? Can I see …?*)
– names of shops (e.g. *clothes shop, chemist*) and things you can buy at them
– places in towns (e.g. *post office, cinema, station*)
– place prepositions (e.g. *opposite, near, between*).
The Reading and Listening activity is about opening and closing times.

1 At the market

This exercise recycles vocabulary that has been presented earlier in the book, and focuses on expressions commonly used in shopping: asking to see something, asking about price and size, and saying whether or not you want something.

➤ Workbook: Exercise A

> *Key expressions:* Can I see …? How much is/are …? What size is …? Can I help you?
> It's too big/small/expensive.   *Recycled language:* everyday objects.

1 Introduction: identifying vocabulary items

● Look at the picture and establish what the items are. They have all appeared in earlier units, but present any that students have forgotten. Answers:

a lamp, mirrors, pictures, jeans, T-shirts, a jacket, shoes, glasses, plates, a camera, a radio, toy planes, clocks, watches, pens, toy cars, lighters, sunglasses, knives.

2 Presentation of key expressions; sequencing task; listening to check

● Look through the conversations and present *How much is …?* and *What size is …?* Present the expressions *It's too expensive* and *It's too big.*

● Working alone or in pairs, students look at the conversations and try to put them in the right order.

● 🔲 Discuss the answers together, then play the recording to check. As you play the conversations, focus on other expressions, e.g. *Can I help you? Thanks anyway. All right, I'll have one.*

> *Language note*
> If necessary, give examples to show the difference between *too* and *very*, e.g.
> It's *very* expensive = it's a lot of money.
> It's *too* expensive = I can't buy it.

> *Practice option*
> Ask students to practise the dialogues in pairs.

3 Activation: making questions

● Ask students to make questions about some of the other objects, e.g. *Can I see that camera? Can I see those shoes? How much are those sunglasses? How much is that picture? What size are the jeans?* Focus on the difference between singular and plural forms.

4 Role-play: buying & selling

● To introduce the activity, take the part of the shopkeeper, and choose a student to be your customer. Have a conversation, and try to sell him/her something. Begin by asking *Can I help you?*

● Students work in pairs, with one person in each pair being the shopkeeper and the other being the customer. They have conversations about the things in the picture.

● As a round-up, ask students whether they bought or sold anything, and how much it cost.

> *Whole class option*
> Students come to the front in turn to take the role of the shopkeeper. Other students 'buy' things from them.

🔲 Tapescript for Exercise 1: *At the market*

A A Can I see that radio?
   B Yes, here you are.
   A How much is it?
   B £25.
   A Oh no, that's too expensive.
   B All right, 20 then.

B A How much are these lighters?
   B They're £1 each.

   A OK, I'll have one, please.
   B What colour do you want? Red, blue, green?
   A Blue, I think.
   B Here you are, then. That's £1, please.

C A Hello. Can I help you?
   B Yes. What size is that jacket?
   A It's size 38.
   B Oh, that's too big. Thanks anyway.

10 Things people buy

1 At the market

1 Look at the market stall. What can you see?

2 Here are three conversations. Put them in the right order.

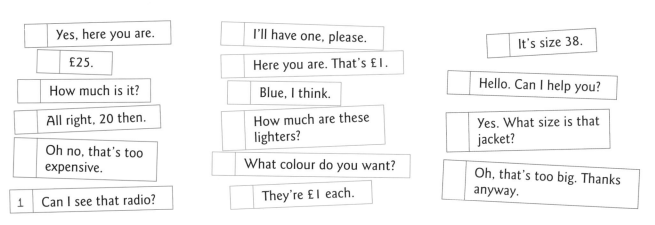

	Yes, here you are.
	£25.
	How much is it?
	All right, 20 then.
	Oh no, that's too expensive.
1	Can I see that radio?

	I'll have one, please.
	Here you are. That's £1.
	Blue, I think.
	How much are these lighters?
	What colour do you want?
	They're £1 each.

	It's size 38.
	Hello. Can I help you?
	Yes. What size is that jacket?
	Oh, that's too big. Thanks anyway.

[cassette icon] Now listen and check your answers.

3 Choose some other things on the market stall. What questions can you ask about them?

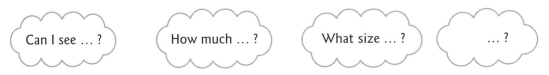

Can I see … ?   How much … ?   What size … ?   … ?

4 Role-play

Student A: You work at the market stall. Sell things to B.
Student B: You're a customer. Buy things from A.

2 Shops

1 Look at the shopping list.
Which things do you buy at each shop?

2 Think of one other thing you buy at
each shop. Use a dictionary to help you.

Together, build up a list on the board.

3 Test your partner.

> Where do
> you buy a jacket?

> At a clothes shop.

potatoes
Time magazine
cigarettes
shampoo
pen
sunglasses
1 kilo beef
aspirins
street map
apples
T-shirt
chocolate cake

3 Is there a bank near here?

1 Here's part of a town map.
Where are places A–F on the map?
Choose sentences from the box.

> It's by the river.
> It's in the next street.
> It's next to the school.
> It's opposite the station.
> It's near the station.
> It's between the school and the cinema.

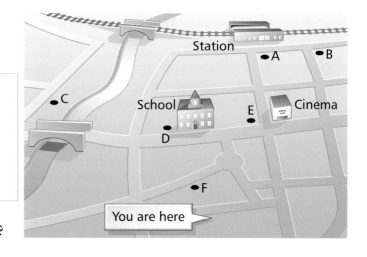

2 ▭ Now listen. What are places A–F?
Where is the bookshop?

supermarket   bank   post office   restaurant   newsagent   chemist   bookshop

3 Work in pairs.

Student A: Turn to page 106. Ask and answer questions.
Student B: Turn to page 108. Ask and answer questions.

> Is there
> a bank near
> here?

> Yes, there's one
> in the next street,
> opposite the cinema.

4 Think about real places near where you are now.
Ask and answer questions.

2 Shops

This exercise introduces the names of common shops, and gives a chance to 'brainstorm' words for things you buy.

➤ Workbook: Exercise B, Listening

> *Shops:* chemist, newsagent, baker, butcher, greengrocer, bookshop, clothes shop, kiosk.   *Other new words:* shampoo, beef, aspirin, map, cake.

1 Presentation of shops & other vocabulary; matching task

- Go through the shopping list. Present any new items (e.g. *shampoo*, *beef*).
- Ask where you can buy each item, and present the names of the shops. Focus on pronunciation of /ˈkemɪst/, /ˈkləʊðz ʃɒp/ and /ˈbʊtʃə/. Possible answers:

potatoes: greengrocer	*beef:* butcher
magazine: newsagent, kiosk	*aspirins:* chemist, kiosk
cigarettes: kiosk, newsagent	*street map:* kiosk, newsagent, bookshop
shampoo: chemist, (kiosk)	*apples:* greengrocer
pen: newsagent, kiosk	*T-shirt:* clothes shop
sunglasses: kiosk, (chemist)	*chocolate cake:* baker

> *Note*
> The answers will of course vary slightly from one country to another. If you have a mixed nationality class, encourage discussion of differences.

> *Language note*
> We sometimes also say *chemist's* (= chemist's shop), *baker's*, *butcher's* and *newsagent's*. A *greengrocer('s)* sells fruit and vegetables.

2 Vocabulary expansion

- Working alone or in pairs, students think of one other item they could buy at each shop. If students think of an item they don't know, let them either look it up in a dictionary or write it in their own language.
- Build up a list of useful words on the board. This is an opportunity to 'brainstorm' vocabulary that students want to know in English.

> *Note*
> Some common items are given in the Reference section, page 119.

3 Practice: asking & answering questions

- Focus on the question *Where do you buy …?* and the use of *at* with shops.
- Pairwork. Students test each other.

3 Is there a bank near here?

In this exercise students learn to ask where places are in a town. It introduces vocabulary for talking about public places in towns, and place prepositions.

➤ Workbook: Exercise C

> *Public places:* supermarket, bank, post office, restaurant, cinema, (bus) station, school.   *Place prepositions:* by, in, next to, opposite, near, between.
> *Recycled language:* newsagent, chemist, bookshop; There's …, Is there …?

1 Presentation of prepositions; matching task

- Look at the box, and try to elicit the correct sentences. As you do so, make sure students understand what the prepositions mean. Answers:

  A is opposite the station.   B is near the station.   C is by the river.   D is next to the school.   E is between the school and the cinema.   F is in the next street.

> *Presentation idea*
> To present the new prepositions, draw simple sketches on the board (e.g. *Look – here's my house. My friend's house is here. It's opposite my house*).

2 Listening & matching; presentation of vocabulary

- 🔲 Play the recording. Pause after each exchange, and establish what the places on the map are. Present any new vocabulary as you go through. Answers (in the order you hear them):

  D = a bank   A = a post office   C = a supermarket   E = a chemist
  F = a newsagent   B = a restaurant
  The bookshop is in the town centre, near the bus station (so it isn't on the map).

> *Language note*
> *Next to* and *by* have almost the same meaning. We usually use *next to* with things of the same type, so we say: *The cinema is next to the school*, but *The cinema is by the river*.

> 🔲 The tapescript is on page T45.

3 Pairwork game: finding places on a map

- Write these structures on the board:
- Divide the class into pairs, and give each student a letter, A or B.

> **Is there a … near here?**
> **Yes. There's one …**
> **No, but there's one …**

  Students ask and answer questions, looking only at their own map.

4 Extension: talking about real places

- Ask the same questions about places near the school, and see if students can answer them.

> *Optional extension*
> Write other places on the board (e.g. *café, hotel, bus stop, disco, kiosk*). Get students to ask and answer about them in the same way.

4 Open and closed

This combined Reading and Listening activity is about opening times of shops in different countries. The reading is about opening times in Britain, and the listening is about particular features of shops in Poland, Greece and Thailand.

Reading skills: *reading for specific information.*
Listening skills: *listening for specific information.*

> *New words (text):* open, closed, bar of chocolate, stamps, post, parcel, sweets, sell, nowadays, petrol station, stay open, late, all night.
> *New words (listening):* close (v.), open (v.).

1 Presentation of vocabulary; reading to answer questions

- Look at the questions, and ask students to give brief answers about their own country. As you do so, present *a bar of chocolate*, *a stamp*, *post a parcel*.
- Present these expressions with *open* and *closed*:

The shops are	open. closed.		The shops stay open	late. till 6.30.

Alternative 1
Leave this until Stage 3.

Alternative 2: Classes in Britain
See if students know the answers to the questions, as applied to Britain.

- Ask students to read the texts about Britain and find answers to the questions.
- Discuss the answers together. Expected answers:

  a At a supermarket or a small food shop, or at a petrol station.
  b Maybe at a supermarket or a small shop.
  c At a petrol station, or maybe at a supermarket.
  d No.
  e No.
  f Go to an all-night petrol station (or an all-night supermarket, in a city).

- Read through the texts together, focusing on any new words or expressions.

2 Listening & gap-filling

- Read the texts below the pictures. If you like, ask students to guess what might go in the gaps. Present the verbs *open* and *close* on the board:

The shops	open close	at 6 o'clock.

Language note
The verbs are *open* and *close*: *The shop opens/closes at 12.* The adjectives are *open* and *closed*: *The shop is open/closed today.*

- 🔲 Play the recording. Pause after each speaker and ask students to complete the texts. (For answers, see tapescript.)

3 Extension: talking about opening times

- Ask students to imagine you are a foreign visitor to their country. Ask them about the same topics that they have read about and listened to, e.g.

  – opening times   – banks and post offices   – markets
  – weekends   – kiosks

Role-play option
Write a list of topics on the board. Then students work in pairs: one student pretends to be a foreign visitor and asks the other student questions.

🔲 Tapescript for Exercise 3:
Is there a bank near here?

1 A Is there a bank near here?
  B Yes, there's one on the main road, next to the school.
2 A Excuse me, where's the post office?
  B Oh, it's just opposite the station.
3 A Excuse me, is there a supermarket near here?
  B Yes, there's one in Bridge Street, just by the river.
4 A Is there a chemist near here?
  B Yes, let's see … Yes, there's one on the main road, between the school and the cinema.
5 A Is there a newsagent near here?
  B Yes, there's one in the next street.
6 A Excuse me, is there a good restaurant near here?
  B Yes, there's a very good one near the station – it's called Dino's.
7 A Excuse me, is there a good bookshop near here?
  B No, there isn't, but there's one in the town centre, near the bus station.

🔲 Tapescript for Exercise 4: *Open and closed*

1 In Poland, the banks are open till 7 o'clock in the evening. And in towns, supermarkets stay open all night, so you can buy bread at 3 o'clock in the morning.

2 In Greece, the shops close at 2 o'clock in the afternoon and open again at 5 o'clock. But there are also lots of kiosks, and they stay open all day.

3 In many cities in Thailand, there are large street markets which stay open in the evening. You can buy lots of things there: watches, cameras, books, clothes – lots of things. And they usually stay open till about 12 o'clock at night.

4 Open and closed

1 Imagine you're visiting Britain, and you want to answer these questions.

a It's 8.30 in the evening. Where can I buy a bar of chocolate?

b It's Sunday morning. Can I buy bread?

c Where can I buy stamps on a Sunday afternoon?

d It's Saturday afternoon. Can I post a parcel?

e It's 7 o'clock in the evening. Can I buy a pair of jeans?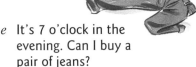

f It's 4 o'clock in the morning, and I want a magazine. What can I do?

Find answers in the texts.

YOU DON'T FIND KIOSKS in Britain. But there are lots of small newsagents. They sell newspapers and magazines, sweets, cigarettes, drinks and sometimes bread. Nowadays, you can usually buy these things at petrol stations too.

MOST SHOPS are open from 9.00 till 5.30, and they're closed all day on Sundays. But a lot of supermarkets and small food shops stay open later – till 9.00 or 10.00 in the evening, and they're also open on Sundays.

In cities, some supermarkets are open 24 hours a day. Petrol stations also stay open late in the evening, and some stay open all night.

POST OFFICES are open from 9.00 till 5.00 on Monday–Friday, and from 9.00 till 12.00 on Saturdays. But you can also buy stamps in newsagents, supermarkets and petrol stations.

2 Three people talk about shopping times in three countries. Listen and fill the gaps.

In Poland the banks are open till .... And in towns, supermarkets stay open .... , so you can buy bread ....

In Greece the shops close .... and open again .... But there are also .... , and they stay open all day.

In Thailand many towns have .... You can buy .... there. They stay open ....

3 Think about your own country. When are shops open and closed?

Focus on ... Days of the week

1 Listen to the days of the week.

Monday

Tuesday

Wednesday

Thursday

Friday

Saturday

Sunday

Practise saying them.

2 Work in pairs. Test your partner.

Thursday,
Friday ...?

What's the second
day of the week?

Saturday.

Tuesday.

3 Look at this table.
What does the person do?

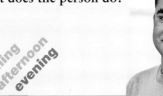

	morning	afternoon	evening	
Mon		✓		I go to the supermarket.
Tues				
Wed			✓	I play table tennis.
Thurs				
Fri			✓	I wash my hair.
Sat	✓			I get up late!
Sun		✓		I go to a football match.

He goes to the supermarket on
Monday afternoon.

4 Think about your own week. Tell other
students what you do on different days.

5 Cover up the days of the week.
Do you remember how to say them?

Sounds: Hello!

1 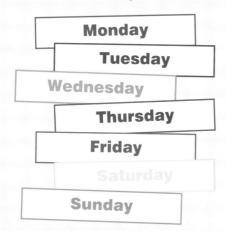 Listen to the sound /h/ in English. Is it
the same in your language?

/h/ Hello. Can I help you?

How much are they?

It's behind the door.

2 Listen and practise.

they have	gets home	half past four
her husband	how much	in a hotel
at home	his brother	behind the door

3 Write a sentence. Use phrases from the box.

4 Read out your sentence.

Phrasebook: What does it mean?

Look at the bubbles. Match the questions
and the answers.

What does
'slow' mean?

Friend.

What does
'millionaire'
mean?

What's 'vino'
in English?

Wine.

It means 'not fast'.

A person with lots
of money.

What's 'amigo'
in English?

 Now listen and check.

Write down three words in English, and
three in your own language. Test other
students.

What does
.... mean?

What's ....
in English?

Study pages E

Focus on ... *Days of the week*

This exercise introduces days of the week, and gives further practice in talking about regular activities.

> *Key language:* days of the week; *on.* *Recycled language:* morning, afternoon, evening; Present simple tense, activity verbs, ordinal numbers.

1 ● Begin by asking *What day is it today?* and write the day on the board.

   ● 🔲 Play the recording of the days of the week, and ask students to repeat them. Focus on pronunciation, especially of /ˈtjuːzdeɪ/ and /ˈwenzdeɪ/.

2 Ask a few test questions round the class. Then let students test each other in pairs.

   Note: This is an opportunity to practise ordinal numbers (*the first day, the second day,* etc.).

3 Show how we use *on* with days:

on	Monday
	Tuesday

Then show how we can add *morning, afternoon* or *evening*:

on Monday	morning
	afternoon
	evening

   ● Look at the table and ask students to say what the person does. Answers:

   He goes to the supermarket on Monday afternoon.
   He plays table tennis on Wednesday evening.
   He washes his hair on Friday evening.
   He gets up late on Saturday morning.
   He goes to a football match on Sunday afternoon.

4 *Either:* Prompt students to talk about when they do things by giving topics, e.g. *What about music? Does anyone play the piano? When? What about football? Any other sports?*
   Or: Students write one or two sentences about themselves, and then read them out to the class. You could write a list of phrases on the board to help give ideas, e.g.

play (the piano)	watch ... on TV
play (football)	go to the cinema
go to the shops	have English lessons
get up late	wash my hair

5 See if students can still remember the days of the week.

Sounds: *Hello!*

> The sound /h/.

1, 2 🔲 Students may have problems with this sound, depending on their own first language.
   – French and Spanish speakers should practise saying the /h/ forcefully enough.
   – Slavonic and Greek speakers should practise saying the /h/ lightly, without a 'kh' sound.

3 Students write a sentence using phrases from the box, and including any other words they like, e.g.
   – His brother works in a hotel.
   – Her husband gets home at half past four.

4 Students read out their sentences in turn. Focus on the pronunciation of /h/.

   Alternative: Dictation. Students dictate their sentence to the person next to them. As a check, ask students to read out the sentence they wrote down.

Phrasebook: *What does it mean?*

This exercise teaches ways of asking what words mean.

> *Key language:* What does ... mean? It means ...
> What's ... in English?
> *Recycled language:* Present simple questions.

   ● Look at the bubbles and ask students to match the questions and the answers. Answers:

   What does 'slow' mean?   It means 'not fast'.
   What does 'millionaire' mean?   A person with lots of money.
   What's 'amigo' in English?   Friend.
   What's 'vino' in English?   Wine.

   ● 🔲 Play the recording.

   ● Write these structures on the board:

What does ... mean?	What's ... in English?
It means ...	(It's) ...

   Point out that *mean* is a verb, and the question is in the Present simple (just like *When does he get up?*).

   ● Write on the board some words in English and some in the students' own language. Get students to find out what they mean by asking questions.

   ● Students write down three words in English, and three (different) words in their own language. They then test each other by asking questions.

> *Idea*
> Write the two questions on pieces of card, and stick them on the classroom wall. Make sure students use them when they want to know what words mean.

Consolidation

A kilo of apples

This exercise focuses on simple quantities used in shopping (kilo, litre, gram), and gives practice in asking for food in shops. This consolidates language from Unit 10.

1 ● Write these structures on the board:

2 kilos	
a kilo	of apples
half a kilo	

Point out any differences from students' own language (e.g. we say *2 kilos*, not ~~2 kilo~~; we say *half a kilo*, not ~~a half kilo~~).

● Read through the sentences and ask how much money the man spends. (Answer: $5.50.)

2 ● Quickly demonstrate the pairwork by having a conversation with one student.

● Pairwork. Students have conversations.

I'd like

This exercise focuses on the difference between I like *and* I'd like. I like *was introduced in Exercise 7.2;* I'd like *was introduced in Exercise 8.3.*

● Look at the examples, and make sure students understand the difference between *I like* and *I'd like*. If possible, give equivalents in students' own language, and also refer back to examples in Unit 7 and Unit 8.

● Choose one of the shops and set up a very simple conversation, taking the role of the shop assistant yourself, e.g.

A I'd like a pen, please.
B OK. What colour?
A Blue.
B Here you are. That's 1.40, please.

● Students write down one thing to buy from each shop.

● Either divide the class into pairs to have conversations, with one customer and one shop assistant in each pair, or choose pairs of students to have conversations in front of the class.

Review

1 Adjectives

Review of adjectives that have appeared in the book so far (especially Exercise 7.2).

1 Look at the adjectives, and ask students to find pairs of opposites. As you do this, remind students of any words they have forgotten. Answers:

big	long	fast	old	weak	hot	high
small	short	slow	new	strong	cold	low

(*Not used*: expensive, beautiful, rich)

If you like, teach the opposite pairs *rich/poor, expensive/cheap, beautiful/ugly* and *old/young.*

2 In pairs, students look at the picture and decide how to use the adjectives to talk about it. Discuss the answers together. Possible answers:

The beach is beautiful/hot.   The mountains are high/cold. The sun is low.   There's a fast boat on the sea.   There's an old man.   The man and woman on the beach are beautiful/rich. The man is strong.   The man has short hair, the woman has long hair.   One car is small/old/slow; one is big/new/beautiful/fast/expensive.

Which word?

Review of articles (Study Pages B Consolidation, Study Pages C Consolidation), this/that/these/those *(Study Pages B Consolidation); some and any (Exercise 5.2).*

Students do the exercise, working alone or in pairs. Then go through it together. If students have any problems, refer back to earlier exercises. Answers:

a I'd like *an* orange juice and *a* cup of coffee, please.
b My flat has *a* balcony. On *the* balcony there's *a* big sofa.
c – Look at *these* jeans. Do you like them?
– Yes. And I like *this* jumper, too.
d I live in *that* house over there, behind *those* trees.
e There are *some* good shops in this town, but there aren't *any* good restaurants.

Words

Review of addresses (Exercise 6.3), and vocabulary from Units 6, 8 and 10.

1 Ask students what the letters are. Answers:

a first name   *b* last name   *c* street (or road)
d town/city   *e* post code   *f* country
g (tele)phone number

2 Students look at the questions alone or in pairs, and write down words. Then go through the answers together. Possible answers:

to keep food cold: a fridge
to cook food: a cooker
to eat a meal: a plate, a knife, a fork, a spoon
to look at yourself: a mirror
to go up to the next floor: a lift, stairs
to find out the time: a clock, a watch, a radio, a phone
to find out the news: a newspaper, a radio, a TV, a computer

Consolidation

A kilo of apples

1 A man goes into this shop and buys

   – a kilo of apples
   – four kilos of potatoes
   – 200 grams of beef
   – a litre of mineral water
   – half a litre of milk

   How much money does he spend?

2 Work in pairs. You're in the shop.

   Student A: Buy something from B.
   Student B: Say how much it is.

> Half a kilo of beef, please.

> That's five dollars.

I'd like ...

I like books.

I'd like this book, please.

I like books =
I think books are good.

I'd like this book =
I want it.

Buy one thing from each shop.

> I'd like ..., please.

| KIOSK |

| NEWSAGENT |

| BOOKSHOP |

| CLOTHES SHOP |

Review

Adjectives

1 Find seven pairs of opposites. Which *three* words are not used?

beautiful	big	short	high
weak	fast	strong	young
expensive	small	rich	long
hot	low	old	cold	slow

2 Choose adjectives to describe things in the picture.

Which word?

Choose the right words.

a I'd like *a/an* orange juice and *a/an* cup of coffee, please.

b My flat has *a/the* balcony. On *a/the* balcony there's *a/the* big sofa.

c – Look at *this/these* jeans. Do you like them?
   – Yes. And I like *this/these* jumper, too.

d I live in *that/those* house over there, behind *that/those* trees.

e There are *some/any* good shops in this town, but there aren't *some/any* good restaurants.

Words

1 What are a–g?

2 What do you use to

   – keep food cold?
   – cook food?
   – eat a meal?
   – look at yourself?
   – go up to the next floor?
   – find out the time?
   – find out the news?

What's going on?

1 Windows

Present continuous

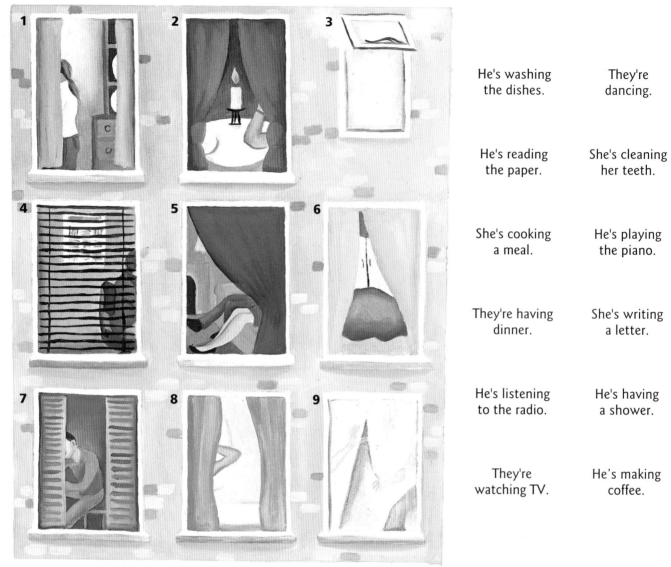

He's washing
the dishes.

They're
dancing.

He's reading
the paper.

She's cleaning
her teeth.

She's cooking
a meal.

He's playing
the piano.

They're having
dinner.

She's writing
a letter.

He's listening
to the radio.

He's having
a shower.

They're
watching TV.

He's making
coffee.

1 Look at the windows. What do you think the people are doing? Choose from the list.

▭ Now listen. Were you right?

2 What are these people doing?

3 Think of an action, and write it on a
piece of paper. Mime the action.
Can other students guess what you're doing?

I'm playing chess.   *I'm making a cake.*

I'm washing my hair.

This unit introduces the Present continuous tense for talking about things going on at the moment of speaking. It focuses on three common uses:
– saying what you can see or hear happening
– asking someone what they are doing
– saying where people are and what they are doing.

1 Windows

This exercise shows partly obscured views through windows. Students guess what the people inside are doing, and then check by listening to sounds. This introduces the Present continuous tense, and a range of common 'activity' verbs (some are new and some are from earlier units).

➤ Focus on Form: Exercises 1 & 2
➤ Workbook: Exercise A

> *New verbs and phrases:* wash the dishes, dance, clean (your) teeth, cook, write a letter, have a bath, make (coffee).   *Recycled verbs:* read, have (lunch), listen to, play, watch, eat, go (to bed).

1 Presentation of Present continuous; guessing task; listening to check

● Look at the sentences. Show the form of the Present continuous tense on the board:

> I'm
> He's
> She's   + verb + -ing
> They're

Point out that we use this tense to talk about what's happening *now* (at this moment, or in this picture).

● Read through the sentences. Present any new items, using gestures if necessary to make the meaning clear (e.g. *washing the dishes, cleaning her teeth*). If you like, build up a list of verbs on the board:

> wash   listen to   play
> read   watch   write
> cook   dance   make
> have   clean

● Ask students to guess what is happening in each of the rooms.

● [recording] Play the recording, pausing after each sound effect to check. Answers:

1 She's cooking a meal.
2 They're having dinner.
3 He's having a shower.
4 She's writing a letter (on a computer).
5 They're watching TV.

6 He's reading the paper.
7 He's playing the piano.
8 She's cleaning her teeth.
9 They're dancing.

> [recording] The recording for this exercise consists of sound effects.

2 Activation: describing pictures

● Look at the drawings. Ask students what the people are doing. Prompt them if necessary by indicating verbs from those on the board. Answers:

A She's playing tennis.   B She's playing the guitar.   C She's eating a burger.
D She's eating an ice-cream.   E He's cleaning a window.   F He's playing a computer game.   G She's drinking coffee.   H He's making a sandwich.
I She's washing her hair.

> *Practice option*
> Practise the form of the Present continuous by giving prompts, e.g.
> – Play the piano – He (He's playing the piano).
>   She (She's playing the piano).
> – Cards – She (She's playing cards).
>   They (They're playing cards).

3 Guessing game: miming actions

● To introduce this part, choose an action from those shown in this exercise and mime it. See if students can guess what you're doing.

● Give time for students think of an action and write a sentence. It can be either one of the actions shown in the pictures or another action that uses one of the same verbs.

● In turn, students mime their action. Other students guess what they're doing.

> *Pairwork option*
> Divide the class into pairs. Students mime their action and their partner tries to guess it.

2 Questions

This exercise introduces common questions in the Present continuous which are used in everyday conversation.

> *New verbs:* sit, do, stay. *Other new words:* anyone; football match.

1 Listening & gap-filling; presentation of questions; practice

- Look at the photo and establish where the people are (in the foyer of a hotel). Ask *What's the woman doing?* (She's reading a book) and *What's the man doing?* (He's talking to her).

- 📼 Play the recording and establish what the man's questions are:

  Is anyone sitting here?   Are you staying at this hotel?   What are you reading? Where are you going?

- Show how we form questions in the Present continuous:

  > *I'm reading.*
  > *Are you reading?*
  > *What are you reading?*

2 Activation: making questions

- If necessary, teach the words *question* and *answer* at this point. Then look at the answers, and ask students to think of a suitable question for each one. Possible questions:

  Where are you going?   What are you watching?   What are you making? Where are you staying?   What are you doing? (*or* What are you writing?)

3 Can I speak to Lisa, please?

This exercise is based on two-line phone conversations. It shows how we use the Present continuous and other phrases with the verb to be *to say where people are and what they're doing (e.g. he's having a shower, she's at work).*

> *Key phrases:* out, away, asleep; at home, at school, at the cinema.
> *Other new expressions:* at the moment, for the weekend, do (your) homework, I'm afraid. *Recycled language:* days of the week.

1 Comprehension task; presentation of key phrases

- Look at the replies, and build up the key expressions on the board:

She's	out away asleep	She's	at school at the cinema (not) at home

- Establish when Lisa is at home. Answers:

  At home: Thursday, Friday, Sunday
  Not at home: Monday, Tuesday, Wednesday, Saturday

- If you like, ask students to quickly practise the conversations in pairs.

2 Role-play: asking for people on the phone

- To introduce the activity, write the names of a few people you know on the board (e.g. *Maria, my brother, my daughter Sara*). Ask students to 'phone' you and ask to speak to one of them. Say where they are or what they are doing (begin *Sorry ...* or *I'm afraid ...*).

- Pairwork. Students write down the names of a few people on a piece of paper and give it to their partner. These people can be either real or invented.

- In turn, students 'phone' their partner and ask to speak to one of the people. Their partner gives a suitable reply.

> ➤ Focus on Form Exercise 3
> ➤ Workbook: Exercise B

> **Language note**
> We usually use *some* in positive sentences and *any* in negatives and questions; the same applies to *someone* and *anyone*. Is *anyone sitting here?* is another way of saying *Is this seat free?*

> **Language note**
> The Present continuous is formed from *be* + verb + *-ing*. So questions are simply the same as for the verb *to be*: *Is he here? – Is he staying here?*

> **Practice option: Yes/no questions**
> Play a game using the pictures in Exercise 1. Choose a picture. Students guess which it is by asking *Is she playing the guitar?, Is he drinking coffee?*, etc.

> ➤ Workbook: Exercise C, Listening

> **Language note**
> *She's out* means 'She's not at home'; *She's away* means 'She's not in this town'; *She's asleep* means 'She's sleeping'.

> **Option**
> Students could also include language from Exercise 1 in their replies, e.g. *Sorry, he's having dinner at the moment.*

📼 Tapescript for Exercise 2: *Questions*

A Is anyone sitting here?
B Er, no.
A Are you staying at this hotel?

B Yes. Yes, I am.
A What are you reading?
B Excuse me.
A Hey, where are you going?

2 Questions

Yes/no & Wh- questions

1 📼 Listen to the conversation.
What are the man's questions?

– ....?

– Er, no.

– ....?

– Yes. Yes, I am.

– ....?

– Excuse me.

– ....?

Practise the conversation.

2 Look at these answers. What do you think the questions are?

To the shops.

A football match.

A chocolate cake.

At the Central Hotel.

I'm writing a letter.

3 Can I speak to Lisa, please?

Saying where people are

Can I speak to Lisa, please?

MONDAY

I'm sorry. She's at school.

TUESDAY

Sorry. She's at the cinema.

WEDNESDAY

Sorry. I'm afraid she's out at the moment.

THURSDAY

Sorry. I'm afraid she's asleep.

FRIDAY

I'm afraid she's having a shower.

SATURDAY

Sorry. She's away for the weekend.

SUNDAY

Sorry. She's doing her homework.

1 On which days is Lisa

– at home?
– not at home?

2 Think of three people you know. Write down their names, and give the list to your partner.

Student A: Phone and ask to speak to someone on the list.
Student B: Say where they are / what they're doing.

Focus on Form

1 Verb + -ing

Group A		
play → playing	do →	
read →	drink →	

Group B		
writ~~e~~ → writing	have →	
smok~~e~~ → smoking	dance →	

Group C		
get → tt → getting		
run → nn → running		
swim →		

Add *-ing* to these verbs.

make	go	wash	live	sit	look

2 Present continuous

am / is / are + **verb** + -ing

Complete the text. Use the Present continuous.

It's Saturday night. The hotel guests (have) a good time. Some people (have) dinner in the restaurant. In the bar, a band (play) slow music. Some guests (sit) at the tables, and others (dance). In the next room, a few people (play) roulette.

In front of the hotel, a man (sit) in a car. He (smoke) a cigarette and he (look) at his watch.
It's two minutes to twelve …

3 Questions

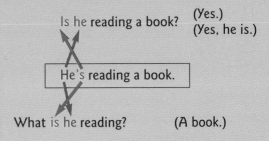

Is he reading a book?   (Yes.)
(Yes, he is.)

He's reading a book.

What is he reading?   (A book.)

Make questions. What are the answers?

a She's watching TV. → .... TV?
→ What ....?

b They're going home. → .... home?
→ Where ....?

c He's making coffee. → ....?
→ ....?

How to say it

1 🔊 Listen to the *s* in these sentences. Practise saying them.

She's asleep.

He's at school.

She's away for the weekend.

He's doing his homework.

She's wearing glasses.

2 🔊 Listen to the rhythm of these questions. Practise saying them.

■ . ■.
What's he doing?

■ . ■.
What's she wearing?

■ . ■.
What's she doing?

■ . ■.
Where are they going?

■ . . ■.
What are you doing?

Focus on Form

1 Verb + -ing

- Look at the examples and establish the basic rules:
  - Group A: Add -ing.
  - Group B: If the verb ends in -e, the -e disappears.
  - Group C: If the verb ends in a single consonant (e.g. t, m, n), we often double the consonant before -ing.

- Ask students to fill the gaps in each group, and write the answers on the board. Answers:

  A: reading, doing, drinking   B: having, dancing
  C: swimming

- Do the last part of the exercise together or as pairwork. Answers:

  making (group B)   going (A)   washing (A)   living (B)
  sitting (C)   looking (A)

2 Present continuous

- Establish why the verbs in the text should be in the Present continuous. Answer: It is describing a scene going on 'at the moment of speaking' (it's Saturday night – this is what is happening now). Compare:

  The hotel guests have a good time (usually).
  The hotel guests are having a good time (now).

- Either do the exercise round the class, or get students to write the verb forms and then go through the answers together. Answers:

  are having … are having … is playing … are sitting … are dancing … are playing … is sitting … is smoking … is looking

3 Questions

- Use the example to show how we make questions in the Present continuous: by changing round the subject and the verb *to be*. Compare:

  He's English → Is he English?
  He's reading → Is he reading?

- Ask students to add the questions and possible answers. Answers:

  a   Is she watching TV? (Yes, she is / No, she isn't.)
     What is (or What's) she watching? (TV.)

  b   Are they going home? (Yes, they are / No, they aren't.)
     Where are they going? (They're going home.)

  c   Is he making coffee? (Yes, he is / No, he isn't.)
     What is (or What's) he making? (Coffee.)

How to say it

1 Pronunciation of short forms: he's, she's, they're

- ▭ Play the recording, pausing and getting students to repeat the phrases. Focus on:
  - the rhythm of the sentences:
    He's <u>do</u>ing his <u>home</u>work.
    She's <u>wear</u>ing <u>glass</u>es.
  - the slightly reduced vowel in /hiz/ and /ʃiz/
  - the running together of /ʃiz_əsliːp/ and /hiz_ət skuːl/.

2 Recognising short forms: 's, 'm, 're

- ▭ Play the example. Focus on the (not very obvious) /s/ in the first sentence, and get students to repeat it.
- Play the other sentences, pausing and getting students to repeat them.

This unit covers a range of language used in describing people:
– clothes (e.g. *jacket, trousers, shirt*)
– jobs (e.g. *secretary, shop assistant*) and the phrases *work in* and *work for*
– physical appearance (e.g. *he's tall, she has dark hair*).
The Reading and Listening activity is about the '60s rock band The Troggs.

1 Clothes

This exercise introduces names of clothes, and also gives further practice in using the Present continuous tense. Students learn the names of clothes, then use these words to guess what people in the pictures are wearing.

▶ Workbook: Exercise A

> *Clothes:* shirt, blouse, T-shirt, jumper, coat, jacket, dress, skirt, suit, trousers, jeans, shorts, hat, tie.   *Recycled language:* colours; is wearing.

1 Presentation of clothes; writing task: making a list

- Look at the small pictures of clothes, read the words and get students to practise saying them. Focus on the pronunciation of /ˈtraʊzəz/, /blaʊz/ and /suːt/ and on the difference between /ʃɜːt/ and /skɜːt/.

- Working alone or in pairs, students write the clothes in three lists, according to whether they think they are for a man, a woman or either.

- Discuss the answers together, and see if students agree. If you like, build up lists on the board. Possible answers:

  Woman: hat, jacket, coat, blouse, skirt, dress   *Man:* shirt, tie, trousers, suit
  Either: jumper, T-shirt, shorts, jeans

2 Guessing game: describing someone in the class

- To introduce this stage, ask students to say what you are wearing, including colour words. Then choose a student in the class, and say what he/she is wearing. See if the class can say who you are describing.

- Pairwork. Students take it in turn to describe someone in the class, and to guess who it is.

3 Discussion activity: guessing what people are wearing

- Look at Picture A, and ask the students what they think the person is wearing. Try to get a range of different ideas, and encourage students to be specific (e.g. *I think she's wearing a light blue jacket*).

- In pairs, students look at the other people in the pictures and decide what they think they are wearing. Then ask round the class to find out what students decided.

- Show the class the pictures on page 129 of the Teacher's Book. Answers:

  A She's wearing a blue jacket and blue jeans.
  B The woman is wearing a black and white dress; the girl is wearing a pink T-shirt and a blue skirt.
  C He's wearing a dark blue hat, a blue and white T-shirt and white shorts.
  D The woman is wearing a light grey jumper and a white blouse. The man is wearing a pink shirt.
  E They're wearing dark grey suits and white shirts.

Language note
Trousers, jeans and *shorts* are all plural nouns in English, so we cannot say e.g. ~~a trousers~~. To talk about one item, we say *a pair of trousers, a pair of jeans*, etc.

Note
There are no 'right' answers. The idea of this exercise is to encourage discussion.

Review option
Quickly review colour words before you begin this stage.

Whole class option
Students take it in turn to describe someone, and the rest of the class guess who it is.

Alternative
If students are all wearing the same clothes (e.g. a school uniform), bring magazine pictures into the class and get students to describe them instead.

🔲 Tapescript for Exercise 2: *Jobs*

1 I'm a singer. I sing with a band. I always wear the same thing when I sing – I wear a red jacket and black trousers.

2 Well, I'm a doctor. I work in a large hospital. And I wear a skirt and a blouse and a white coat.

3 I'm a shop assistant. I work in a bookshop. And I usually wear just a jumper and jeans.

🔲 Tapescript for Exercise 3: *Who do you mean?*

1 Anna? She's got blond hair, quite short, and she wears glasses. She's about 25, quite attractive.

2 You know Anna – she drives a blue Volkswagen. She's quite tall, usually wears jeans.

3 You must know Anna – she lives in the next street. She teaches maths, and she's got those two small children.

Describing people

1 Clothes

1 Look at these clothes.
Which do you think are

– for a woman?
– for a man?
– for either a woman or a man?

Make three lists.

Show your list to other
students. Do they agree?

2 Choose a student in the class. Say what he/she is wearing.

Can other students guess who you're talking about?

This person's wearing a dark green blouse and blue jeans.

I think that's …

hat   tie   trousers   coat   jacket   suit

shirt   jumper   blouse   T-shirt

skirt   shorts   jeans   dress

3 Look at these people. What do
you think they're wearing?

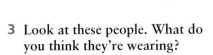

A

B

D

E

2 Jobs

1 Seven people talk about their jobs. Fill the gaps with jobs from the box.

a doctor
an engineer
a singer
a secretary
a shop assistant
a student
a waiter

a I'm ....
I study French.

b I'm ....
I work in a bookshop.

c I'm ....
I sing in a band.

d I'm .... I work
in a Thai restaurant.

e I'm .... I work
in a large hospital.

f I'm .... I work
for British Telecom.

g I'm .... I work for
an insurance company.

2 Three of the people wear these clothes to work. Which people do you think they are?

1

2

3

Now listen and check.

3 Talk about someone in your family. Use a dictionary to help you.

He
She works in …

He's
She's …

He
She works for …

He
She usually wears …

3 Who do you mean?

tall   hair
long   fair   grey
short   dark

1 Make sentences about the people at the bus stop.

He's
She's …

He
She has …

2 Three people describe a woman. What do they say about her?

She's about ☐ 25 ☐ 35 years old, and she has ☐ two ☐ three small children. She's quite ☐ tall ☐ short and

she has ☐ long ☐ short ☐ fair ☐ dark hair. She ☐ wears ☐ doesn't wear glasses, and she usually wears ☐ jeans. ☐ a skirt.

She drives ☐ a Mercedes ☐ a Volkswagen and she works in ☐ a bank. ☐ a school.

3 Look at the pictures on page 106. Which is the woman? How do you know?

4 Think of someone your partner knows (e.g. another student, a teacher, a friend, someone on TV). Write three sentences about him or her.

Does your partner know who you mean?

2 Jobs

This exercise introduces common names of jobs, and also teaches other ways to talk about jobs, using the verbs work in, work for, study *and* play.

> *Jobs:* (doctor), engineer, singer, secretary, shop assistant, (student), (waiter).
> *Other new words:* sing, band, hospital, insurance company.

1 Presentation of jobs; matching task

- Read the sentences and ask students to fill the gaps. As you do this, present names of jobs that students don't know. Focus on the pronunciation of /ˈsekrətərɪ/ and /endʒɪˈnɪə/. Answers:

  a a student *b* a shop assistant *c* a singer *d* a waiter *e* a doctor
  f an engineer *g* a secretary

2 Activation: guessing what people wear; listening to check

- Look at the sets of clothes and establish what they are:

  1 a jacket, trousers 2 a coat, a skirt, a blouse 3 jeans, a jumper

- Discuss which of the people wear them to work.
- 🔲 Play the recording to check. Answers:

  1 singer 2 doctor 3 shop assistant

3 Extension: writing sentences

- To show what to do, tell the class about someone in your family.
- Students choose someone in their family and prepare a few sentences about them. If you like, ask them to write their sentences down.
- In turn, students talk about the person they chose.

3 Who do you mean?

This exercise shows ways of describing people by saying what they look like and what they do. It introduces adjectives for describing general appearance.

> *New words:* tall, short; long/short hair; fair/blond/dark hair; drive (a car).
> *Recycled language:* age, clothes, family relationships; wears, works, has; usually.

1 Presentation of adjectives; practice: describing people

- Look at the picture, and use it to establish the meaning of *tall* and *short*, *long* and *short hair*, and *fair* and *dark hair*. Answers (L to R):

  1 She's short and she has long fair hair.
  2 He's tall and he has short dark hair.
  3 She's tall and she has long dark hair.
  4 She's short and she has long grey hair.
  5 He's short and he has short grey hair.
  6 She's tall and she has short dark hair.
  7 He's tall and he has short fair hair.

2 Listening & reading

- 🔲 Read the sentences, then play the recording. Students listen and mark the correct choice by the sentences in the box. Answers:

  25 years old, two small children, quite tall, short fair hair, wears glasses, wears jeans, drives a Volkswagen, works in a school

3 Discussion activity: interpreting a picture

- Look at the pictures (page 106). Ask which is the correct one, and why. Answer:

  B. (A has brown hair and has three children. C has long hair and drives a Mercedes.)

4 Guessing game: writing a description

- To demonstrate this part, choose someone everyone in the class knows. Write sentences on the board about their appearance and what they do, as in the examples in the box. See if the class can guess who you mean.
- Alone or in pairs, students choose someone and write sentences about them.
- Students read their sentences. The rest of the class try to guess who the person is.

➤ Workbook: Exercise B

> *Language note*
> Notice these relationships:
> – A *singer* is someone who *sings*.
> – A *student* is someone who *studies*.

> *Optional extension*
> Go through the list, and ask if students know people who do any of these jobs.

> 🔲 The tapescript is on page T51.

> *Note*
> The idea is for students to learn to make a simple statement about someone's job (or possibly their own). They should talk about the job in the simplest way, e.g. *My father works for a bank*, rather than *My father is an assistant accounts manager*!

➤ Workbook: Exercise C, Listening

> *Language note*
> *Short* is the opposite of *tall* (a tall/short man) and also of *long* (long/short hair).

> *Language note*
> The Present simple tense is used here and in Exercise 2 because we are talking about what people do *in general* or *usually*.

> 🔲 The tapescript is on page T51.

> *Homework option*
> Students write the sentences for homework, and read them out in the next lesson.

4 Love is all around

This combined Reading and Listening activity is about the '60s rock musician Reg Presley and his band The Troggs. In the reading, students put paragraphs about his life in the right order. The listening is a verse from one of his songs.

Reading skills: *reading to understand the sequence of events.*
Listening skills: *listening to the words of a pop song.*

New words (reading): later, go back, contract, song, hit (n.), suddenly, rock star, tape, send, producer, busy, come back, tell, leave, club, garage, builder, version, film, copies, next, get to, change.
New words (listening): feel, finger, toe, everywhere, written, wind, feeling, grow, really, love (n.), love (v.).

---

1 Presentation of vocabulary; reading & sequencing task

- To introduce the activity, explain to students that they're going to read the story of a rock star. Look at the diagram at the top, and tell the class that this shows the rock singer's life – it starts from nothing, goes up, goes down, and then goes up again. Ask if anyone has heard of The Troggs (a '60s band) or of Wet Wet Wet (an '80s band).

- Give time for students to read through the paragraphs. They should do this fairly quickly and without trying to understand every word, just to get the general meaning, and using the pictures to help them.

- Ask students which they think is the first paragraph (Answer: B). Read through it together, presenting new words (*leave school, a builder*) as you go.
  Then ask students to identify the next paragraph, and so on, reading through each paragraph in turn. The order of the story is:

  1 B   2 F   3 G   4 A   5 E   6 C   7 D

2 Listening & matching task

- 📼 Play the recording once through. Then ask students to match the lines. As you do so, explain key words and expressions (many of these, e.g. *fingers, toes, all around me, it's written* can easily be shown by gestures). Answer: see tapescript.

- Play the recording again, and let students just listen to it for enjoyment.

Idea
Get hold of a copy of the complete song *Love is all around* (either the original Troggs version or the Wet Wet Wet version). Play it at the beginning of the lesson to create a good atmosphere.

Optional lead-in
Talk in general about bands and rock music with the class, and build up key words and phrases on the board, e.g. *a pop singer, a rock singer, a band, a song, a hit, Number 1, a tape, a producer.* This will help students to read the paragraphs.

Note
This is the first verse of the Troggs' original version of *Love is all around.*

📼 Tapescript for Exercise 4: *Love is all around*

I feel it in my fingers, I feel it in my toes.
Well, love is all around me, and so the feeling grows.
It's written on the wind, it's everywhere I go.
So if you really love me, come on and let it show.

4 Love is all around

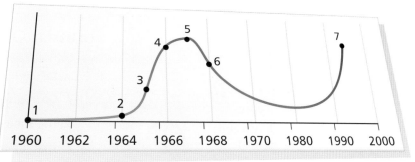

1 Read the story of the 1960s rock singer Reg Presley. Put the seven paragraphs in the right order.

A

A year later, they go back to Larry Page, and he gives them a contract. Their second song, *Wild thing*, is a big hit, and suddenly the Troggs are rock stars!

B

Reginald Ball leaves school at 16 and gets a job as a builder. He wants to be a singer in a rock band.

C

The Troggs leave Larry Page. They don't have any more hits. They play in clubs, but they aren't big stars any more.

D

The band Wet Wet Wet make a new version of *Love is all around* for the film *Four Weddings and a Funeral*. The song sells five million copies, and suddenly Reg Presley is a millionaire.

E

Reg Presley writes their next hit – *With a girl like you* – which gets to Number 1 in Britain. In the next two years, Reg writes three more hit songs for the Troggs. One is called *Love is all around*.

F

He starts a rock band with three friends. They call the band 'The Troggs'. Reginald Ball changes his name to Reg Presley.

G

The Troggs make a tape of their songs. They send the tape to producer Larry Page in London. Page likes the songs, but he's very busy. He tells them 'Come back in a year.'

2 Here are four lines of the song *Love is all around*. Can you match the first and second parts of each line?

 Now listen and check.

I feel it in my fingers, …   … it's everywhere I go

Well, love is all around me, …   … come on and let it show

It's written on the wind, …   … and so the feeling grows

So if you really love me, …   … I feel it in my toes

Focus on ... Imperatives

1 Listen to your teacher.
Do what he/she says!

Open your bag and give me £10

Now it's your turn. Tell other students to do things.

Give ...　　Open ...　　　　　　　Put ...
　　　　　　　　Look at ...

Close ...　　　　Take ...　　　　............

2 Look at these examples.

Look!　　　　　　Don't look!

Don't drink that!

Drink that.

3 Now look at these sentences. Which are correct? Write ✓ or add *Don't*.

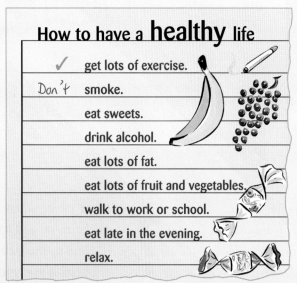

How to have a **healthy** life

✓	get lots of exercise.
Don't	smoke.
	eat sweets.
	drink alcohol.
	eat lots of fat.
	eat lots of fruit and vegetables.
	walk to work or school.
	eat late in the evening.
	relax.

Sounds: Coffee on Sunday

1 Listen to these sounds.

/ɒ/　Do you want coffee?

The shop's opposite my office.

/ʌ/　That jumper's a lovely colour.

Are you coming on Sunday or Monday?

2 Listen and practise.

doctor watch long shop opposite orange hot o'clock	brother colour lovely how much jumper umbrella Monday

3 Write a sentence. Use words from both boxes.

4 Read out your sentence.

Phrasebook: Hurry up!

Match these expressions with the pictures.

1

Hurry up!
Sit down.
Wait a minute.
Come in!
Be quiet.

2

3

4

Listen and check. Practise saying the expressions.

Study pages F

Focus on ... *Imperatives*

This exercise introduces positive and negative imperatives, used for giving instructions and stating rules.

> *Key language:* imperative forms. *New verbs:* put, give, take. *Recycled language:* common verbs.

1 ● Give instructions to various students round the class, using the verbs *open, close, give, take, look at* and *put*. If necessary, use gestures to make the meaning clear. Possible instructions:

Open your book.
Close your book.
Give me your book.
Give (Maria) your pen.
Put your book on the floor.
Take (Maria's) pen and give it to me.
Look at (Karl).

● Focus on the new verbs *give, take* and *put*. If necessary, give other examples to show what they mean.

● Choose other students to give similar instructions, using the same verbs.

2 Look at the examples. Establish that:

– we use imperatives to tell people to do things or not to do things (if possible, refer to imperatives in students' own language).
– the imperative is just the simple form of the verb (*look, give*, etc.).
– to tell people not to do things, we say *Don't* + verb.

3 ● Read through the sentences about how to have a healthy life. Establish what *a healthy life* is, and also the meaning of *fat* and *relax*.

● In pairs, students look at the sentences. They decide which ones are correct, and which ones should begin *Don't ...*

● Discuss the answers together. If you like, build up an agreed set of sentences on the board. Expected answers:

Get lots of exercise.
Don't smoke.
Don't eat sweets.
Don't drink alcohol.
Don't eat lots of fat.
Eat lots of fruit and vegetables.
Walk to work or school.
Don't eat late in the evening.
Relax.

> *Optional extension or homework*
> Choose another set of rules, e.g. *How to be happy, How to be successful, How to make friends, How to be a good husband/wife/friend/student*. Students think of sentences. Pool your ideas and build up a list on the board.

Sounds: *Coffee on Sunday*

> The vowel sounds /ɒ/ and /ʌ/.

1, 2 🖳 If students have problems, focus on these features:

– /ɒ/ is short, with lips slightly rounded.
– /ʌ/ is short, close to the sound /a/ in many languages (e.g. German *ja*, French *la*, Slavonic *da*). It is pronounced with mouth open and lips not rounded.

Get students to say both sounds and notice how their lips change.

3 Students write a sentence using words from both boxes, and including any other words they like, e.g.

– My brother has an orange jumper.
– How much is that lovely watch?

4 Students read out their sentences in turn. Focus on the pronunciation of /ɒ/ and /ʌ/.

Alternative: Dictation. Students dictate their sentence to the person next to them. As a check, ask students to read out the sentence they wrote down.

Phrasebook: *Hurry up!*

This exercise teaches common conversational phrases which use the imperative.

> *Key language:* Hurry up, Sit down, Wait a minute, Come in, Be quiet.

● Use the pictures to establish what the phrases mean. Students may be able to guess some of them. If not, tell them the answers, and give other examples. Answers:

1 Sit down.
2 Wait a minute.
3 Come in!
4 Hurry up!
5 Be quiet.

● 📼 Play the recording and ask students to repeat the phrases. Focus especially on intonation.

Consolidation

Expressions with 'have'

This exercise focuses on expressions with the verb have *for talking about everyday activities, including eating and drinking. This consolidates language from Exercise 7.1, Exercises 9.1 and 9.3, and Exercises 11.1 and 11.3.*

1 Look at the examples. Point out that we usually use *have* in these expressions, rather than *eat, drink, take, give,* etc.

2 • Ask the questions round the class, getting answers from one or two students each time.

   • Students ask and answer the questions in pairs.

   • As a round-up, ask a few students what they found out about their partner (e.g. *She has breakfast at 7 o'clock, She has a shower every morning …*).

at …

This exercise focuses on the use of at *for talking about places. This consolidates language from Exercises 8.1 and 8.2 and Exercise 11.3.*

1 Look at the examples. Point out that with some common phrases with *at*, we leave out *the* (*at school, at work, at home*).

2 Ask the questions round the class. Encourage students to give precise answers based on their knowledge of the local area (e.g. *At the Café Roma – it's near the station, and they have very good lemonade*).

3 • Give time for students to think about members of their family and make notes.

   • Either let students talk in pairs, or choose students to tell the whole class where members of their family are.

Review

Present simple tense

Review of Present simple positive, negative and questions (Units 7 and 9).

Do Part *a* with the whole class. Then let students do the other parts alone or in pairs, and go through the answers together. Answers:

   a I *study* French and she *studies* maths. She *has* a room at the university, but I *live* at home …
   b I *don't like* wine … I sometimes *have* a glass of beer.
   c My brother *works* in a fast food restaurant. He *makes* about 50 burgers … he *doesn't eat* meat.
   d What time *do you get up* in the morning? *Do you have* a big breakfast?
   e How many languages *does he speak*? I know he *speaks* French but *does he speak* Italian?

me, my …

Review of object pronouns and possessives (Study Pages C Focus, Study Pages D Consolidation).

• Write on the board:

I	**me**	**my**
he	**him**	
she	**her**	
it		
we		
you		
they		

Ask students to find the missing words and, in pairs, to put them in the diagrams. (Only the correct answers will fit the diagrams.)

• Go through the answers and build them up in the table on the board. The pairs are:

him	his
her	her
it	its
us	our
you	your
them	their

Mixed-up words

Review of vocabulary from Units 1, 8 and 10.

1 • Look at the first word together, and establish what it is. (Answer: *chemist*.)

   • Working alone or in pairs, students work out the other words. Let them look back at Units 1, 8 and 10 if they need help.

   • Go through the answers together. Answers:

   Things to eat: fruit, potato, cheese
   Shops: chemist, baker, butcher
   Countries: Brazil, Japan, Germany

2 • Students look through previous units to find a word. They write it in a jumbled form and add a clue.

   • They give their word to another student to solve.

Consolidation

Expressions with 'have'

1 We often use *have* to talk about food or drink.

have breakfast

have a sandwich

have a cup of coffee

We also say:

have a bath

have a shower

have a party

2 Ask your partner:

> When do you have breakfast? lunch? dinner?

> What do you have for breakfast?

> If you go to a café, what do you usually have?

> When do you have a shower? a bath?

at …

1 Notice these expressions.

> She's at home, at work, at school, at a friend's house.
>
> I usually eat at Dino's Restaurant.
>
> You can buy it at the market, at a chemist's, at The Book Centre.

2 Answer these questions.

> Where can I get a drink near here?

> Where can I buy some stamps?

> Where can I get a cheap meal near here?

> Where can I buy a pair of jeans?

3 Think about people in your family. Where are they at the moment?

Review

Present simple tense

Choose verbs from the boxes and fill the gaps.

a My girlfriend and I are both students. I ▢ French and she ▢ maths. She ▢ a room at the university, but I ▢ at home with my parents.

> live
> study
> have

b I ▢ *(not)* wine, but if it's very hot I sometimes ▢ a glass of beer.

> have
> like

c My brother ▢ in a fast food restaurant. He ▢ about 50 burgers an hour. The funny thing is, he's a vegetarian – he ▢ *(not)* meat.

> eat
> work
> make

d What time ▢ *(you)* in the morning? ▢ *(you)* a big breakfast?

> get up
> have

e How many languages ▢ *(he)* ? I know he ▢ French, but ▢ *(he)* Italian?

> speak

me, my …

Make pairs and write them in the right diagrams.

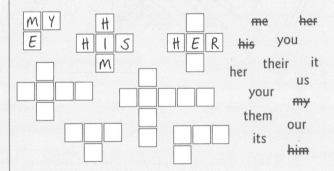

~~me~~   ~~her~~   ~~his~~   you   her   their   it   your   us   ~~my~~   them   our   its   ~~him~~

Mixed-up words

1 Look at these mixed-up words. Can you make

- three things to eat?
- three shops?
- three countries?

CEHIMST   FIRTU
ABEKR   ABILRZ
AANJP   AOOPTT
BCEHRTU
CEEEHS   AEGMNRY

How do you spell them?

2 Now you write a mixed-up word. Show it to your partner.

> ENTIHKC
> (This is a room)

13 How much?

1 Useful things

Count & non-count nouns • a & some

~~bowl~~
~~bread~~
coffee
cup
~~eggs~~
envelope
flour
flowers
keys
knife
~~matches~~
money
paper
~~pen~~
soap
radio
shampoo
spoon
stamps
~~water~~

There's …	There are …	There's …
a bowl	some eggs	some bread
a pen	some matches	some water
…	…	…

1 What is there in the picture? Add to the three lists. Use words from the box.

What is the difference between the three lists?

2 Cover the picture. How many things can you remember?

 There's a …

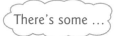 There are some …

There's some …

3 Work with a partner. You want to

– light a fire
– write a letter
– make a cake
– make some coffee.

What do you need? Write four lists.

Show your lists to other students. Do they have the same things?

13

This unit is concerned with ways of talking about quantity. It focuses on these main areas:
– count and non-count nouns
– *a, some* and *any*
– quantifiers: *(not) much/many, lots of*
– questions with *how much/how many?*
– the use of *have got* as an alternative to *have*.

1 Useful things

This exercise focuses on words for common household items and food, some of which are count (e.g. a spoon, matches), and some non-count (e.g. soap, flour). Students practise talking about the objects, using There's ... *and* There are ...

> ➤ Focus on Form: Exercise 1
> ➤ Workbook: Exercise A

Key structures: count and non-count nouns; a, some.
New words and phrases: key, money, bowl, paper, envelope, soap, matches; need, light a fire.
Recycled language: food, common objects; there is/are.

---

1 Task: putting words in categories; presentation of count/non-count nouns

- Look at the items already given in the three lists (*bowl, pen, eggs*, etc.) and ask students to find them in the picture.
- Establish the difference between the three lists:
  - *bowl* and *pen* are singular nouns. They have *a* or *an* in front of them.
  - *eggs* and *matches* are plural nouns. They have *-s* (or *-es*) at the end. These words are all *count nouns*: they have a singular and a plural form (*a pen / pens, a match / matches*).
  - *water* and *bread* are *non-count nouns*. They have no plural form (we cannot say *a water / waters* – it's just *water*).

  Point out that we often use *some* with non-count nouns and with plural nouns.
- Ask students to identify other items in the picture. Write them on the board in three lists. Expected answers:

  There's (a bowl, a pen,) a cup, an envelope, a knife, a radio, a spoon.
  There are (some eggs, some matches,) some flowers, some keys, some stamps.
  There's (some water, some bread,) some coffee, some flour, some money, some paper, some soap, some shampoo.

2 Practice: memory game

- Ask students to cover the picture and see how many things they can remember. Get them to use the structures *There's a ...*, *There are some ...* and *There's some ...*

3 Activation: making a list

- Look at the activities in the list. Teach *light a fire* (use gestures or a drawing). Ask students what you need to light a fire, and write a list on the board. (Expected answer: some paper, some matches, maybe some wood.)
- Ask students to write similar lists of things they need for the other activities. They could do this alone or in pairs.
- Discuss the answers together. Focus on the difference between count and non-count nouns. Possible answers:

  to write a letter: a pen, some paper, an envelope, some stamps.
  to make a cake: some flour, some eggs, some water, some sugar, a bowl, a spoon.
  to make some coffee: some coffee, some water, a spoon, a cup, some milk.

Language note
Some words can be either count or non-count, with a difference in meaning. So the picture shows *paper*, but we can also say *a paper* (= a newspaper); we can see *coffee* in the picture, but we can also say *a coffee* (= a cup of coffee).

Presentation option
Teach the words *bag, jar* and *bottle*, and show how we can say *some coffee* or *a jar of coffee, some flour* or *a bag of flour*, etc. If you like, teach *a piece* (or *sheet*) *of paper* and *a loaf of bread* in the same way.

Pairwork option
Students work in pairs. One student covers the picture and tries to remember the items.

---

2 Shopping list

This exercise practises have/haven't got, *and quantity expressions. Students listen to people making a shopping list and work out what they have and haven't got.*

> *Key language:* not much, not many; we've got, we haven't got.
> *Recycled language:* food and drink; lots of, some/any.

1 *Listening & note-making; presentation of 'have/haven't got'*

- Look at the food and drink items. Ask which are count nouns and which are non-count nouns. (Answer: *orange juice*, *bread*, *rice*, *coffee* and *sugar* are non-count; the others are count.)
- Write these structures on the board:

> **We've got some tomatoes.**
> **We haven't got any tomatoes.**

  Point out that *we've got* (= we have got) means the same as *we have*.
- 🔊 Play the recording. Students mark the items the people need. Answer:

  orange juice, tomatoes, eggs, potatoes, apples, bananas, coffee, sugar

2 *Listening & sentence completion. Presentation of quantity expressions*

- 🔊 Play the recording again, and complete the sentences. Expected answers:

  They've got lots of bread.   They haven't got many potatoes.
  They haven't got much sugar.   They haven't got any eggs/coffee.

3 *Activation: talking about food at home*

- Tell students what you've got and what you haven't got at home. Use the structures from Part 1.
- Ask students if they know what food they've got at home. Prompt them, e.g. *What about tomatoes? What about milk? What have you got in the fridge?*

3 How much ...?

This exercise shows how we use How much? *with non-count nouns and* How many? *with count nouns. It takes the form of a multiple choice quiz.*

> *New words:* quiz, pages, copies, use, blood, human, body, average, fuel, journey, basketball, team, jam, state, tonne, lifetime, elephant.

1 *Reading; presentation of 'how much/many'*

- Read through the quiz, presenting any new words as you go. Ask the class to guess the answers, then tell them. Answers:

  1 c   2 b   3 a   4 c

- Establish that the red questions use *How many* and the blue ones use *How much*. Write these phrases on the board:

| **How many** | trees?
people? | **How much** | blood?
fuel? |

  Point out that with count nouns (*trees*, *people*) we use *How many*; with non-count nouns (*blood*, *fuel*) we use *How much*.

2 *Activation: making questions*

- Look at the other quiz items. Ask students to make questions with *How much* or *How many*, and see if anyone can guess the answers (in brackets):

  A How many players are there in a basketball team? (5)
  B How much sugar is there in a kilo of jam? (600 grams)
  C How many letters are there in the English alphabet? (26)
  D How many states are there in the USA? (50)
  E How much food/How many tonnes of food does the average person eat? (13 tonnes)
  F How much water/How many litres of water does an African elephant drink a day? (50 litres)

> ➤ Focus on Form: Exercises 2 & 3
> ➤ Workbook: Exercise B

> 📼 The tapescript is on page T58.

> *Language note*
> *I've got*, etc. is often used instead of *I have* in conversational English. Students can learn it at this stage as a set expression.

> *Language note*
> *Some* is usually used in positive sentences, *any* in negative ones:
> – I've got some bread.
> – We haven't got any bread.
> In the same way, we usually say *lots of* (or *a lot of*) in positive sentences, and *much/many* in negative sentences:
> – We've got lots of bread.
> – We haven't got much bread.

> *Pairwork option: role-play*
> Students make a shopping list in pairs, as in the dialogue.

> ➤ Focus on Form: Exercise 2
> ➤ Workbook: Exercise C

> *Option*
> Get 'majority guesses' from the class and write them on the board.
> Obviously, students are not expected to know the answers to the questions.

> *Practice option*
> Give other nouns and ask students to add *How much/many*, e.g.
> water – How much water?
> books – How many books?

> *Homework option*
> Students think of a question at home. They then ask their questions in the next lesson.

2 Shopping list

lots of • not many/much • not any

1 Two people are making a shopping list. Which of these things do they need? Write them on the shopping list.

tomatoes	rice	bananas
eggs	potatoes	coffee
bread	apples	sugar

shopping list
Orange juice

2 Listen again and complete these sentences.

They've got lots of …

They haven't got many …

They haven't got much …

They haven't got any …

3 Do you know what you've got in your own kitchen? Talk about the things in the list.

We've got some …

We haven't got any …

We've got lots of …

We haven't got many/much …

3 How much …?

How many …? • How much …?

1 Here are four quiz questions. Can you guess the answers?

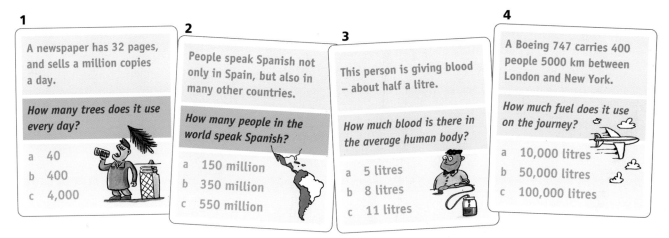

1

A newspaper has 32 pages, and sells a million copies a day.

How many trees does it use every day?

a 40
b 400
c 4,000

2

People speak Spanish not only in Spain, but also in many other countries.

How many people in the world speak Spanish?

a 150 million
b 350 million
c 550 million

3

This person is giving blood – about half a litre.

How much blood is there in the average human body?

a 5 litres
b 8 litres
c 11 litres

4

A Boeing 747 carries 400 people 5000 km between London and New York.

How much fuel does it use on the journey?

a 10,000 litres
b 50,000 litres
c 100,000 litres

What's the difference between the red questions and the blue questions?

2 Make questions with *How many …?* and *How much …?* Do you know the answers?

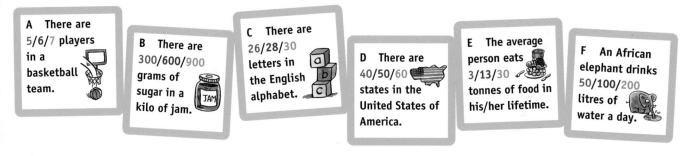

A There are 5/6/7 players in a basketball team.

B There are 300/600/900 grams of sugar in a kilo of jam.

C There are 26/28/30 letters in the English alphabet.

D There are 40/50/60 states in the United States of America.

E The average person eats 3/13/30 tonnes of food in his/her lifetime.

F An African elephant drinks 50/100/200 litres of water a day.

Focus on Form

1 Count & non-count

Count nouns

a boy   two boys   a cup   three cups

Non-count nouns

sugar   a kilo   water   two glasses
of sugar   of water

Count or non-count?

shirt	beef	wine	ketchup
picture	lake	oil	cigarette

2 many & much

Count nouns	Non-count nouns
There aren't many cups.	There isn't much salt.
How many cups are there?	How much salt is there?

Fill the gaps with *much* or *many*.

a How .... wine do we need?

b I don't eat .... white bread, but I eat a lot of brown bread.

c How .... cigarettes do you smoke a day?

d How .... sugar is there?

e They've got a lot of books in their house, but not .... pictures.

f I haven't got .... money in the bank.

3 have got

have		*have got*
I have a bike.	↔	I've got a bike.
I don't have a car.	↔	I haven't got a car.
My sister has a car.	↔	My sister's got a car.
She doesn't have a bike.	↔	She hasn't got a bike.

> I've got = I have got   He's got = He has got

Read out this paragraph using *have got*.

My brother and I are very different. He has dark hair and black eyes; I have fair hair and green eyes. He has a flat in the city centre; I have a small house in the country. He has a fast car, but he doesn't have any children. I have three children, but I don't have a car. He doesn't have any problems. And I don't have any money.

Think of a person in your family. How are you different? Make sentences with *have got*. Think about these things.

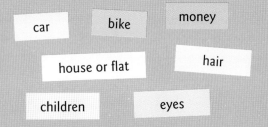

car   bike   money

house or flat   hair

children   eyes

How to say it

1 🔊 **Listen to *'ve got* and *haven't got* in these sentences. Practise saying them.**

I've got a new bike.

I've got brown hair.

We've got some money.

We haven't got much sugar.

I haven't got a car.

2 🔊 **Listen to the /ə/ sound in these phrases. Practise saying them.**

ə ə
∎ ■ ∎ ∎ ■
a kilo of rice

ə ə ə
∎ ■ ∎ ∎ ■
a litre of milk

ə ə ə
∎ ■ ∎ ∎ ■
a glass of water

ə ə
∎ ■ ∎ ∎ ■
a bag of sugar

ə ə ə
∎ ■ ∎ ∎ ■
a bottle of wine

Focus on Form

1 Count & non-count

● Look at the examples and establish that:

– count nouns have a singular and plural form; in the singular they have *a* or *an*.

– non-count nouns are singular only, without *a* or *an*.

– to make non-count nouns countable, we can use phrases like *a glass of*, *a kilo of*.

● Do the exercise round the class. Answers:

shirt: count   beef: non-count   wine: non-count
ketchup: non-count   picture: count   lake: count
oil: non-count   cigarette: count

2 many & much

● Look at the examples.

● Either do the exercise round the class, or let students do it in pairs and then go through the answers together. Answers:

a How *much* wine …?
b I don't eat *much* white bread …
c How *many* cigarettes …?
d How *much* sugar …?
e … not *many* pictures.
f I haven't got *much* money …

3 have got

● Look at the examples. Point out that:

– *have* and *have got* are two different structures that mean the same.

– *have* is a normal verb. We say *I have*, *he has*. The negative is *I don't have*, *he doesn't have*.

– *have got* is really a form of the verb *get*. We say *I have got* (*I've got*), *he has got* (*he's got*). The negative is *I haven't got*, *he hasn't got*.

● Go through the paragraph. Ask students to use forms of *have got*. Answers:

… He's got dark hair and black eyes; *I've got* fair hair and green eyes. *He's got* a flat in the city centre; *I've got* a small house in the country. *He's got* a fast car, but *he hasn't got* any children. *I've got* three children, but *I haven't got* a car. *He hasn't got* any problems. And *I haven't got* any money.

● To introduce the second part of the exercise, tell the class some things about yourself and other people in your family, saying how you are different.

● Either ask students to make some sentences orally round the class, or give them time to write sentences and ask them to read out what they have written.

How to say it

1 The sound of ''ve got' and 'haven't got'

● ▭ Play the sentences, and ask students to repeat them. Focus on the (not very obvious) /v/ sound in /aɪv_gɒt/, /wiːv_gɒt/.

2 Reduced /ə/ in phrases like 'a glass of water'

● ▭ Play the recording, pausing and getting students to repeat the phrases. Focus on:

– the rhythm of the phrases:
  a glass of water
  a kilo of rice
– the /ə/ sounds: /ə glɑːs əv/, /ə ˈkiːləʊ əv/.

▭ Tapescript for Exercise 2: *Shopping list*

A Let me see … We need some orange juice, and some tomatoes, and … we haven't got any eggs … What else?
B What about bread?
A No, we've got lots of bread … Rice? No, we've got rice … Ah, we haven't got many potatoes.
B Potatoes, OK. What about fruit?

A Oh, yes. Get some apples – and some bananas, maybe. What else? Ah yes, we haven't got any coffee.
B We haven't got much sugar, either.
A OK, sugar. Is that everything?
B I think so, yes.

14

This unit covers a range of topics to do with seasons and climate:
– names of seasons
– names of months
– vocabulary for describing the climate of a country (e.g. *wet, cold, rain*)
– expressions for talking about the weather (e.g. *it's raining, it's windy*).
The Reading and Listening activity is about festivals.

1 Seasons

This exercise introduces the names of the seasons, and vocabulary for talking about climate. Students extract key vocabulary from the texts, then write sentences about the climate in their own country.

➤ Workbook: Exercise A

> *Seasons:* summer, winter, spring, autumn; wet season.
> *Climate words:* hot, cold, warm, cool, wet, dry, humid; rain, snow; temperature.

1 Reading to answer questions

- Read through the questions. Ask students to look at the pictures and try to guess the answers.

- Give time for students to read the texts, then discuss the answers together. Answers:

  Always hot: Alice Springs, Jakarta
  Very cold in winter: Moscow
  Dry in August: Alice Springs, Istanbul, Moscow, Jakarta

2 Vocabulary task; presentation of vocabulary

- Ask students to find pairs of opposites in the texts. Write them on the board, and explain the meaning of any new words:

wet	dry	summer	winter
hot	cold	spring	autumn
warm	cool	day	night

- Show how we use *rain* and *snow* either as verbs or as nouns:

  | It often | rains / snows | in the winter. | | There is often | rain / snow | in the winter. |

- Read through the texts together, presenting any other new items, e.g. *humid, temperature, 20° (= 20 degrees), all year round.*

3 Activation: writing sentences

- Give time for students to write sentences about their own country. They can do this either alone or working together in pairs.

- Students read out their sentences. If the class all come from the same country, you could build up sentences on the board.

Optional lead-in
Talk about where the places in the pictures are, and ask what students know about them, e.g. Jakarta is the capital of Indonesia, in South-East Asia. (You could do this in the students' own language.)

Note
Students should just read to answer the questions at this stage, not to understand every word in the texts. They will read them more closely in Stage 2.

Note
Do not spend too much time on the names of months at this point. They are practised more fully in Exercise 2.

14 Around the year

1 Seasons

1 Here are four places from around the world.
Which places are

- always hot?
- very cold in the winter?
- dry in August?

Read the texts and find out.

In the summer, Istanbul is quite hot, about 25–30°, and in the winter it is cool. It often rains in the autumn and winter, and it sometimes snows.

Alice Springs is hot and dry all year round. From October to March it is very hot, often 40° or more. From May to August it is clear and warm by day, but cool at night.

Moscow has hot and mainly dry weather in the summer, with temperatures of 25–30°. In the winter it is very cold, and it snows a lot. Temperatures can be below –20°, and there is often snow from November to March. Spring comes late in Moscow, usually in April or May.

Jakarta is hot all year round, and the temperature is about the same in January and July. November to April is the wet season, and in January there is a lot of rain. From July to September it is mainly dry, but the air is always humid.

2 Find pairs of opposites in the texts. Make a list.

COLD   SUMMER

HOT   WINTER

3 Write a few sentences about the weather in your own country around the year.

2 January, February …

1 What are the missing months? Find them in Exercise 14.1 and write them in the table.

2 What month is your birthday? What about other people in the class? Which month has the most birthdays?

3 These two lists are about months in Britain.
Which months do you think they are?

dark nights
cold
jumpers and coats
TV
Christmas

school finishes
swimming
holidays
ice-cream
shorts

Now you choose a month and write a list.

Read out your list. Can other students guess the month?

January
February
June
December

3 What's the weather like?

1 These four people are talking about the weather.
Here are some of the things they say. Match the sentences with the pictures.

a ☐ It's cloudy.   *f* ☐ It's hot and humid.

b ☐ It's very windy. *g* ☐ It's quite warm.

c ☐ It's sunny.   *h* ☐ It's quite cool.

d ☐ It's raining.   *i* ☐ It's very cold.

e ☐ It's snowing.

☐ Listen and check your answers.

2 Look out of the window. What's the weather like?

3 Guess what the weather's like today in these places.

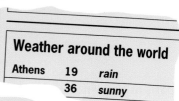

Weather around the world

Athens	19	rain
	36	sunny

London   Singapore   Moscow   Rio de Janeiro

Get a newspaper and find out!

2 January, February ...

This exercise focuses on the months of the year. Students compile a list of months, then use this as a basis for practice.

> *Key vocabulary:* months of the year. *Other new words:* night, Christmas, holiday.

➤ Workbook: Exercise B, Listening

1 Vocabulary task; presentation of months

● Look at the table of months. Ask students to look at the texts in Exercise 1 again, and fill in the missing months. Build up a list on the board and get students to practise saying the words. Answers:

January, February, March, April, May, June, July, August, September, October, November, December

2 Activation: birthdays

● Ask students round the class which month their birthday is in. Mark crosses beside the list on the board to find out the most popular month for birthdays.

3 Writing & guessing game

● Look at the two lists of words and present any new vocabulary; each is a list of things that someone in Britain associates with this month. Ask students which months they think they are. (Answer: December, July.)

● Working alone, students choose a month and write a list of words and phrases. As far as possible, they should keep to vocabulary that they know already, although they could also use dictionaries to help with new words.

● Pairwork. Students read out their list. Their partner tries to guess the month.

● As a round-up, ask a few students to read out their list.

> *Note*
> The names of the months may be very similar in the students' own language. Focus on differences in spelling and pronunciation (especially /ˈdʒænjʊərɪ/, /ˈfebrʊərɪ/, /ˈeɪprɪl/, /dʒʊˈlaɪ/, /ˈɔːɡəst/).

> *Alternative*
> Ask students to keep count of the number of times they hear their own birthday month. Then go through the months, and find out the total 'scores'.

> *Homework idea*
> Ask students to learn the names of the months at home. Test them in the next lesson by asking questions, e.g. *January, February ... what comes next? What is before September?*

3 What's the weather like?

This exercise teaches simple ways of talking about the weather at the moment. It builds on vocabulary from Exercise 1 and introduces some new expressions.

> *New expressions:* it's sunny, it's windy, it's cloudy; it's raining, it's snowing.
> *Recycled language:* hot, warm, cool, cold, humid.

➤ Workbook: Exercise C

1 Matching task; presentation of vocabulary; listening to check

● Read through the sentences and see if students can match them with the pictures. Use the pictures to present new vocabulary, and write key expressions on the board:

It's	cloudy windy sunny	It's	raining snowing

● [cassette] Play the recording and check the answers. (Answers: see tapescript.)

2 Activation: today's weather

● Ask students to describe the weather where you are now. Build up sentences on the board.

3 Extension: world weather

● Take each city in turn, and discuss what the weather might be like. Help students to focus by prompting them, e.g. *What do you think? Is it hot or cold there? Or warm? What's the temperature? Is it sunny there at the moment?* If you like, make notes for each place on the board.

● To find out the answers, either look in the world weather report of a national newspaper or (if your school has a computer) look on the Internet.

> *Language note*
> *Rain* and *snow* are used as verbs, so we can say *It usually rains in July* (Present simple) and *It's raining at the moment* (Present continuous – see Unit 11).
> The adjectives *sunny, cloudy* and *windy* all come from nouns: sun → sunny; wind → windy; cloud → cloudy.

> [cassette] The tapescript is on page T61.

> *Homework option*
> Ask students to find out the answers at home. They report back in the next lesson.

4 Festivals

This combined Reading and Listening activity is about festivals associated with particular times of the year. Students read short texts about festivals in different parts of the world, and then they listen to people saying how they spend New Year's Eve.

Reading skills: *reading for general idea.*
Listening skills: *listening for main points.*

> *New words (reading):* statues; celebrate, carnival, the best known, parade, fantastic, costumes, samba; festival, coloured, powder; everyone, during, keep, because; match, team, player, century, costume, dangerous, rules; visit, sausage; last, spend, midnight.
> *New words (listening):* meal, early, fireworks.

1 Presentation of vocabulary; reading & matching task

- Give time for students to read the texts, and match them with the pictures. They should not try to understand every word at this stage, but just understand enough to identify the festivals from the pictures.

- Go through the answers together. Ask students to say what words helped them to identify each festival (e.g. Oktoberfest: *drink, beer, eat, people*). Read through each text, making clear any new words and expressions.
  Answers:

  A Snow Festival   B New Year's Eve   C Gioco del Calcio   D Carnival
  E Songkran   F Holi   G Oktoberfest

> *Pre-reading option*
> Write key vocabulary on the board, e.g. *statues, costumes, powder, football match, sausages, midnight.* Either give the words in the students' own language or give examples to show the meaning.

2 Listening

- Read through the list of activities. Then play the recording. Pause after each speaker and establish what things he/she does. Answers:

  1 They go to a party, go out into the street, watch fireworks.
  2 She goes to a restaurant, dances.
  3 He goes to bed early, (stays at home).
  4 They stay at home, watch TV.
  5 They stay at home till midnight, then visit friends.

> *Alternative: pre-listening discussion*
> Read through the list and ask students which of the things they do on New Year's Eve. Then play the recording as a final stage.

3 Extension: New Year's Eve

- Ask students what they do on New Year's Eve. Either simply ask round the class, prompting to encourage students to talk (e.g. *Do you go out? Where do you go? Does anyone watch TV?*), or let students talk briefly in pairs, then ask what they found out from their partner.

> *Alternative*
> If students come from a country where New Year is not celebrated at the end of December, they should of course talk about their own New Year celebrations or another important festival.

Tapescript for Exercise 3: *What's the weather like?*

1 …Yes, it's quite warm here, but it's raining …

2 It's nice and sunny, but it's very windy, and quite cool …

3 It's very, very cold. And it's snowing …

4 It's really hot here, quite humid … No, it isn't sunny at all, it's cloudy – cloudy and very hot …

Tapescript for Focus on … *Can*

OK, I can make a cup of coffee, I can make toast, yes … 'Can you cook rice?' Yes, I can cook rice, no problem … I can make an omelette, not a very good omelette, but yes, I can make an omelette. Barbecue a chicken … Yes, I can barbecue a chicken, I can do that. I can't make a cake, no, not really. But I can make my own pasta. I have a pasta machine and I often make my own pasta, yes, so I can do that. But I can't make bread, no.

Tapescript for Exercise 4: *Festivals*

1 Well, we usually go to a party and then at midnight we all go out into the street and we watch fireworks.

2 Well, I usually go out to a restaurant with a lot of friends and we all have a nice meal together and we listen to music and dance and have a good time.

3 I don't do anything. Actually, I don't like New Year's Eve very much so I go to bed early.

4 Well, we stay at home, but we stay up till midnight, and we watch New Year on television.

5 We stay at home till midnight, and then we usually go and visit friends, and we have a few drinks with them.

4 Festivals

1 Read about these festivals. Which festivals do the pictures show?

SNOW FESTIVAL (February – Sapporo, Japan)
At the Sapporo Snow Festival people make statues from snow. Some of the statues are *very* big. You can just look at the statues – or you can make one yourself.

CARNIVAL (February – Brazil)
People celebrate Carnival in many countries, but the best known is in Brazil. In Rio de Janeiro, many thousands of people parade through the streets. They wear fantastic costumes and dance to samba music.

HOLI (March – India)
This is a Hindu festival. On the last day of the festival, people sell coloured powder in the street. You can buy the powder, and throw it over other people.

SONGKRAN (April – Thailand)
Songkran – the Water Festival – is the Thai New Year. If you're in Thailand during Songkran, keep your car windows closed, because everyone throws water at everyone.

GIOCO DEL CALCIO (June – Florence, Italy)
This is a 16th-century version of a football match. There are four teams, each with 27 players. The players wear 16th-century costumes. The game is quite dangerous, because there aren't many rules.

OKTOBERFEST (September! – Munich, Germany)
If you like beer, this is the festival for you. Seven million people visit the Oktoberfest. They drink five million litres of beer, and eat a million sausages and half a million chickens.

NEW YEAR'S EVE (end of December)
In most parts of the world, December 31 is the last day of the year. People go out with their families and friends, and at 12.00 midnight, everyone says 'Happy New Year'.

2 ▢ **Five people say what they do on New Year's Eve.**

Which things does each speaker do? Choose from the list.

a stay at home
b watch TV
c go to a party
d go to bed early
e visit friends
f go to a restaurant
g go out into the street
h dance
i watch fireworks

3 What do you do on New Year's Eve?

G | Study pages

Focus on ... Can

Look! I can swim!

Help! I can't swim!

She can ride a horse.

He can't ride a horse.

They can ski.

They can't ski.

1 Look at the examples and complete the table.

✓	✗
I can	I can't
He/She	He/She ....
They	They ....

2 🔲 A man answers these questions. Listen and write his scores in column A.

Can you cook?

		A	B
Can you make a cup of coffee?	(1 point)		
Can you make toast?	(1 point)		
Can you cook rice?	(3 points)		
Can you make an omelette?	(4 points)		
Can you barbecue a chicken?	(4 points)		
Can you make a cake?	(6 points)		
Can you make your own pasta?	(8 points)		
Can you make bread?	(10 points)		
	Total score		

3 Now find out your partner's scores. Write them in column B.

Sounds: Lovely weather

1 🔲 Listen to these sounds.

/v/ It's never very cold in November.

/w/ What's the weather like in winter?

Listen to the two sounds together.

I want to watch TV this evening.

It's twenty past twelve.

2 🔲 Listen and practise.

seven have very	wet windy winter
lovely vegetables	Wednesday watch
November TV	sandwich weather

3 Write a sentence. Use words from both boxes.

4 Read out your sentence.

Phrasebook: Would you like ...?

Match the questions with the pictures.
What do you think the replies are?

1 ☀️

Would you like another drink?

Would you like a lift?

Would you like an ice-cream?

2

3

🔲 Listen and check.

A friend is staying with you. Offer him/her the things in the pictures.

Study pages G

Focus on … *Can*

This exercise teaches the use of can *and* can't *for talking about ability, and questions with* Can you …?

> *Key language:* can, can't.   *New verbs:* swim, ride, ski.
> *Recycled language:* cook, make; food vocabulary.

1 Use the pictures to present the verbs *swim*, *ride* and *ski*. Look at the examples and complete the table on the board:

I can	I can't
He/She can	He/She can't
They can	They can't

Establish that:
– the negative of *can* (/kæn/) is *can't* (/kɑːnt/).
– all the forms of *can* and *can't* are the same (so we say *I can* and *he can*).

2 ● Read through the questionnaire. Present any new items (e.g. *toast*, *barbecue*, *omelette*).

 ● ▭ Play the recording (tapescript on page T61). Students listen and give points. Then discuss together what score the speaker should have (probably 21).

 ● Play the recording again, pausing after each part, and establish exactly what the person can and can't do.

3 ● Write the question form on the board:

Can you	make toast?
	cook rice?

If necessary, point out that after *can* we do not use *to* (so we don't say ~~Can you to make toast?~~).

 ● In pairs, students take it in turns to ask each other the questions and note down a score.

 ● As a round-up, find out who had the highest (and lowest!) score.

> ▭ Tapescript for Phrasebook: *Would you like …?*
>
> 1 A Would you like an ice-cream?
>   B Oh, yes please.
>   A OK, what kind?
>   B Chocolate.
> 2 A Hello! Would you like a lift?
>   B Oh, yes. Thank you very much.
>   A That's OK. Where are you going?
>   B Just to the next village.
>   A OK.
> 3 A Would you like another drink?
>   B Ooh, yes please.
>   A Orange juice, wasn't it?
>   B Yes, orange juice with ice.

Sounds: *Lovely weather*

> The sounds /v/ and /w/.

1, 2 ▭ If students have problems, focus on these features:
 – To pronounce /v/, the upper teeth should touch the lower lip, and the lips are not rounded.
 – To pronounce /w/, the lips and teeth should not touch, and the lips should be rounded. Students could practise by saying /ʊ/: /ʊ – aɪ/, /ʊ – en/, /ʊ – ɪntə/.

Get students to alternate the sounds /v/ and /w/ and notice how their lips change.

3 Students write a sentence using words from both boxes, and including any other words they like, e.g.

 – We have lovely weather in November.
 – It was very wet on Wednesday.

4 Students read out their sentences in turn. Focus on the pronunciation of /v/ and /w/.

Alternative: Dictation. Students dictate their sentence to the person next to them. As a check, ask students to read out the sentence they wrote down.

Phrasebook: *Would you like …?*

This exercise teaches students how to offer things to other people.

> *Key language:* Would you like …?
> *Recycled language:* food and drink, common objects.

● Establish the meaning of *Would you like …?*
 – I say it if I want to give you something.
 – It means 'Do you want …?' but it is more polite.
 Give the equivalent in the students' own language if possible.

● Look at the pictures and ask students to match them with the remarks. Explain *a lift* (*have a lift* = to go with someone in their car; *give someone a lift* = to take them in your car). Ask students to suggest replies, e.g. *Yes, please. No, thank you. That's very nice of you.*

● ▭ Play the recording, and establish what the people actually say. (Answers: see tapescript.)

● Look at the pictures. Ask students to make sentences with *Would you like …?* Expected answers:

 Would you like a cup of coffee (some coffee)?
 Would you like a shower?
 Would you like an apple?
 Would you like some milk (a glass of milk)?
 Would you like a sandwich?
 Would you like some sugar?

● Pairwork. Students offer their partner the things in the pictures. The other student gives suitable replies.

Consolidation

have and have got

This exercise focuses on the two equivalent forms have *and* have got. *The verb* have *was introduced in Unit 2 and was used in Units 1–12. The form* have got *was introduced and practised in Unit 13.*

1 Look at the examples. Point out that *have* and *have got* mean the same (= *have*), but they have a different form. If you like, give some quick practice by saying a sentence in one form and asking students to change it to the other.

2 Look at the examples. In these sentences *have* means *eat* or *take*. In sentences like this we cannot say *have got*.

3 *Either:* Help students to make sentences about themselves by giving prompts, e.g. *a car, a bike, brothers and sisters, a big bedroom, a black T-shirt.*

   Or: Give time for students to write a few sentences about themselves. Then they read out their sentences to the class.

A hundred, a hundred and one ...

This exercise focuses on numbers over 100. It picks up on items which have appeared earlier in the book (in reading texts and in Exercise 13.3) and shows how large numbers are formed.

1 Look at the examples, and see if students can guess what should go in the gaps. Answers:

   137 = a hundred and thirty seven
   205 = two hundred and five
   851 = eight hundred and fifty-one
   1,054 = one thousand and fifty-four
   2,500 = two thousand five hundred
   3,651 = three thousand six hundred and fifty-one
   200,000 = two hundred thousand

2 ● Give time for students to read the sentences and think how to say the numbers. They could do this alone, or with a partner.

   ● Ask students to read out sentences round the class. Focus on the numbers. Answers:

   a twelve thousand years old
   b five thousand and five rooms
   c four thousand seven hundred and eighty-six metres
   d eight thousand eight hundred and forty-eight metres high
   e a hundred passengers, two thousand three hundred kilometres an hour

> **Idea for further practice**
> At the beginning or end of lessons after this, write a few numbers on the board (or sentences containing numbers, e.g. *I've got 562 books*) and ask students to say them.

Review

Present simple and continuous

Review of Present simple and continuous tenses (Units 7 and 11).

1 ● Look at the two questions. Establish that:
   – the blue question is Present simple (= in general, usually).
   – the red question is Present continuous (= now, at this moment).

   ● Students match the answers to the questions. Answers to the blue question:

   I wear shorts in hot weather.
   I don't wear shorts. (= never)
   I wear shorts when I play tennis.
   I always wear shorts.

   Answers to the red question:

   I'm not wearing shorts. (= now, at the moment)
   I'm wearing shorts. (= now, at the moment)

   ● Ask a few students round the class: *When do you wear shorts? Are you wearing shorts now?*

2 Look at the prompts and establish what the questions might be, e.g. *Do you smoke? Are you smoking now? When do you wear a hat? Are you wearing a hat now?* Then get students to answer them.

Where's the supermarket?

Review of shops and place prepositions (Exercises 10.2 and 10.3).

Look at the map. Students say where the places are. Answers:

1 The supermarket is near the railway station.
2 The post office is between the school and the bus station.
3 The bank is next to the cinema.
4 The chemist is opposite the railway station.
5 The kiosk is opposite the market.
6 The bookshop is opposite the school.

Time

Review of expressions for telling the time (Study Pages D, Focus).

1 Look at the clocks and ask students what times they show. Answers:

   seven o'clock, a quarter past twelve, half past three, ten past eight, ten to twelve.

2 ● To show what to do, choose a day of the week yourself. Imagine each clock time in turn and say what you are doing, e.g. *It's seven o'clock on Tuesday morning. I'm just getting up. Now it's a quarter past twelve. I'm teaching English at school ...*

   ● Students talk about themselves in the same way, either round the class or in pairs.

Consolidation

have and have got

1 We can often use *have* or *have got*. In these sentences, they mean the same.

I have a radio, but I don't have a TV. ↔ I've got a radio, but I haven't got a TV.

He has long hair. ↔ He's got long hair.

2 Sometimes you can't use *have got*:

✓ I have breakfast at 8 o'clock.
✗ I've got breakfast at 8 o'clock.

✓ I don't have a shower in the morning.
✗ I haven't got a shower in the morning.

3 Say a few true things about yourself.

I have …

I've got …

I don't have …

I haven't got …

A hundred, a hundred and one …

1 Look at these numbers. Can you fill the gaps?

100 a hundred	101 a hundred and one	137 ....
200 two hundred	205	851 ....
1,000 one thousand	1,011 one thousand and eleven	1,054 ....
1,200 one thousand two hundred	2,500	3,651 ....
100,000 a hundred thousand	200,000	1,000,000 a million

2 Read out these sentences.

a 'Eternal God', a tree in California, is 12,000 years old.

 b The MGM Grand Hotel in Las Vegas has 5,005 rooms.

c The railway station at Condor in Bolivia is 4,786 metres above the sea.

d Mount Everest, in the Himalayas, is 8,848 metres high.

The plane Concorde can carry exactly 100 passengers. It can travel at 2,300 kilometres an hour.

Review

Present simple and continuous

When do you wear shorts?

Are you wearing shorts now?

1 Look at these sentences. Which answer the blue question? Which answer the red question?

I wear shorts in hot weather.

I don't wear shorts.

I'm not wearing shorts.

I'm wearing shorts.

I wear shorts when I play tennis.

I always wear shorts.

What about you? When do you wear shorts? Are you wearing shorts now?

2 Ask and answer questions. Use these ideas.

| – smoke | – drink coffee | – speak English |
| – wear a hat | – wear jeans | – wear glasses |

Where's the supermarket?

Look at the map. Where's

1 the supermarket?	4 the chemist?
2 the post office?	5 the kiosk?
3 the bank?	6 the bookshop?

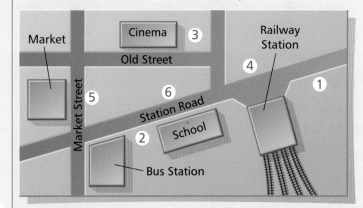

Time

1 Look at the clocks. What time is it?

2 Choose a day of the week. Imagine yourself at these times. Where are you? What are you doing?

15 In the past 1

1 Bedtime story

1 Here is a story. The red words are verbs in the *Past tense*.
Read Part 1 of the story and complete the table.

Past simple

Present	Past
is	was
are	
ask	asked
look	
open	
play	
smile	
want	
give	gave
go	
have	
put	
say	
see	
take	.

Part 1

I was about five years old. It was very late at night, and my parents were asleep. I was awake because I wanted to go to the toilet. I went to the toilet, and I saw a light under the living room door. So I opened the door and went in, and I saw a man in the living room. He was about 20 years old.

I looked at him, and he looked at me, and he smiled at me and said, 'Hi! What's your name?' And I said, 'Sam'. 'Do you want to play a game, Sam?' he asked, and I said, 'Yes.' He had a big bag in his hand, and he said, 'OK. Let's put things in this bag.'

So we played the game. I gave things to him, and he put them in his bag. I took my father's wallet out of his jacket, and I took my mother's purse out of her coat, and the man put them in his bag.

Part 2

Then I (1) .... into my parents' bedroom – very quietly – and (2) .... their watches and rings, and my mother's earrings, and (3) .... them to the man.

I (4) .... him some other things too – the silver knives, forks and spoons, two clocks and some old books – and he (5) .... everything in his bag. It (6) .... a great game.

And in the end he (7) .... , 'OK, Sam. It's bedtime. You go back to bed now. Goodnight.' So I (8) .... goodnight and (9) .... back to bed.

2 Read Part 2 of the story. Fill the gaps with verbs from the table.

🔲 Now listen to Sam telling the whole story.

3 Cover the text, and try to tell the story yourself. Use the verbs in the table to help you.

64   *Unit 15* In the past 1

15

This unit introduces the Past simple tense. It focuses on:
– Past simple regular and irregular forms
– *was* and *were*
– past time expressions with *on, in, at.*

1 Bedtime story

This exercise is based on a true story about a boy who helped a burglar. It introduces the Past tense forms of common verbs, some regular and some irregular, and also the Past tense of the verb to be.

➤ Focus on Form: Exercises 1 & 2

➤ Workbook: Exercise A, Listening

Key structures: Past simple tense.   *New verbs:* smile, give.

Irregular past forms: gave, went, had, put, said, saw, took; was, were.

Other new words: awake, light, game, thing, wallet, purse, silver, bedtime.

---

1 Reading & completing a table; presentation of Past tense forms

- Look at the picture and establish what's happening in it: there's a boy, a man with a bag, the boy is giving him things, he's putting things in the bag, it's night. But try not to give the story away at this point.

- Read through Part 1 of the story, presenting key words as you go (e.g. *light, smile, wallet, purse*) and focusing on the verb forms. Establish that:
  – some verbs add *-ed* in the past (e.g. *play – played*).
  – some verbs change their form in other ways (e.g. *give – gave, go – went*).

- As you read through, ask students to add verbs to the table, and write them on the board. Answers:

  (was), were; (asked), looked, opened, played, smiled, wanted; (gave), went, had, put, said, saw, took

- Show how most verbs have only one Past tense form, but the verb *to be* has two: *was* and *were*:

I He They	played cards. went home.	I He	was at home.	You We They	were at home.

> *Alternative: better classes*
> Let students read through the story themselves and try to work out which verbs the past forms go with. Then go through the answers together.

> *Presentation option*
> Give other examples, showing how the verbs are used in the past, e.g.
> My friend *had* a birthday yesterday. I *went* to his house. I *took* a present.

2 Reading & gap-filling; listening to check

- Read through Part 2 of the story. Pause at each gap and ask students to suggest a verb from the table. Answers:

  1 went   2 took   3 gave   4 gave   5 put   6 was   7 said   8 said   9 went

  🔲 Play the recording of the story. Make sure students understand the point of the story: that the man was a burglar. If you like, teach the words *burglar* and *steal* at this point.

> *Note*
> *Give* and other verbs with indirect objects are practised in Study Pages H Consolidation, page 71.

3 Activation: telling the story

- Ask students to cover the story, but to look at the table of verbs (or to look at the table on the board). Students retell the story round the class, taking turns to say a sentence or two. They should not of course try to repeat the story word for word: the idea is to retell the main events and to use verbs in the Past tense.

> *Pairwork option*
> Students practise telling the story in pairs, one student telling Part 1 and the other telling Part 2.

🔲 Tapescript for Exercise 3: *Childhood places*

1 Our flat was on the third floor, and it was very small – it was really just one room. It had a kitchen and a bathroom, but they were very, very small – they were like cupboards, really. The room had one big window, and outside there was a small balcony. And in the room there were two sofas, one on each side. And at night these sofas were our beds – my parents slept in one, and I slept in the other with my little sister.

2 I remember my grandmother's house, where I stayed every summer. It was in the country, and it was quite small – it only had a living room and two bedrooms – but it had a really big garden, and there were lots of trees, and it was very quiet. It was an old house, and it had lovely old wooden furniture. And I remember there was a large veranda which went all round the house, so there was always a sunny place to sit. I loved it.

2 Yesterday ...

This exercise gives further practice in Past tense forms, and also focuses on time expressions with in, on *and* at.

> Key language: in, on, at; yesterday.   New Past tense forms: read, wrote, bought.
> Recycled verbs: saw, went, gave, played, had.

➤ Focus on Form: Exercise 3
➤ Workbook: Exercise B

1 *Presentation of new verbs*

● Read the sentences. Ask students to identify the verbs (some will be known from the previous exercise), and write the new forms on the board:

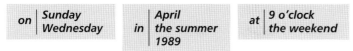

buy	read	write
bought	**read**	**wrote**

2 *Presentation of 'in/on/at'*

● Look at the sentences again. Ask which words come after *on*, *in* and *at*, and write examples on the board:

on	Sunday Wednesday		in	April the summer 1989		at	9 o'clock the weekend

Language note
We use *on* with days; *in* with months, seasons and years; *at* with times, and in special phrases like *at the weekend*, *at New Year*. There is no preposition before *yesterday*: *I saw her yesterday.*

3 *Activation: writing sentences; guessing game*

● To introduce this part, write five sentences about yourself on the board (or simply say them), e.g. *I read a very good book yesterday. I bought a new car at the weekend.* See if students can guess which are true and which are false.

● Students write sentences about themselves.

● Students read out their sentences. Other students guess which ones are true.

Pairwork option
Students read out their sentences to their partner, who guesses which are true. As a round-up, find out which sentences students guessed correctly.

3 Childhood places

This exercise gives practice in describing things in the past, using there was, there were, it was *and* it had.

> New words: quiet, veranda.   Recycled language: rooms, houses, adjectives.

➤ Focus on Form: Exercise 2
➤ Workbook: Exercise C

1 *Reading & matching task*

● Read through the notes, presenting the new words *quiet* and *veranda* (shown in the picture). Discuss which go with photo A and which with photo B. Expected answers:

A: just one room, one big window, a small balcony, on the third floor
B: very quiet, a big garden, lots of trees, in the country, a large veranda

2 *Listening & making sentences*

● ▭ Play the recording. Then ask students to make sentences from the notes. Expected answers:

A It was just one room. The room had one big window. There was a small balcony. It was on the third floor.

B It was very quiet. It had a big garden. There were lots of trees. It was in the country. There was a large veranda.

▭ The tapescript is on page T64.

● Establish what else the speakers say. If necessary, replay the tape. Answers:

1 Rooms: There was a small kitchen and a bathroom.
Sofas: There were two sofas. The sofas were their beds.

2 Rooms: There was a living room and there were two bedrooms.
Furniture: It had lovely old wooden furniture.
Veranda: It went all round the house, there was always a sunny place to sit.

3 *Activation: writing notes*

● Students choose a place they remember and write notes. These can either be complete sentences or phrases as in the example.

● Ask students in turn to say a few things about the place they remember.

Homework option
Students write the sentences for homework.

2 Yesterday …

Past simple • time expressions

I saw some old friends on Sunday.

I read nine novels in the summer.

I played football at the weekend.

I went to Istanbul in April.

I wrote a novel in 1989.

I had breakfast at nine o'clock.

I gave my mother some flowers on Wednesday.

I bought a new coat yesterday.

1 Read these sentences. What is the present tense of the red verbs?

2 What can come after *on*, *in* and *at*? Continue these sentences.

I saw her on …

I saw her in …

I saw her at …

3 Write five sentences about yourself (three *true* sentences and two *false* sentences).
Use the red verbs.

Read out your sentences. Can other students guess which are true and which are false?

3 Childhood places

(there) was/were • had

… very quiet

… just one room

… a big garden

… one big window

… a small balcony

… lots of trees

… on the third floor

… in the country

… a large veranda

1 Read the notes in the box. Which go with picture A, and which with picture B?

2 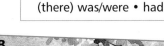 Two people remember the places in the pictures.
Listen and make the notes into complete sentences.

It was …   There was …
It had …   There were …

What do they say about these things?

Speaker 1 – the rooms   – the sofas
Speaker 2 – the rooms   – the furniture   – the veranda

3 Choose one of these places:

– the place where you lived as a young child
– a place you often visited as a young child

What can you remember about it?

Focus on Form

1 Verb + -ed

play	→	played	smile	→	smiled
stay	→	stayed	like	→	liked
watch	→	....	dance	→	....
wash	→	....	smoke	→	....
listen	→	....	live	→	....

Fill the gaps with a past form from the list.

a When I was a child, we .... in London.

b On Saturday evening, I .... at home and .... television.

c When I was young, I .... the Beatles. I .... to them them all the time.

d He .... 20 cigarettes yesterday.

e I .... my hair this morning.

2 Irregular verbs

Match the present and past forms.

PRESENT
see go put
give write
say buy
have take

PAST
bought said
took went gave
wrote put
saw had

Now test your partner.

What's the past of 'see'?

'Saw'.

3 Time expressions

He went out yesterday.

I saw her at the weekend. 8 o'clock.

We went there in September. the winter. 1975.

I washed my hair on Tuesday.

Fill the gaps with at, on, in or – (= nothing).

a They bought a new car .... Thursday.

b I stayed in bed all day .... yesterday.

c He started the book .... January and finished it .... July.

d I drank a cup of coffee .... 8 o'clock, and I had another cup .... 8.30.

e They went to Australia .... 1998.

4 was & were

Change this description to the past tense.

I live in an old house in the village of Ashley. It's a very small village – there are about 25 houses, and there's a small shop, too. The school's in the next village. There are 21 children at the school, and there's only one teacher. The teacher is my mother, so we walk there together every morning.

When I was a child, I lived in ...

How to say it

1 **Listen to the -ed endings. Practise saying the sentences.**

He looked at me.

I smiled at her.

He opened the door.

She asked me a question.

I wanted to go.

2 **Listen to the difference between *there are* and *there were*.**

There are lots of people at the game.

There were lots of people at the game.

Listen and choose the sentence you hear. Then practise saying it.

There are / There were flowers in the room.

There are / There were two trees near the house.

There are / There were some pictures on the wall.

Focus on Form

1 Verb + -ed

- Students complete the list with past forms. Answers:
  watched, washed, listened, danced, smoked, lived

- Point out that:
  – most verbs add -ed.
  – if the verb ends in -e, we just add -d.

- Students fill the gaps. Then go through the answers together. Answers:
  a lived *b* stayed, watched *c* liked, listened *d* smoked
  e washed

2 Irregular verbs

- Ask students to match the present and past forms. Answers:
  see – saw   go – went   put – put   give – gave
  write – wrote   say – said   buy – bought   have – had
  take – took

- Pairwork. Students take it in turns to test each other.

3 Time expressions

- Look at the examples. Point out that:
  – we use *at* with times and in the expression *at the weekend*.
  – we use *in* with months, seasons and years.
  – we use *on* with days.

- Students fill the gaps. Then go through the answers together. Answers:
  a on   *b* –   *c* in, in   *d* at, at   *e* in

4 was & were

- Establish that we use:
  – *there was* with singular nouns.
  – *there were* with plural nouns.

- Students do the exercise in pairs. Then go through the answer. Answer:

  When I *was* a child, I *lived* in an old house in the village of Ashley. It *was* a very small village – there *were* about 25 houses, and there *was* a small shop, too. The school *was* in the next village. There *were* 21 children at the school and there *was* only one teacher. The teacher *was* my mother, so we *walked* there together every morning.

How to say it

1 Pronunciation of -ed ending

- ▭ Play the recording, pausing and getting students to repeat the sentences. Focus on:
  – the consonant clusters in /lʊkt/, /smaɪld/, /ˈəʊpənd/, /ɑːskt/
  – the /ɪd/ sound in /wɒntɪd/
  – the way the *d* ending runs onto the next sound (/lʊkt‿æt/, /ɑːskt‿miː/).

2 Difference in sound between 'there are' and 'there were'

- ▭ Play the example. Focus on the two phrases: /ðeərə lɒts əv ˈpiːpl/ and /ðeəwə lɒts əv ˈpiːpl/.

- ▭ Play the other sentences. Pause after each one to establish which sentence it is, and get students to repeat it. Answers:
  There were flowers in the room.
  There were two trees near the house.
  There are some pictures on the wall.

16

This unit covers a range of related topics to do with the world: geographical features, countries and languages. It focuses on the following vocabulary areas:
- *north, south, east, west*
- geographical features (e.g. *river, coast, mountains, lake*)
- types of town (e.g. *port, capital, village*)
- names of countries, continents and languages.

The Reading and Listening activity is about a business trip to Miami.

1 On the map

This exercise introduces compass points, expressions with in *and* on *(e.g.* on the coast), *and vocabulary for talking about towns and other features.*

➤ Workbook: Exercise A

> *Compass points:* north, south, east, west.   *Types of town:* town, village, capital, port, resort.   *Geographical features:* mountain, lake, river, sea, coast, island.

1 Reading & vocabulary task; presentation of vocabulary

- Look at the map, and read the text beside it to establish the situation (the family are coming to the island on holiday, A–L are all towns or villages on the island). Teach the words *island, tourist, holiday* and *ferry (boat)*.
- Either read through the six descriptions with the students, or give time for them to read them on their own. Build up lists of vocabulary on the board:

village	port	capital		north	south		sea	lake	river
town	resort			east	west		mountain	coast	

Language notes

The *capital* is the main town of a country or region (London is the capital of Britain).
A *port* is a town on the sea or a river, which ships go to.
A *resort* is a place where people go on holiday.
We can say that a town is *on the sea* or *on the coast*: these mean roughly the same.

2 Reading & matching task

- Working alone or in pairs, students read the descriptions again. Ask them to find the places on the map, and decide the best route for the family.
- Discuss the answers together. Answers:

Newport = E   Belmonte = L   Iguana = H   Johnstown = G   Salvador = B
Laguna = D   *Possible routes (starting from A):* B, D, H, L, G, E; *or* B, G, E, L, H, D

3 Activation: describing places

- Point out that we say:
  - *in* the north, south, east, west; *in* the mountains.
  - *on* the sea, *on* the coast, *on* a lake, *on* a river.
- Choose other places on the island, and ask students to describe them, e.g.

A is a large port on the north coast.
F is a village in the west of the island. It's near the sea, and it's on a lake.
I is a small village in the mountains in the centre of the island. It's on a river.
K is a port in the south of the island. It's on a river and it's near the coast.

4 Extension: writing sentences

- If you like, introduce this part by choosing a place that the whole class knows and building up sentences about it on the board.
- Working alone, students write sentences about a place in their own country.
- Students read out their sentences.

Alternatives

1 *Game.* Students read out their sentences without naming the place (*X is a* …). Other students guess which place they are describing.

2 *Homework.* Students write the sentences for homework and read them out in the next lesson.

🔲 Tapescript for Exercise 3: *Which country?*

1 India – well, it's a large country, very large. It's also a very poor country, at least most people are poor. What else? It's in Asia ... the capital is New Delhi, I think, and the River Ganges flows through it. It's very hot in the summer and the winter, I think – but not in the north, of course. In the north there are mountains, very high mountains – the Himalayas.

2 What do I know about Switzerland? Well, it's in Europe, in the centre of Europe, it isn't on the sea. It has a lot of lakes, and a lot of mountains –- it's very cold in the winter. It's a very rich country – a very beautiful country as well. And there are three main languages, I think – French, German and Italian.

3 Argentina is in South America, and people speak Spanish there. It's a very big country. The south of the country is very cold – I'm not sure about the north, but the south is certainly cold. And the capital is Buenos Aires.

16 Around the world

1 On the map

1 Look at the six descriptions and find words to add to the lists.

village, town, ...

north, ...

mountain, sea, ...

2 Can you solve the puzzle?

Places to visit

NEWPORT is a large town in the west of the island. It's on the coast.

BELMONTE is a village in the mountains, near the south coast.

IGUANA is the capital of the island. It's a port on the Iguana River, and it's in the east of the island.

JOHNSTOWN is the old capital. It's in the mountains in the centre of the island, and it's on a lake.

SALVADOR is a small town on a river in the north of the island. It's near the coast.

LAGUNA is a small tourist resort on the north coast. It isn't on a river.

What's the best route?

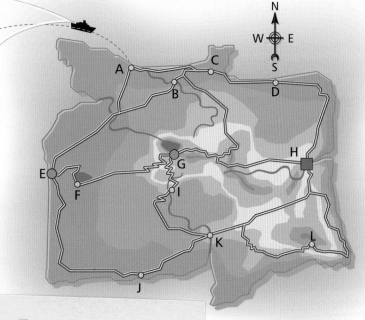

This family of tourists are on a ferry boat, at the start of a week's holiday on the island. They want to go to all six places to visit, and then get the boat home again.

3

4

... s a large port in the ... he River Shannon.

2 I love you

1 All the gaps in this text are the names of languages. Which language goes in each gap?

Arabic	Greek	Portuguese
Chinese	Italian	Russian
French	Japanese	Spanish
German	Polish	Turkish

2 Here is *I love you* in seven different languages. Can you guess the languages?

Te quiero

Je t'aime

Ich liebe dich

君が好きだよ。

Seni seviorum

я люблю тебя

أحبك

Can you say *I love you* in any other languages?

The names of languages are often like the countries where people speak them. So (1) .... is the language of Italy, (2) .... is the language of Russia, and (3) .... is the language of Greece. In Turkey people speak (4) .... and in Poland they speak (5) .... In Japan, people speak (6) .... , and in China they speak (7) ....

But some languages are not so simple. People speak (8) .... in many countries in the Middle East and North Africa. People speak (9) .... in Germany, but they also speak it in Austria and part of Switzerland. You can hear (10) .... in France, but also in Canada, Belgium and in many countries in Africa. (11) .... is the language of Portugal, but also of Brazil. And people speak (12) .... not only in Spain, but also in most of South and Central America.

3 Which country?

1 How much do you know about these countries? Match them with the sentences. (Write *I*, *S* or *A*.)

India

Switzerland

Argentina

S	It isn't on the sea.
	It's in Asia.
	The capital is Buenos Aires.
	People speak Spanish there.
	It's a very rich country.
	People speak French, German and Italian there.
	It's a poor country.
	Most of the country is hot in summer and winter.
	It's in Europe.
	The south of the country is very cold.
	The capital is New Delhi.
	It has a lot of lakes and mountains.
	It's in South America.
	The River Ganges flows through it.

2 🔲 Three people say what they know about India, Switzerland and Argentina. Listen and check your answers.

3 Think of a country. Write three or four sentences about it.

Then read out your sentences. Can other students guess the country?

2 I love you

This exercise is based on a text about major languages in the world and where they are spoken. The second part presents I love you *in seven of the languages mentioned in the text. The main focus of this exercise is on the names of languages: the countries where they are spoken are for comprehension only.*

> ➤ Workbook: Exercise B, Listening

Languages: Arabic, Chinese, French, German, Greek, Italian, Japanese, Polish, Portuguese, Russian, Spanish, Turkish.   *New countries:* Austria, Belgium, Canada, Portugal, Switzerland; Middle East.   *Recycled language:* names of countries.

1 *Reading & gap-filling task; presentation of languages*

- Read through the text, and use the names of the countries (most of which are known) to teach the names of the languages. Focus on pronunciation, especially of /ˈpəʊlɪʃ/, /pɔːtjʊˈgiːz/, /ˈrʌʃən/, /ˈspænɪʃ/. Answers:

  1 Italian   2 Russian   3 Greek   4 Turkish   5 Polish   6 Japanese   7 Chinese
  8 Arabic   9 German   10 French   11 Portuguese   12 Spanish

- After establishing which languages go in the gaps, ask students to read the text aloud round the class, adding the languages as they read.

> *Presentation option*
> Build up a list of countries and their languages (France – French, Italy – Italian, etc.) on the board. Add other pairs that students find important.

2 *Activation: guessing languages*

- Look at the expressions in the heart, and see if students can guess what languages they are. Answers:

  Left side (top to bottom): Spanish, German, Russian
  Right side (top to bottom): French, Japanese, Turkish, Arabic

- Ask students if they can say *I love you* in any other languages. Use this as an opportunity to teach the names of languages that may be important for students (e.g. languages from nearby countries).

3 Which country?

This exercise teaches simple ways of describing a country, and introduces the names of continents. Students hear people describing the countries in the pictures, then they describe a country themselves.

> ➤ Workbook: Exercise C

Continents: Europe, Asia, America.   *Other new words:* rich, poor; flow.
Recycled language: languages; climate; geographical features; compass points.

1 *Reading & matching task; presentation of continents*

- Read through the sentences, introducing new words as you go.
- Pairwork. Students match the sentences with the countries. Then discuss the answers together.

> *Vocabulary option*
> Write the names of these continents on the board:
>
> | | |
> |---|---|
> | **Europe** | **North America** |
> | **Asia** | **South America** |
> | **Africa** | **Australia** |

2 *Listening to check*

- 🔲 Play the recording, pausing to check the answers:

  India: It's in Asia. It's a poor country. Most of the country is hot in summer and winter. The capital is New Delhi. The River Ganges flows through it.
  Switzerland: (It isn't on the sea.) It's a very rich country. People speak French, German and Italian there. It's in Europe. It has a lot of lakes and mountains.
  Argentina: The capital is Buenos Aires. People speak Spanish there. The south of the country is very cold. It's in South America.

> 🔲 The tapescript is on page T67.

3 *Writing & guessing game: countries*

- To introduce the activity, think of a country yourself and say a few sentences about it, e.g. *It's in Asia. It's a very big country. It's on the sea. The capital is Beijing.* Ask students to say the name of the country. (Answer: China.)
- Working alone or in pairs, students choose a country and write a few sentences about it.
- In turn, students read out their sentences. The rest of the class try to guess which country it is.

> *Vocabulary option*
> Present the names of any countries that come up during the activity. (But do not give too much emphasis to the names of countries here; the main point of the activity is to practise ways of describing countries.)

> *Homework option*
> Students write the sentences for homework. Then play the guessing game in the next lesson.

4 International travel

This combined Reading and Listening activity is about a business trip. The reading text describes the trip, and the listening is a series of short scenes.

Reading skills: *organising information.*
Listening skills: *understanding a dialogue; listening for key points.*

> *Key words (pictures):* room service, reception, international departures, passport, check-in, flight, ticket. *New words (text):* business trip, flight, excellent, view, quickly, tired; left (v.), landed, phoned, decided, ordered. *New words (listening):* smoking, non-smoking, reserved, key.

1 Introduction: interpreting pictures; presentation of vocabulary

- Look at the pictures and establish what they show. Expected answers:

  A a sign at an airport; shows where to get a taxi or a bus.
  B a sign at an airport; shows where you check in (get your seat and give them your bags).
  C a sign in a hotel; shows where reception is (where you get your key).
  D a sign at an airport; shows which flights are leaving.
  E a key for a hotel room; shows the room number.
  F a menu; shows food and drink you can have in your room.
  G a passport.
  H a list of phone numbers in the hotel.
  I a plane ticket; shows where the person is going.

Note
Focus only on key words (e.g. *reception*, *departures*). Try not to get involved in details (e.g. of the passport) which students do not need to understand.

2 Reading & gap-filling

- Read through the text. Pause at each green gap and ask students to complete it, using information from the pictures. Answers:

  a Brown *b* Miami *c* 9.25 *g* Miami Beach

Option
Ask students to guess what might go in the blue gaps at this stage.

3 Listening & gap-filling

- 🖭 Play the recording, pausing after each scene. Ask students to complete the blue gaps. Answers:

  d window *e* 3.20 *f* taxi *h* ninth *i* husband *j* London *k* hot and sunny *l* room service *m* a chicken sandwich *n* a cold beer

4 Answering questions; listening to check

- See if students can answer the questions.

- 🖭 Play the tape again and check the answers. Answers:

  a One *b* No *c* Three *d* Two *e* It's raining

🖭 Tapescript for Exercise 4: *International travel*

1 A Good morning.
   B Good morning.
   A Could I see your ticket and passport, please? … Thank you. Just one bag to check in, is it?
   B Yes, just one.
   A OK … Would you like a smoking or a non-smoking seat?
   B Non-smoking, please, by the window.
   A A window seat, OK. There you are.
   B Thank you.
   A Thank you. Have a good flight.

2 Ladies and gentlemen, welcome to Miami, where the time is exactly 3.20 in the afternoon. We hope you had a good flight and …

3 B Miami Beach Hotel, please.
   C Miami Beach Hotel. OK.

4 D Good afternoon.
   B Hello. You've got a room reserved for Brown.
   D Mrs Brown – Just a moment … Yes, here we are, ma'am. Three nights, is that right?
   B Yes, that's right.
   D OK … Your room number is 926. It's on the ninth floor. Here's your key, ma'am.
   B Thank you.

5 B Hello? Richard? It's me, Karen.
   E Karen, hi. Are you in Miami? Did you have a good flight?
   B Yes, fine. Is everything OK? How are the children?

   E Oh, they're fine. They're both asleep. What's it like there? Is it hot?
   B Yes, it is. Sunny and very hot. What's it like in London?
   E Oh, still raining.
   B OK, look. I'll phone again tomorrow, OK?
   E OK. Bye.

6 F Room service. Can I help you?
   B Yes, I'd like a chicken sandwich, please.
   F Yes, ma'am. Anything to drink?
   B Yes, a cold beer, please.
   F OK. What's your room number?
   B 926.
   F 926. Fine. Thank you.

4 International travel

1 These pictures all have a connection with international travel. What do they show?

A TAXIS → BUSES →

B CHECK-IN
All flights to the USA and Canada

C ▽ RECEPTION ▽

D

INTERNATIONAL DEPARTURES

Flight no	Destination	Time	Status	Gate no
1B512	MADRID	0914	Delayed	
AA246	MIAMI	0925	Flight now boarding	15
BA413	BUENOS AIRES	0950	Wait in lounge	

E 926 MIAMI BEACH HOTEL

F Room Service
Sandwiches
Beef
Turkey
Chicken
Cheese
Drinks
White wine
Red wine
Beer

G United Kingdom of Great Britain and Northern Ireland
Passport
BROWN
KAREN
BRITISH CITIZEN
22 JUL/JUL 71

H
01 Operator
02 Room service
03 Reception
04 Porter
05 Laundry
9 Outside line
00 International

I BRITISH AIRWAYS FLIGHT TICKET
NAME OF PASSENGER : BROWN, K
TRAVEL DETAILS
FROM LONDON
TO MIAMI
TO LONDON
ARRIVE 14 MAY
DEPART 17 MAY

2 This text is about a business trip.
Fill the green gaps, using information from the pictures.

3 🔲 You will hear six short scenes. Listen and fill the blue gaps.

4 How well did you listen?
Can you answer these questions?

a How many bags does Karen check in?
b Does Karen smoke?
c How many nights is she staying at the hotel?
d How many children has she got?
e What's the weather like in London?

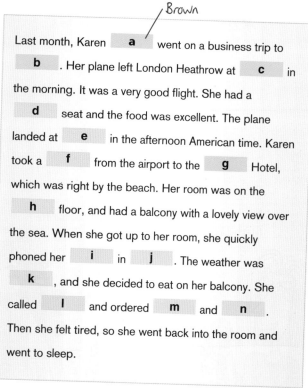

Brown

Last month, Karen [**a**] went on a business trip to [**b**]. Her plane left London Heathrow at [**c**] in the morning. It was a very good flight. She had a [**d**] seat and the food was excellent. The plane landed at [**e**] in the afternoon American time. Karen took a [**f**] from the airport to the [**g**] Hotel, which was right by the beach. Her room was on the [**h**] floor, and had a balcony with a lovely view over the sea. When she got up to her room, she quickly phoned her [**i**] in [**j**]. The weather was [**k**], and she decided to eat on her balcony. She called [**l**] and ordered [**m**] and [**n**]. Then she felt tired, so she went back into the room and went to sleep.

Focus on ... Dates

1 Can you remember these numbers?

1st	2nd	3rd	4th	5th

first .... third .... fifth

6th	7th	8th	9th	10th

.... eighth ....

2 Now try these. What are the missing numbers?

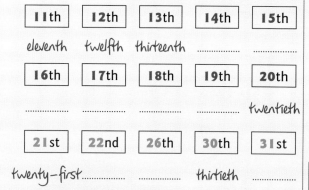

11th	12th	13th	14th	15th

eleventh twelfth thirteenth ....

16th	17th	18th	19th	20th

.... twentieth

21st	22nd	26th	30th	31st

twenty-first.............. .... thirtieth ....

3 [cassette] Six people say the date of their birthday. Write down the dates.

Henry	1st March
André	
Hazel	
Chris	
Natasha	
Gabi	

4 When is your birthday?

Does anyone in the class have the same birthday?

HAPPY BIRTHDAY!

Sounds: Russia, China, Japan

1 [cassette] Listen to these sounds.

/ʃ/   She speaks Spanish, Russian and Polish.

/tʃ/   How much chocolate do the children want?

/dʒ/   In June and July we stayed in a small village in Germany.

2 [cassette] Listen and practise.

> fish wash shop shirt Russian
> teacher children Chinese watch
> Japan jeans engineer fridge July

3 Write a sentence. Use words from the box.

4 Read out your sentence.

Phrasebook: I'm not sure

What's the capital of India?

1 [cassette] Four people answer this question. What do they say?

– .... Bombay.
– .... Calcutta?
– ....
– .... Delhi.

Which answer is correct?

2 Can you answer these questions? Use the expressions in the box.

> I think ...   I don't know.
> I'm not sure.   I have no idea.

1 Where is Helsinki?
2 Where is Mount Everest?
3 Where can you see a gondola?
4 Where can you hear Koto music?
5 What is Madagascar? Where is it?
6 What is Potocatapetl? Where is it?
7 What is a kiwi? Where can you find one?

Study pages H

Focus on ... *Dates*

This exercise teaches dates, and recycles ordinal numbers and months.

> *Key language:* dates; ordinal numbers 11th to 31st.
> *Recycled language:* months, ordinal numbers 1st to 10th.

1 ● Look at the numbers 1st to 10th. See if students can remember the missing words. Answers:

   second, fourth, sixth, seventh, ninth, tenth

   ● Show how we write the short forms of ordinal numbers, by adding the last two letters of the word:

fi**rst**	= 1st
seco**nd**	= 2nd
thi**rd**	= 3rd
four**th**	= 4th

2 Look at the numbers 11th to 31st and see if students can guess the missing words. Answers:

14th = fourteenth	19th = nineteenth
15th = fifteenth	22nd = twenty-second
16th = sixteenth	26th = twenty-sixth
17th = seventeenth	31st = thirty-first
18th = eighteenth	

3 ● Check that students remember the names of the months. Then show how we normally write dates, and how we say them:

   Written: 19th April (*or* April 19th)
   Spoken: the nineteenth of April (*or* April the nineteenth)

   ● 🔊 Play the recording. Students listen and note down the dates.
   ● Go through the answers. Answers:

André: 26th July	Natasha: 26th December
Hazel: 22nd April	Gabi: 20th February
Chris: 9th June	

4 Go round the class, asking students to say the date of their birthday. The others listen to see if they have the same birthday.

   Note: With a small class, you could ask a student to come to the front and write the dates on the board as students say them.

Sounds: *Russia, China and Japan*

> The sounds /ʃ/, /tʃ/ and /dʒ/.

1, 2 🔊 If students have problems, try these ideas:

   – To pronounce /ʃ/, try saying /s/ and then round the lips and move the tongue back away from the teeth.
   – To pronounce /tʃ/, say /t/ and /ʃ/, and then run them together.
   – To pronounce /dʒ/, say /d/ and /ʒ/ and then run them together.

3 Students write a sentence using words from the box and including any other words they like, e.g.

   – He's a Russian engineer.
   – Most children in Japan eat fish.

4 Students read out their sentences in turn. Focus on the pronunciation of /ʃ/, /tʃ/ and /dʒ/.

   Alternative: Dictation. Students dictate their sentence to the person next to them. As a check, ask students to read out the sentence they wrote down.

Phrasebook: *I'm not sure*

This exercise teaches students how to say that they don't know or they are not sure of something.

> *Key language:* I think, I'm not sure, I don't know, I have no idea. *Recycled language:* Wh- questions.

1 🔊 Play the recording and ask students to fill the gaps. (The correct answer is Delhi or, more strictly, New Delhi.)

2 ● Either ask the questions round the class or let students discuss the answers in pairs first, and then talk about them together. Emphasise that they shouldn't expect to know the answers: the point of the exercise is to practise the expressions in the box!

   ● When students have tried to answer (or have guessed answers to) all the questions, tell them the answers:

   1 In Finland.
   2 In Nepal.
   3 In Venice.
   4 In Japan.
   5 It's an island. It's in Africa, in the Indian Ocean.
   6 It's a volcano/a mountain. It's in Mexico.
   7 It's a bird. In New Zealand. (It's also a green fruit. You can find one at the greengrocer or supermarket!)

> 🔊 Tapescript for Focus on ... *Dates*
>
> My name's Henry. My birthday is on 1st March.
> My name's André. My birthday's on 26th July.
> My name's Hazel, and my birthday is 22nd April.
> OK, my name's Chris, and my birthday is 9th June.
> Hello, my name's Natasha, and my birthday's on 26th December.
> My name is Gabi, and my birthday is on 20th February.

> 🔊 Tapescript for Phrasebook: *I'm not sure*
>
> A What's the capital of India?
> B I think it's Bombay.
> A What is the capital of India?
> C I don't know. Is it Calcutta?
> A What's the capital of India?
> D I have no idea. Sorry.
> A What is the capital of India?
> E I'm not sure, but I think it's Delhi.

Consolidation

Give me the book!

This exercise focuses on common verbs with two objects. This consolidates and expands on language from Exercise 15.1.

1 Look at the verbs in the box, and check that students know what they mean. Then read the examples and show that they are different ways of saying the same thing:
   – We can either mention the thing first or the person first.
   – If we mention the thing first, we say *to* the person.

2 Ask students to fill the gaps. Then go through the answers:
   a wrote him   *b* give me   *c* sent her   *d* show me
   e bring us   *f* give them

in and on

This exercise focuses on the use of in *and* on *with places. This consolidates language from Exercises 16.1 and 16.3.*

1 Use the examples to show that we use:
   – *in* with countries, continents and regions
   – *on* with rivers, lakes, coasts, etc.

2 Students fill the gaps. Then go through the answers together.
   a ... in the north ... on the Amazon River
   b ... in the west ... on Lake Geneva
   c ... on the east coast ... in East Asia
   d ... in South America ... in the north ... in the Andes ... on the coast

Review

Which word?

Review of count/non-count nouns, some/any *and* much/many *(Exercises 13.1, 13.2 and 13.3).*

- Students do the exercise alone or in pairs.
- Go through the answers. If students have any problems, look back at the exercises where the items were first introduced. Answers:
   a ... *some* pasta, *some* cheese, *a* large onion, *some* tomatoes and *a* bottle of white wine.
   b ... *some* soap ... *any* shampoo ... *any* hot water.
   c ... *much* fruit ... *many* vegetables.
   d How *many* computer games ... Not *many*.
   e How *much* money ... Not *much*.

Describing people

Review of ages (Exercise 2.2); Present continuous tense (Unit 11), clothes (Exercise 12.1) and physical appearance (Exercise 12.3).

Look at the pictures in turn, and ask the questions. Get students to describe the people. Expected answers:

1 *a* He's young, and he has short black hair.
   b He's wearing blue jeans, a red T-shirt and trainers.
   c He's about 16.
2 *a* She has long dark hair.
   b She's wearing a green jacket and skirt (a green suit) and green shoes.
   c She's about 35.
3 *a* He's quite old, and he has grey hair.
   b He's wearing a blue jumper, a white shirt, grey trousers and brown shoes.
   c He's about 70.

Words

Review of vocabulary, especially from Units 7 and 8.

1 Look at the first sentence (*You can drink ...*). Ask students to think of possible endings, and write them on the board, e.g.

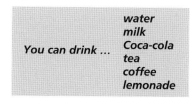

You can drink ...	water milk Coca-cola tea coffee lemonade

2 • Students look at the other sentences and note down endings for them. They could do this either alone or in pairs.
   • Ask a student to read out one of his/her endings (e.g. ... *a book*). Other students guess which sentence it goes with (Answer: *You can read it*).

Consolidation

Give me the book!

1 Look at these verbs.

give	send	bring	show	write

We can use them like this:

I gave some money to the man.
I gave some money to him.
I gave him some money.

I sent a present to my aunt.
I sent some money to her.
I sent her some money.

Bring the book to me!
Bring me the book!

2 Fill the gaps with phrases from the box.

a I .... a letter, but he never answered.

b Can you .... some money? I need to buy some food.

c It was my girlfriend's birthday, so I .... some flowers.

d Why don't you .... your photos? I'd love to see them.

e Waiter, we'd like two coffees, please. And can you .... some more water?

f The children come home at one o'clock. Can you .... something to eat?

sent her
give them
give me
wrote him
bring us
show me

in and on

1 Look at the examples.

in **Spain**	on **the coast**
in **Europe**	on **the (west) coast**
	on **the sea**
in **the north/south/east/west**	
	on **a lake**
in **the mountains**	on **Lake Victoria**
in **the centre**	on **a river**
	on **the River Ganges**

2 Fill the gaps with *in* or *on*.

a Manaus is .... the north of Brazil. It's .... the Amazon River.

b Geneva is .... the west of Switzerland. It's .... Lake Geneva.

c Tokyo is .... the east coast of Japan, ... East Asia.

d Ecuador is a small country .... South America. The capital, Quito, is .... the north of the country, high .... the Andes. The second city, Guayaquil, is .... the coast.

Review

Which word?

Choose the right words.

a OK – we need *a/some* pasta, *a/some* cheese, *a/some* large onion, *a/some* tomatoes and *a/some* bottle of white wine.

b We've got *some/any* soap, but we haven't got *some/any* shampoo. And I'm afraid there isn't *some/any* hot water.

c My children eat a lot of bread, but they don't eat *much/many* fruit and they don't eat *much/many* vegetables.

d – How *much/many* computer games have you got?
– Not *much/many*.

e – How *much/many* money have you got?
– Not *much/many*.

Describing people

Look at these people and answer the questions.

a What do they look like?

b What are they wearing?

c How old do you think they are?

Words

1 Write sensible endings for these sentences. How many endings can you think of for each one?

| A You can drink ... |

| B You can play ... |

| C You can listen to ... |

| D You can watch ... |

| E You can read ... |

2 *Student A*: Read out one of your endings.
Student B: Which sentence does it go with?

17 In the past 2

1 Did and didn't

> Past simple • positive & negative

1 Do these quiz questions, then check your answers with the teacher. What's your score?

ART AND ARTISTS

Michelangelo

> **painted**
> **didn't paint**

the Mona Lisa.

SCIENCE

The Chinese

> **made**
> **didn't make**

the first fireworks.

FILMS

Steven Spielberg

> **made**
> **didn't make**

the films *Jaws* and *ET*.

HISTORY

Margaret Thatcher

> **was**
> **wasn't**

Britain's first woman Prime Minister.

FAMOUS PEOPLE

Marilyn Monroe

> **had**
> **didn't have**

red hair.

MUSIC

The Beatles

> **were**
> **weren't**

American.

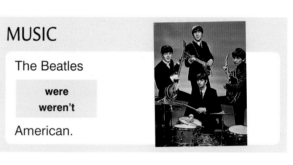

2 Complete these questions, using verbs from the box. What are the answers?

die	died
play	played
start	started
win	won
write	wrote

SPORT

England

the 1998 football World Cup.

FAMOUS PEOPLE

Frank Sinatra

in a plane crash.

MUSIC

Jimi Hendrix

the guitar.

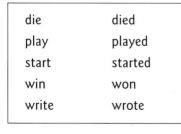

HISTORY

The First World War

in 1914.

BOOKS AND PLAYS

Charles Dickens

the play *Hamlet*.

3 Work with a partner. Choose one of the topics and write a question of your own.

Can other students answer it?

17

This unit introduces Past simple negatives and questions. It focuses on:
– positive and negative sentences
– *yes/no* questions
– *Wh-* questions.

1 Did and didn't

This exercise is in the form of a general knowledge quiz with a choice of positive or negative answers. It introduces the Past simple negative.

➤ Focus on Form: Exercises 1 & 2
➤ Workbook: Exercise A

> *Key structures:* Past simple negative. *New verbs:* paint, die.
> *New irregular past forms:* made, won. *Recycled verbs:* was, were, had, wrote.
> *Other new words:* prime minister, space, plane crash, war, play (n.).

1 *Presentation of 'didn't'; reading & choosing sentences*

● Read the first quiz item, and show how we form the Past tense negative. Do this by comparing it with the Present tense:

> **He _paints_ pictures.**   **He _doesn't_ paint pictures.**
> **He _painted_ this picture.**   **He _didn't_ paint this picture.**

● Go through the quiz item by item. Make sure students understand the sentences and present any new words. Ask students to choose the sentences they think are correct. They could either note down what they think, or you could build up a 'class answer' on the board.

● Give the answers, and see how many students got them right. Answers:
Michelangelo didn't paint the Mona Lisa (Leonardo da Vinci painted it).
Steven Spielberg made the films *Jaws* and *ET*.
Marilyn Monroe didn't have red hair. (She had fair/blond hair).
The Chinese made the first fireworks.
Margaret Thatcher was Britain's first woman Prime Minister.
The Beatles weren't American. (They were English/British.)

● Show how we form the negative of *was* and *were* by simply adding *n't*:

> **She was English.**   **They were English.**
> **She wasn't English.**   **They weren't English.**

2 *Activation: making sentences*

● Look at the verbs in the table. Present the verb *die*, and check that students remember the others.

● Look at each quiz item in turn. Ask students to complete them by adding positive and negative verb forms, and write the verbs on the board. The items should be:
England won/didn't win …
Frank Sinatra died/didn't die …
Jimi Hendrix played/didn't play …
The First World War started/didn't start …
Charles Dickens wrote/didn't write …

● See if students know the answers. Answers:
England didn't win the 1998 football World Cup. (France won it.)
Frank Sinatra didn't die in a plane crash. (He died in hospital, aged 82.)
Jimi Hendrix played the guitar.
The First World War started in 1914.
Charles Dickens didn't write the play *Hamlet*. (Shakespeare wrote it.)

> *Note*
> If students don't know any of these people, explain who they were. Charles Dickens was a 19th century English novelist. Frank Sinatra was an American singer; he died in 1998. Jimi Hendrix was a black American rock guitarist of the '60s.

3 *Extension: making up a quiz question*

● In pairs, students choose someone who is no longer alive and write a question like those in the quiz.

● Students read out their question. Other students try to answer them.

> *Help option*
> Write names of famous people on pieces of paper and give one to each pair.

2 Did you see ...?

This exercise introduces Past simple yes/no questions, used in talking about TV programmes, concerts and sports events.

> Key language: yes/no questions.
> New words: programme, match, concert, interesting, boring.

➤ Focus on Form: Exercise 3
➤ Workbook: Exercise B

1 Listening & gap-filling; presentation of yes/no questions; practice

- Read the dialogues, and present the words *programme*, *football match*, *concert*, *interesting* and *boring*. As a way of focusing, ask students to guess what the questions are. They probably won't actually be able to form the questions, but may be able to suggest what the verbs are (*see*, *watch*, *go to*).

- 🔲 Play the recordings, pausing after each dialogue. Establish what the questions were and write them on the board. Answers:

  A Did you see ...? Did you like it?   B Did you watch ...? Was it good?
  C Did you go to ...? Did you enjoy it?

- Show how we form Past tense questions:

  > **I saw it.**
  > **Did you see it?**

  > **It was good.**
  > **Was it good?**

- Practise each conversation with one or two students. Then divide the class into pairs to practise the conversations.

🔲 The tapescript is on page T74.

Language note
Past simple questions are formed with *did* + verb, just as Present simple questions are formed with *do/does* + verb:

Do you like music?
Did you like the concert?

Did is used in all persons:

Did you see it?
Did he see it?

2 Activation: asking questions

- Working alone or in pairs, students think of something they saw recently, e.g. a film, a TV programme, a concert, a sports match. They think of a question to ask about it, using one of the question forms on the board.

- In turn, students ask their question, and other students answer.

Pairwork option
Students prepare questions alone, then have conversations in pairs. As a round-up, ask a few students what question they asked and what they found out.

3 Memory test

This exercise practises past simple Wh- questions. It is in the form of a memory test, in which students see if they can remember events in the past.

> New verbs: arrive, leave.   New irregular past forms: wore, cost, ate, got up, left.
> Recycled language: clothes, prices, weather, food and drink, times.

➤ Focus on Form: Exercise 2
➤ Workbook: Exercise C, Listening

1 Presentation of Wh- questions; listening

- Read the first section, and use this to present Wh- questions in the past:

  > **I wore a dress**
  > **Did you wear a dress?**
  > **What did you wear?**

- 🔲 Play the recording. Students listen and give each person a score out of 6 (3 for each question). Then discuss the scores.

🔲 The tapescript is on page T74.

2 Reading & making questions

- Read through the questions in Parts 2 and 3, then establish what the Part 4 and 5 questions should be. Possible answers:

  4 What did you wear? When (What time) did you arrive? When (What time) did you leave?
  5 Where did you go/eat? What did you eat/drink/have? How much was it / How much did it cost / How much did you pay?

3 Presentation of Past tense forms

- Establish the past forms of the verbs, and write them on the board (they will be needed to answer the questions):

  > **wear → wore**   **drink → drank**
  > **buy → bought**   **get up → got up**
  > **cost → cost**   **arrive → arrived**
  > **eat → ate**   **leave → left**

4 Activation: doing the test

- To introduce the activity, get the students to ask you the questions. Give answers using the verbs. Ask the class to give you a score.

- Pairwork. Students ask each other the questions, and note down their partner's score. As a round-up, find out who scored the most points.

Note
Parts 2–5 have three questions each, so students should give two points for each question.

2 Did you see …?

Yes/no questions

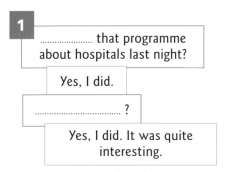

1

…………… that programme about hospitals last night?

Yes, I did.

…………………… ?

Yes, I did. It was quite interesting.

2

…………… the football match on Sunday?

No, I didn't.
………………… ?

Yes, it was.
We won 2–0.

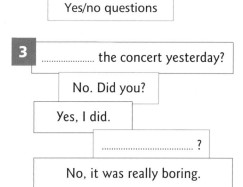

3

…………… the concert yesterday?

No. Did you?

Yes, I did.

………………………… ?

No, it was really boring.

1 ▭ Listen to the three conversations and fill the gaps.

Practise the conversations.

2 Think of something you saw recently. Ask other students about it.

3 Memory test

Wh- questions

Can you remember …

1 *… your first day at school?*
- What did you wear?
- What was your teacher's name?

2 *… the last time you bought some clothes?*
- What did you buy?
- Where did you buy it?
- How much did it cost?

3 *… last Sunday?*
- What was the weather like?
- What did you eat and drink for breakfast?
- What time did you get up?

4 *… the last time you went to a party?*
- … wear?
- … arrive?
- … leave?

5 *… the last time you ate in a restaurant?*
- Where …?
- What …?
- How much …?

SCORE UP TO 6 POINTS FOR EACH SECTION. TOTAL: 30 POINTS

1 ▭ Two people do Part 1 of this memory test. Listen and give each person a score out of 6.

2 Read the whole test. What are the questions for Parts 4 and 5?

3 Here are some verbs from the test. What are their past forms?

wear   buy   cost   eat   drink   get up   arrive   leave

4 Do the test with a partner. Give your partner a score out of 30.

Focus on Form

1 Irregular verbs

Match the present and past forms.

Present
get make wear
buy cost leave
drink win eat

Past
left cost won
wore made bought
ate got drank

Now test your partner.

What's the past of 'get'?

'Got'.

2 I went ↔ I didn't go

Fill the gaps in this table.

Yesterday I …

watched TV	↔	didn't watch TV
went to the cinema	↔	didn't go to the cinema
bought a newspaper	↔	.... a newspaper
got up early	↔	.... up early
played cards	↔	.... cards
made a cake	↔	.... a cake
had a big lunch	↔	.... a big lunch
wore a white shirt	↔	.... a white shirt

Which sentences are true of you?

3 Questions in the past

Choose question words from the box, and make *Wh-* questions.

Example:
Did you eat *at home/in the park/in a restaurant?*
→ Where did you eat?

a Did you see *Peter/Mary/John?*
b Did they drink *water/milk/wine?*
c Did she go *home/to the cinema/ to a party?*
d Did they win *£100/£1,000/ £1,000,000?*
e Did he leave on *Tuesday/at the weekend/yesterday?*

What
Who
When
Where
How much

4 was(n't) & were(n't)

Change these sentences to the past.

a He's at school.	→	He was at school.
b They're asleep.	→	....
c I'm not in Class 1.	→	I wasn't in Class 1.
d She isn't at home.	→	....
e We aren't married.	→	....
f Is she at work?	→	....
g Where is she?	→	....
h Are you there?	→	....
i Where are you?	→	....

Note: didn't = did nøt   wasn't = was nøt   weren't = were nøt

---

How to say it

1 🔲 Listen to *didn't* and *wasn't* in these sentences. Practise saying them.

I didn't see you at the party.

We didn't go to London.

He wasn't there last night.

The film wasn't very interesting.

2 🔲 Listen to the rhythm of these sentences. Practise saying them.

■ . . ■
What did you wear?

■ . . ■ .
Where did you buy it?

■ . . ■ .
Why did you go there?

■ . ■ . . ■
How much did it cost?

Focus on Form

1 Irregular verbs

- Students match the present and past forms.
  Answers:

  get – got   make – made   wear – wore   buy – bought
  cost – cost   leave – left   drink – drank   win – won
  eat – ate

- Pairwork. Students take it in turns to test each other.

2 I went ↔ I didn't go

- Students fill the gaps in the table. Establish that we form
  the Past simple negative with *didn't* + verb.
  Answers:

  didn't buy a newspaper
  didn't get up early
  didn't play cards
  didn't make a cake
  didn't have a big lunch
  didn't wear a white shirt

- Go through the list, asking students to choose sentences
  that are true of them (e.g. either *I watched TV yesterday* or
  I didn't watch TV yesterday).

3 Questions in the past

- Look at the example. Then give time for students to do
  the exercise alone or in pairs.
- Go through the answers together. Answers:

  a Who did you see?
  b What did they drink?
  c Where did she go?
  d How much did they win?
  e When did he leave?

4 was(n't) and were(n't)

- Establish that in the past:
  – *am* and *is* change to *was*.
  – *are* changes to *were*.
- Students do the exercise round the class or in pairs.
  Answers:

  a (He was at school.)   f Was she at work?
  b They were asleep.   g Where was she?
  c (I wasn't in Class 1.)   h Were you there?
  d She wasn't at home.   i Where were you?
  e We weren't married.

How to say it

1 The sound of 'didn't' and 'wasn't' in sentences

- ▭ Play the recording, pausing and getting students to
  repeat the sentences. Focus on:
  – the consonant clusters in /dɪdnt_siː/, /dɪdnt_gəʊ/,
  /wɒznt_ðeə/, /wɒznt_verɪ/
  – the rhythm of the sentences.

2 Rhythm of Wh- questions

- ▭ Play the recording. Ask students to repeat the
  sentences. Point out that:
  – the question words and verbs are stressed (*What –
  wear, Where – buy, Why – go, How much – cost*)
  – *did you, did it* are unstressed.

▭ Tapescript for Exercise 2: *Did you see …?*

1 A Did you see that programme about hospitals last night?
  B Yes, I did.
  A Did you like it?
  B Yes, I did. It was quite interesting.

2 A Did you watch the football match on Sunday?
  B No, I didn't. Was it good?
  A Yes, it was. We won 2–0.

3 A Did you go to the concert yesterday?
  B No. Did you?
  A Yes, I did.
  B Did you enjoy it?
  A No, it was really boring.

▭ Tapescript for Exercise 3: *Memory test*

A OK, can you remember your first day at school?
B My first day at school …
A What did you wear?
B I wore … I don't know. Jeans and a T-shirt, probably, but I
  don't really remember.
A OK, and what was your teacher's name?
B Oh, I remember that. It was Mr Fish.
A Mr Fish?
B Yes.

A Can you remember your first day at school?
C Yes, I think so.
A OK, what did you wear?
C I wore a dress, a summer dress – it was a very hot day, and
  I wore a red and white dress.
A What was your teacher's name?
C My first teacher? Mrs … Mrs Grey, I think.

18

This unit covers a range of language connected with movement and direction:
– direction prepositions (*along, down, up, into, through, over, across*)
– verbs of motion (e.g. *go, climb, get into*)
– words and expressions connected with transport (e.g. *go by bus, drive, station*)
– giving directions (e.g. *turn left, go straight on*).
The Reading and Listening activity is about the island of Ithaki in Greece, and
how to get there.

1 From A to B

*This exercise is in the form of a visual puzzle: students have to work out how the
prisoner can escape from his prison. This involves understanding and using direction
prepositions (e.g.* up, along, through), *verbs of motion (*go, climb), *and nouns (e.g.*
rope, steps).

➤ Workbook: Exercise A, Listening

> *Direction prepositions:* up, down, across, over, into, out of, through, along.
> *Other new words:* prisoner, wall, bridge, ladder, rope, hut, path, tunnel; climb.

1 *Presentation of prepositions & vocabulary; practice*

- Use the first picture to establish the meaning of the direction prepositions. Do
  this by going through the picture stage by stage and eliciting the actions, using
  gestures to help show the meaning (e.g. *Look – this is a path. Where does the
  man go? He goes <u>along</u> the path. Then he climbs ... <u>over</u> the wall.*). If you like,
  write sentences on the board. Answers:

  He goes along the path; climbs over the wall; goes up the steps; goes over/across the
  bridge; goes down the steps; climbs up the ladder; climbs down the rope; goes
  through the tunnel; goes into the hut; climbs out of / through the window.

- To practise this language, ask students round the class to say what the man does
  at each stage.

> *Pairwork option*
> Students test each other in pairs,
> taking it in turns to describe the
> picture. Alternatively, they could
> ask questions using the Present
> continuous:
> – What's he doing here?
> – He's climbing up the ladder.

2 *Activation: finding the escape route*

- Look at the second picture and establish the situation: there is a prisoner, and
  there is only one way for him to escape. Identify key words in the picture, but
  not following any particular route (e.g. *Can you see a bridge? How many huts
  are there?*).
- Divide the class into pairs or groups. Together, they try to work out the
  prisoner's escape route.
- Discuss the answer together. Get students to explain the route stage by stage,
  using the language you have practised (e.g. *First he climbs out of the window,
  then he climbs down the rope, ...*).

3 *Listening to check*

- 🖭 Play the recording to check. (Answer: see tapescript below.)

🖭 Tapescript for Exercise 1: *From A to B*

Well, the prisoner climbs through the window on to the
balcony, and then he climbs down the rope. Then he goes
along the path until he comes to the hut. Then he goes into
the hut and he goes down the ladder, and then down the
second ladder. Then he goes down the steps, and he goes
across the bridge, and he goes on until he comes to the lake.
Then he gets into the boat and goes across the lake. When he
reaches the other side, he climbs up the tree. Then he goes
through a short tunnel, climbs up the ladder, and climbs over
the wall – and he's free.

1 From A to B

1 Where does the person go? Use words from the box.

up	into	over	through
down	out of	across	along

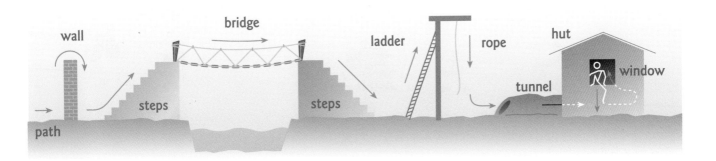

2 Look at this picture. How does the prisoner escape?

He goes …   He climbs …

3 Now listen. Is your answer the same?

2 Getting to work

1 Three people say how they get to work in the mornings.
Change the pictures into words. Use the expressions in the box.

go by train	drive
go by bus	cycle
go by taxi	walk
station	leave home
bus stop	get to work

A I usually [bus] . There's a [bus stop] just outside my

house. If I'm late I sometimes [taxi] , but it's quite expensive.

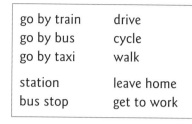

C I usually [car] , but if it's a nice

day I sometimes [bicycle] .

I [door] [computer] at 8.30.

B I [train] . I always [walk] to the [station] , as it's

only five minutes from my house. I always [leave home] at 7.30.

2 How do you get to work or school in the mornings? What about other people in your family?

3 It's on the left

1 Look at these directions. Can you put them in the right order?

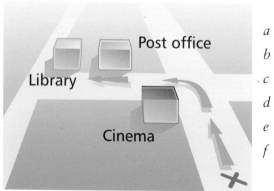

Post office

Library

Cinema

a [ ] The library is at the end of the street, on the right.

b [ ] Then carry straight on.

.c [ ] There's a cinema on the corner.

d [ ] Go past the post office.

e [1] Go straight along this road.

f [ ] Turn left at the cinema.

2 [cassette] You will hear two people giving directions. Listen and answer the questions.

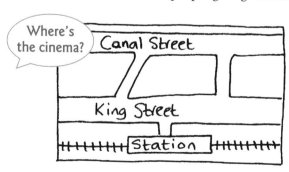

Where's the cinema? Canal Street

King Street

Station

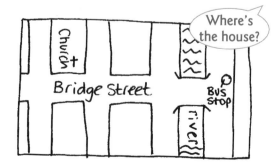

Where's the house?

Church

Bridge Street

river

BUS STOP

3 Choose one of the maps. Can you give the same directions?

4 Imagine you're meeting a friend somewhere (e.g. at your house, at a restaurant).
Draw a simple map, and tell your friend how to get there.

2 Getting to work

This exercise introduces basic language for talking about transport and how you travel to work or school.

> **Key words and phrases:** go by train/bus/taxi; drive, cycle, walk; leave home, get to work; station, bus stop. **Recycled language:** times; usually, sometimes.

1 Reading & gap-filling; presentation of key phrases

- Read through the texts, and get students to use expressions from the box to replace the pictures. Answers:

  A I usually *go by bus*. There's a *bus stop* just outside my house. If I'm late I sometimes *go by taxi*, but it's quite expensive.
  B I *go by train*. I always *walk* to the *station*, as it's only five minutes from my house. I always *leave home* at 7.30.
  C I usually *drive*, but if it's a nice day I sometimes *cycle*. I *get to work* at 8.30.

- Focus on these two ways of saying how you travel:

I go to	work school	by bus. by train. by taxi.		I	walk drive cycle	to	work. school.

2 Activation: going to work/school

- As a lead-in, tell the class how you get to work in the morning, and about other people in your family.
- Ask students how they get to work or school. Try to get a variety of responses (ask e.g. *Does anyone cycle? Who goes by bus?*).

3 It's on the left

This exercise teaches students to understand simple street directions and to give simple directions themselves.

> **Key phrases:** turn left/right, go/carry straight on.
> **Other new words and phrases:** road, past, on the corner, at the end.

1 Presentation of street directions; sequencing task

- Introduce the basic expressions (do this with gestures), and write them on the board:

Turn	left right	Go Carry	straight on

- Read through the sentences. Ask students to put them in order. Answer:

  Go straight along this road. There's a cinema on the corner. Turn left at the cinema. Then carry straight on. Go past the post office. The library is at the end of the street, on the right.

2 Listening & following a route

- 🔲 Play the first recording and ask the students to mark the cinema. Then do the same with the house in the second recording. Answers:

  Cinema: on either corner of Canal Street and the small street on the right
  House: anywhere in the street at top left

3 Practice: giving street directions

- Choose each of the maps in turn and ask students to try to give directions to the same place. Play the recording again to compare with what students said.

4 Activation: giving directions

- Pairwork. Students think of a place, then draw a simple sketch map and show their partner how to get there. The directions should start from somewhere nearby (e.g. a bus stop, an underground station, a nearby landmark).
- As a round-up, find out how many students understood their partner's directions!

➤ Workbook: Exercise B

> *Language note: bicycles*
> In conversational English, people often say *bike* instead of *bicycle*. The verb is *to cycle* or *to go by bike*.

> *Pair- or groupwork option*
> Students sit in pairs or groups to talk about themselves and members of their family. As a round-up, ask a few students to tell the class what they (or other students in their group) said.

➤ Workbook: Exercise C

> *Pairwork option*
> In pairs, students decide on the correct order. Then discuss the answer together.

> 🔲 The tapescript is on page T77.

> *Optional lead-in*
> Choose a place yourself, and draw a simple sketch map, showing the class how to get there.

> *Homework option*
> Students draw a fair copy of their map for homework, and write a set of directions to go with it.

4 The island of Odysseus

This combined Reading and Listening activity is about the island of Ithaki (or Ithaca) in Greece. The reading is a magazine-style travel article, which describes the island and what to do there. In the listening students hear someone describe different ways of getting to the island.

Reading skills: *reading to find answers to specific questions.*
Listening skills: *listening for main points.*

> *New words (text):* mountainous, harbour, accommodation, camp-site, stony, sandy, monastery, statue, museum, disco.

1 Reading to answer questions; presentation of vocabulary

- Establish what the article is about: an island in Greece called Ithaki (the island that Odysseus came from).
- Look at the questions at the top and make sure students understand them.
- Working alone, students read fairly quickly through the article (if you like, set a time limit, e.g. five minutes). Let them use dictionaries, but encourage them to guess words from the context.
- Discuss the questions together. As you do so, focus on the parts of the text that give the answers. Possible answers:

  Tourists: No, except in August (Most of the year it's very quiet, but in August the tourists arrive).
  Beaches: They're stony, not sandy.
  Places to eat: Only in the summer (A few stay open all year round, but in summer there are lots of places to eat).
  At night: Go to a disco or a bar, or sit in a café.
  Roads: Yes (It's very mountainous, but has good roads).
  Camp: Yes (There are several beaches with cheap camp-sites).
  During the day: You can swim, go to the beach, walk, visit museums, monasteries, etc.

- Ask students whether they would like to have a holiday there, and to say why or why not.

2 Listening & gap-filling

- Look at the map. Ask students how they think you can get to Ithaki.
- 🔲 Play the recording, pausing after each section. Students fill the gaps.
- Go through the answers together. Answers:

  From Athens: take a bus or train, take a ferry
  From Kefalonia: get a taxi, take a ferry
  From Italy: get a ferry, get off, drive, get a ferry

- 🔲 Play the recording again to establish the times. Answers:

  From Athens: about 8 hours   *From Kefalonia:* About 2 hours
  From Italy: about 30 hours (a day and a half)

🔲 Tapescript for Exercise 3: *It's on the left*

1 You come out of the station and turn right into King Street. Then you turn left into this little road here, and the cinema's at the end, just here on the corner of Canal Street. OK?

2 OK. You get off the bus here, opposite the bridge. Then you go across the river and just carry straight on – you're in Bridge Street now, so just carry on along Bridge Street and you come to a church. Go past the church and turn right, and the house is just along there.

🔲 Tapescript for Exercise 4: *The island of Odysseus*

Most people go to Greece by plane. So if you fly into Athens, first of all you need to get down to Patras. So you take a bus or a train down to Patras. That takes three or four hours. Then you can take a ferry boat that calls in at Kefalonia and then goes to Ithaki, and that takes maybe four or five hours.

You can also fly in to Kefalonia, there's an airport on Kefalonia. But there aren't any buses at the airport, so you have to take a taxi. You take a taxi right across the island and that takes maybe forty-five minutes or an hour. And then from there you can take a ferry over to Ithaki, and that takes about one hour.

A lot of people drive down to Greece, and you can get a ferry across to Greece from Italy, which takes about 24 hours, about one day. And then you get off the ferry at Igoumenitsa, drive down the coast for two or three hours, and then you can get a ferry across to Ithaki.

So that's three ways of getting to Ithaki.

4 The island of Odysseus

1 Read the article about the Greek island of Ithaki. Find answers to these questions.

Are there many tourists?

What are the beaches like?

Are there many places to eat?

What can you do at night?

Are the roads good?

Can you camp?

What can you do during the day?

Islands in the Sun

Ithaki *the island of Odysseus*

Ithaki is a small island – just 30 kilometres long. It's very mountainous, but has good roads. Most of the year, it's very quiet, but in August the tourists arrive, and the harbour in the main town, Vathi, is full of boats. If you want a quiet holiday with warm sunny weather, go in May, June or July.

Accommodation
Most people stay in rooms, but in August this can be expensive. There are several beaches with cheap camp-sites.

Beaches
The beaches are stony, not sandy. You can drive to some of them, but you need a boat to get to the best beaches on the island.

Eating out
Restaurants are cheap. A few stay open all year round, but in the summer there are lots of places to eat all over the island.

Other places to visit
Drive up the mountain to Kathara Monastery. On a good day, there is a beautiful view of Vathi. Then have coffee in Stavros, see the statue of Odysseus there and visit the museum. And then go on to Frikes or Kioni for a walk by the sea and a meal.

Nightlife
In August there is a music festival, and there are also a few discos and bars with music. In the evenings the main road in Vathi is closed, and children play football and ride their bikes while their parents sit in cafés. In the summer, most places stay open until one or two o'clock.

Statue of Odysseus, Stavros

Vathi

A beach in Ithaki

Kioni

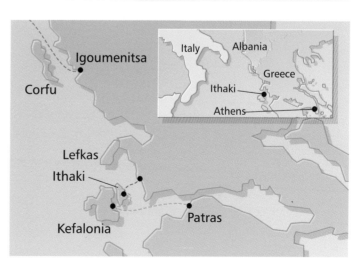

2 Someone describes three ways of getting to Ithaki. Listen and fill the gaps.

From Athens
You .... down to Patras. Then you .... to Ithaki.

From Kefalonia
You .... across the island. Then you .... to Ithaki.

From Italy
You .... from Italy to Greece. You .... at Igoumenitsa, and .... down the coast, and then you .... to Ithaki.

Listen again. How long is each journey?

Study pages

Focus on ... Short answers

1 Look at these questions and answers.

Does she smoke?	Yes, she does. No, she doesn't.
Are they having lunch?	Yes, they are. No, they aren't.
Did he give you the money?	Yes, he did. No, he didn't.

2 Here are some more questions and answers. What are the missing answers?

a Do your children like pizza?   Yes, they do.
 No, ...

b Did you enjoy the party?   Yes, ...
 No, I didn't.

c Are you married?   Yes, ...
 No, I'm not.

d Can he speak German?   Yes, he can.
 No, ...

e Is there any coffee?   Yes, ...
 No, there isn't.

3 Give true answers to these questions.

Did you come here by bus?

Are you wearing black shoes?

Is there a TV in the class?

Do you have a bike?

Can you play chess?

Does your teacher smoke?

Do you like James Bond films?

Sounds: July and April

1 🔲 Listen to the 'l' sound in English.

He climbed down the ladder.

She left on the eleventh of July.

We stayed in a small hotel.

2 🔲 Listen and practise.

> like flowers play yellow
> England usually salad
> girl small April vegetables
> children beautiful school

3 Write a sentence. Use words from box.

4 Read out your sentence.

Phrasebook: Let's ...

Match the expressions with the pictures.

Let's ask for the bill.

Shall we take a taxi?

Let's get some petrol.

Shall we dance?

🔲 Listen. What does the other person say?

Imagine it's the end of the lesson. What do you want to do? Suggest things to another student.

Study pages I

Focus on ... *Short answers*

This exercise focuses on yes/no questions and short answers, using the various verb forms introduced in the book so far. This consolidates language already introduced in Units 9, 11 and 17.

> *Key language:* short answers.
> *Recycled language:* yes/no questions.

1 ● Look at the examples. Show how in short answers we just repeat the first part of the verb (the 'auxiliary verb'): *does, are, did*, etc.

  ● If you like, give other questions using the same verb forms, and ask students to give short answers (e.g. *Does he like music? Are they English? Did they write to us?*).

2 Look at the questions, and ask students to give the missing answers. Answers:

  a No, they don't.
  b Yes, I did.
  c Yes, I am.
  d No, he can't.
  e Yes, there is.

3 *Either:* Ask the questions round the class, getting students to give true answers.

  Or: Prepare for the activity by looking at each question in turn, and establishing what the *Yes* and *No* answers are. Then students ask the questions in pairs and give true answers.

  Possible answers:

  Did you come here by bus? Yes, I did. No, I didn't.
  Are you wearing black shoes? Yes, I am. No, I'm not.
  Is there a TV in the class? Yes, there is. No, there isn't.
  Do you have a bike? Yes, I do. No, I don't.
  Can you play chess? Yes, I can. No, I can't.
  Does your teacher smoke? Yes he/she does. No, he/she doesn't.
  Do you like James Bond films? Yes, I do. No, I don't.

> 🔲 Tapescript for Phrasebook: *Let's ...*
>
> 1 A Let's get some petrol.
>   B Yes, that's a good idea.
> 2 A Shall we dance?
>   B No, I don't want to just at the moment.
> 3 A Let's ask for the bill.
>   B Not yet. I'd like another drink.
> 4 A Shall we take a taxi?
>   B No. Let's walk.

Sounds: *July and April*

> The /l/ sound

1, 2 🔲 The /l/ sound in English is quite varied: it ranges from 'light' (pronounced with the tip of the tongue at the front of the mouth) to 'dark' (pronounced further back in the mouth), depending on the sounds that come before and after. This may be worth pointing out (the first two sentences have 'light /l/' sounds, the third sentence has 'dark /l/' sounds), but do not make too much of this distinction. It is enough for students to produce an approximation of the sound.

3 Students write a sentence using words from the box, and including any other words they like, e.g.

  I like salad in April.
  The children go to school in England.

4 Students read out their sentences in turn. Focus on the pronunciation of the /l/ sound.

  Alternative: Dictation. Students dictate their sentence to the person next to them. As a check, ask students to read out the sentence they wrote down.

Phrasebook: *Let's ...*

This exercise teaches students how to make suggestions using Let's ... *and* Shall we ...?.

> *Key language:* Let's ..., Shall we ...?

● Show these two ways of making suggestions in English:
  Point out that *Let's go* = *Let us go.*

  > **Let's go to the cinema.**
  > **Shall we go to the cinema?**

● Look at the pictures. Establish what is happening in them, and ask students to match them with the remarks. Answers:

  1 Let's get some petrol. (*They're driving along a road, they see a petrol station, they haven't got much petrol.*)
  2 Shall we dance? (*They're at a party or a restaurant, other people are dancing.*)
  3 Let's ask for the bill. (*They're in a restaurant, they want to pay.*)
  4 Shall we take a taxi? (*They're in the street, it's late, there aren't any buses.*)

● 🔲 Play the recording. Establish what the other people say. (Answers: see tapescript.) If you like, ask students to practise the dialogues in pairs.

● Give time for students to think of a suggestion for after the lesson. If they like, they could write it down.

● Students make their suggestions, and other students reply.

Consolidation

It isn't very …

This exercise focuses on ways of describing things using very, not very *and* quite, *and opposite adjectives. This consolidates adjectives from earlier units (especially Units 7, 12 and 16).*

1 ● Look at the expressions, and check that students understand the meaning of *very* and *quite* (if possible, use students' own language for this; otherwise give simple examples).

  ● Ask students to describe the dogs. Expected answers:

    Bonzo is very small.   Chico is quite small / not very big.
    Gigi is quite big.   Lulu is very big.

2 Ask students to complete the sentences. Then go through the answers. Answers:

  b expensive *c* fast *d* new *e* young *f* tall *g* long *h* rich.

3 *Either:* Get students to make sentences round the class, using the ideas as prompts (e.g. *Have you got a watch? What's it like? Cheap? Expensive? Old? New?*).

  Or: Let students talk about the topics in pairs. As a round-up, ask students what they found out from their partner.

Years

This exercise focuses on the way we say years in English. This builds on work already done on numbers and dates.

1 ● Ask students to fill the gaps. Answers:

    1906   nineteen hundred and six
    1960   nineteen sixty
    1993   nineteen ninety-three
    2007   two thousand and seven

  ● Use the examples to show that:
    – we say most years as pairs of numbers (so *1993* is *nineteen – ninety-three*);
    – early numbers in the century we say as normal numbers (*2001* is *two thousand and one*, not 'twenty 0 one').

2 ● Look at the years in the table, and establish how to say them. Then give students time to read the sentences and choose the answers.

  ● Go through the answers together, asking students to read the sentences aloud. Answers:

    The first Mickey Mouse cartoon was in 1928 (nineteen twenty-eight).
    Steven Spielberg made the film *Jaws* in 1975 (nineteen seventy-five).
    Columbus went to America in 1492 (fourteen ninety-two).
    Henry Ford made his first car in 1903 (nineteen hundred and three).
    Marilyn Monroe died in 1962 (nineteen sixty-two).

Review

Climate and weather

Review of months, seasons, and weather (Exercises 14.1, 14.2 and 14.3).

Look at each place in turn. Discuss answers to the questions. Possible answers:

New York in April: It's spring. It's quite warm, sunny.
Moscow in September: It's the end of the summer. It's quite hot, dry, sunny.
London in December: It's winter. It's quite cold, it's raining, it's wet (*or* It's cold, it's snowing).
Sydney in January: It's summer. It's hot, sunny.

Countries

Review of countries and languages (Exercises 16.2 and 16.3).

Look at the countries in the boxes in turn. Ask students to suggest words that go with them and use them in sentences. If you like, build up sentences about each country on the board. Expected answers:

Canada: Canada is in North America. Ottawa is the capital. It's cold in winter. People speak English and French there. It's a very large country.
Saudi Arabia: Saudi Arabia is in the Middle East. People speak Arabic there. It's very dry. The capital is Riyadh.
Poland: Poland is in Europe. People speak Polish there. The capital is Warsaw. It's cold in winter.

Mixed-up words

Review of vocabulary, especially from Units 6, 8 and 14.

1 ● Look at the first word together, and establish what it is. (Answer: *November.*)

  ● Working alone or in pairs, students work out the other words. Let them look back at Units 6, 8 and 14 if they need help.

  ● Go through the answers together. Answers:

    Things to drink: water, juice, lemonade
    Months: November, March, February
    Things in a room: cupboard, carpet, sofa

2 ● Students look through previous units to find a word. They write it in a jumbled form and add a clue.

  ● They give their word to another student to solve.

Consolidation

It isn't very …

1 Choose expressions to describe these dogs.

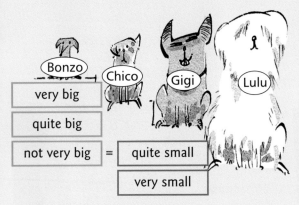

very big	
quite big	
not very big =	quite small
	very small

2 Write in the missing adjectives.

a Our flat isn't very big = It's quite small
b Our TV isn't very .... = It's quite cheap
c Our car isn't very .... = It's quite slow
d Their car isn't very old = It's quite ....
e My brother isn't very old = He's quite ....
f My sister isn't very .... = She's quite short
g Her hair isn't very .... = It's quite short
h We aren't very .... = We're quite poor

3 Now talk about one of these:

– your town/village   – your mother/father
– your flat/house   – your brother/sister
– your car/bike   – your boyfriend/girlfriend
– your TV/watch   – your husband/wife

Years

1 Look at the examples. Can you fill the gaps?

1900 nineteen hundred
1901 nineteen hundred and one
1906 ....
1910 nineteen (hundred and) ten
1911 nineteen eleven
1948 nineteen forty-eight
1960 ....
1993 ....
2000 two thousand
2001 two thousand and one
2007 ....

2 Make true sentences. Read out your answers.

The first Mickey Mouse cartoon was		1492.
Steven Spielberg made the film *Jaws*		1903.
Columbus went to America	in	1928.
Henry Ford made his first car		1962.
Marilyn Monroe died		1975.

Review

Climate and weather

Imagine you're in these places.

New York in April   London in December   Moscow in September

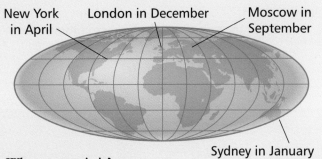

Sydney in January

What season is it?
What do you think the weather's like?

Countries

Which words go with which countries?
Make two or three sentences about each one.

Warsaw   Ottawa   Riyadh

very dry | CANADA |

            French   The Middle East

Polish | SAUDI ARABIA |

                        very large

cold in winter   North America   Arabic

Europe | POLAND | English

Do you know anything else about these countries?

Mixed-up words

1 Look at these mixed-up words. Can you make

BEENMORV   AERTW

– three things to drink?   ACHMR   ABCDOPRU
– three months?
– three things in a room?   ACEPRT   CEIJU

How do you spell them?

ABEFRRUY

ADEELMNO   AFOS

2 Now you write a mixed-up word. Show it to your partner.

YOUCDL (The weather)

19 You mustn't do that!

1 You must stay in your car

must & mustn't • can

1 Read the text about the Kruger National Park.

a Where is the Kruger National Park?
b Why do people go there?
c Where can you stay in the Park?

THE KRUGER NATIONAL PARK covers 20,000 square kilometres. It is the largest wildlife park in South Africa, and a wonderful place to see animals in their natural home. You can drive through the park in your own car, and look at lions, zebras, giraffes, elephants and crocodiles – and you can sometimes see a leopard or a rhinoceros. You can visit the park just for a day, or you can stay overnight at one of the many Rest Camps.

2 Look at the six sentences. Which do you think are true? And which are false?

a You must stay in your car.

b You must take a gun with you.

c You mustn't stop the car.

d You mustn't feed the animals.

e You can take photos.

f You can bring pets into the park.

3 Here is some more information about the Park. Fill the gaps with *can, must* or *mustn't*.

1 The Park is very large, so all visitors .... carry a road map. You .... buy a map at the entrance gate.

2 You .... keep to 50 km/h on the main roads, and 40 km/h on the small roads. You .... leave the roads.

3 Day visitors .... leave the Park before 6.00. If you want to stay overnight at a Rest Camp, you .... reserve a room.

4 You .... drive in the Park at night, but if you are staying in a Rest Camp, you .... go on a group tour to see the animals at night.

4 Think about your English class. What are the rules?
Write sentences saying what you *can, must* and *mustn't* do.

19

This unit introduces ways of talking about obligation and permission, using:
– *must/mustn't*
– *can/can't*
– *have to/don't have to*.

1 You must stay in your car

This exercise is about the Kruger National Park in South Africa. It introduces the modal verbs must, mustn't *and* can *for talking about rules.*

> ➤ Focus on Form: Exercise 1
> ➤ Workbook: Exercise A

> *Key structures:* must, mustn't, can.
> *New words and phrases:* gun, feed, take photos, entrance, visitor, tour, overnight.
> *For comprehension only:* wildlife park, wonderful, natural; lion, zebra, giraffe, elephant, crocodile, leopard, rhinoceros.

1 Reading to answer questions; presentation of vocabulary

- Look at the picture and use it to introduce the idea of a *wildlife park* (a place where you can go to see wild animals).
- Look at the questions. Then ask students to read the text and find answers to them. They should be able to do this without understanding every word of the text.
- Discuss the answers together. Answers:

  a It's in South Africa.   *b* People go there to see wild animals.
  c You can stay at a Rest Camp.

Presentation option
Read through the text again, making sure students understand everything.

2 Presentation of 'must/mustn't/can'; reading true/false sentences

- Show the meaning of *must, mustn't* and *can* on the board:

  > **You must ...   = Do it!**
  > **You mustn't ... = Don't do it!**
  > **You can ...   = It's OK to do it.**

- Look at the six sentences, and ask students whether they think they are true. Answers:

  a True (except in Rest Camps).   *b* False: You mustn't take a gun with you.
  c False: You can stop the car.   *d* True.   *e* True.   *f* False: You mustn't bring pets into the park.

Presentation option
Give other simple examples to make the meaning clear, e.g.

You *must* clean your teeth.
You *mustn't* play football in the road.

Note: Avoid giving examples from the classroom or school, as these are used in Stage 4.

3 Reading & gap-filling

- Students read the texts, either alone or in pairs, and decide which verbs should go in the gaps.
- Go through the answers together. Answers:

  1 ... all visitors *must* carry a road map. You *can* buy a map ...
  2 You *must* keep to 50 km/h ... You *mustn't* leave the roads.
  3 Day visitors *must* leave the park ... you *can* reserve a room.
  4 You *mustn't* drive ... you *can* go on a group tour ...

4 Activation: writing sentences

- Ask the class for one or two rules in the English class and write them on the board as examples (e.g. *You must speak English, You mustn't eat sweets*).
- Working alone or in pairs, students think of other rules and write them down.
- Ask students to read out their rules. If you like, write them up on the board.

Homework option
Students write rules for homework, and read them out in the next lesson.

🔊 Tapescript for Exercise 2: *Can I ...?*

1 A Can I use the phone?
  B Of course. It's in the hall.

2 A Can I smoke?
  C No, sorry, you can't, not in here. But you can smoke on the balcony.

3 A Can I listen to the news?
  B Yes, of course you can. There's a radio in the kitchen.

4 A Can I have a glass of beer?
  C Sorry, we haven't got any beer. You can have fruit juice or lemonade.

2 Can I ...?

This exercise shows how we use can *and* can't *in everyday conversation, when asking for, giving and refusing permission to do things.*

> *Key language:* can, can't; Can I ...?

1 Listening; presentation of 'can/can't'

- Write these examples on the board:

  Get students to read them out, focusing on the pronunciation of /juː kən/, /juː kɑːnt/ and /kæn aɪ/.

  > **You can go now.**
  > **You can't go now.**
  > **Can I go now?**

- 🔊 Play the conversations. Pause after each one, and establish what the woman can and can't do. Answers:

  a She can use the phone.   b She can't smoke in the flat.
  c She can listen to the news.   d She can't have a glass of beer.

2 Listening: focus on questions & answers

- 🔊 Ask students what the questions and answers were. Then play the conversations again to check. (Answers: see tapescript on page T80.)

3 Activation: asking and answering questions

- Divide students into pairs and give them letters, A or B. Ask students to turn to page 109 and look only at their part of the page.

- Students take it in turns to ask questions with *Can I ...?* and to give answers according to the information on his/her page.

- As a round-up, ask students to repeat some of their questions and answers.

3 All in a day's work

This exercise introduces have to *and* don't have to *for obligation. Students hear three people talking about their jobs, then write sentences about themselves.*

> *New words and phrases:* early, polite, careful, dangerous, away from home; cleaner, fishing boat, waitress.

1 Presentation of 'have to / don't have to'; presentation of vocabulary

- Look at the first two sentences, and use them to establish the meaning of *I have to ...* and *I don't have to ...* You could do this by expanding the examples to make the meaning clear, e.g.

  – I start work at 7 o'clock, so I *have to* get up very early – at about 6 o'clock. I don't want to get up early, but I *have to* get up then because of my job.
  – I don't work in the morning. So sometimes I get up early, sometimes I get up late. I *don't have to* get up early.

- Read through the other sentences, presenting any new words.

2 Matching task; listening to check

- Look at the bubbles and present *cleaner, fishing boat,* and *waitress.*

- Ask students which sentences they think each person will say.

- 🔊 Play the recording and check the answers. Answers:

  1 I have to get up early. I have to be polite. I don't have to work very long hours.
  2 You have to be very careful when the weather's bad. I have to be away from home a lot. I don't have to work all year.
  3 I don't have to get up very early. I have to be nice to everyone and smile a lot. I have to work late in the evening.

3 Activation: students' own obligations

- To introduce the activity, say a few things about your own job.

- Students write a few sentences about what they have to or don't have to do.

- As a round-up, ask students to read out their sentences.

> ➤ Focus on Form: Exercise 2
> ➤ Workbook: Exercise B, Listening

> 🔊 The tapescript is on page T80.

> *Language note*
> *You can't* often has a similar meaning to *you mustn't* (e.g. *You can't/mustn't smoke here*), but *mustn't* is much stronger.

> *Optional preparation*
> Establish with the whole class what the questions for A and B should be.

> ➤ Focus on Form: Exercise 3
> ➤ Workbook: Exercise C

> *Language note*
> *Must* and *have to* mean almost the same; we usually use *must* for giving rules or saying what they are (as in Exercise 1).
> But *mustn't* (= it's forbidden, don't do it) does *not* mean the same as *don't have to* (= it isn't necessary).

> 🔊 The tapescript is on page T82.

> *Pairwork option*
> If students have similar circumstances (e.g. they're all school pupils of the same age, or they have similar jobs), they could brainstorm ideas together in pairs.

2 Can I …?

can • questions with 'can'

1 ⬜ You will hear four short conversations.
What can the woman do? What can't she do?

a She can/can't use the phone.
b She can/can't smoke in the flat.
c She can/can't listen to the news.
d She can/can't have a glass of beer.

2 ⬜ Listen again. What were the questions?
What were the answers?

3 Work in pairs. Turn to page 109. Ask and
answer questions.

3 All in a day's work

have to • don't have to

1 Look at these sentences. What does *I have to …* mean? What does *I don't have to …* mean?

a ⬜ I have to get up very early.
b ⬜ I don't have to get up very early.
c ⬜ I have to be polite.
d ⬜ You have to be very careful when the weather's bad.
e ⬜ I have to be nice to everyone and smile a lot.
f ⬜ I have to be away from home a lot.
g ⬜ I don't have to work long hours.
h ⬜ I don't have to work all year.
i ⬜ I have to work late in the evening.

I work in an Italian
restaurant – I'm a waitress.
It's quite a nice job …

I work as a cleaner
in a big hotel. It's not a
very nice job …

2 Three people talk about their jobs.
What do you think they say?
Match the sentences with the people.

I work on a fishing boat.
It's a hard job and it's
quite dangerous …

⬜ Now listen and check your answers.

3 Think about what you do. What are the good things
about it? What are the bad things? Tell your partner.

I have to …   I don't have to …

Focus on Form

1 must & mustn't

You must	=	Do it!
You mustn't	=	Don't do it!

What do these signs mean?
Make sentences from the table.

A — HARD HAT AREA
B
C — SLOW
D
E
F
G

You must You mustn't	wear a hard hat. stop. smoke. drive slowly. turn left. park your car. turn your lights on.

2 can & can't

In Britain, you can often buy food at petrol stations (but you can't buy petrol at the supermarket).

Think about your own country. Are these sentences true or false?

a You can buy food at petrol stations.
b You can smoke on buses and trains.
c You can buy alcohol on Sundays.
d You can smoke in restaurants.
e You can carry a gun.
f Children can buy cigarettes and alcohol.
g You can buy petrol at the supermarket.

3 have to & don't have to

I have to go.	They don't have to go.
She has to go.	He doesn't have to go.

Fill the gaps with *have to*, *has to*, *don't have to* or *doesn't have to*.

a I love Sundays because I .... get up and go to work. My husband's a taxi driver, so he often .... work at the weekend.
b Sorry, I can't come out tonight – I .... clean the flat.
c My son's seven years old. He .... go to school, but he .... do any homework.
d You can stay here – you .... go.

How to say it

1 🔲 **Listen to *must* and *mustn't* in these sentences. Practise saying them.**

You must take a coat.

You must tell me about it.

You mustn't take photos.

You mustn't feed the animals.

You mustn't say anything.

2 🔲 **Listen to the sound of *can* and *can't*. Practise saying the sentences.**

ə
You can come with us if you like.

æ
– Can I come?

æ
– Of course you can.

ɑː
Sorry, you can't come with us.

æ
– Can I watch the news?

ɑː
– No, sorry, you can't.

Focus on Form

1 must & mustn't

- Look at the signs, and ask students to make sentences.
  Answers:

  A You must wear a hard hat.
  B You mustn't smoke.
  C You must drive slowly.
  D You mustn't turn left.
  E You must stop.
  F You must turn your lights on.
  G You mustn't park your car.

2 can & can't

- Read through the example.
- Students read the sentences and change them if necessary so that they are true of their own country. They could either do this in pairs, or they could write the sentences.

  (Answers will of course vary from one country to another.)

3 have to & don't have to

- Look at the table. Establish that *have to* is formed just like the verb *have*, so we say *He/she has to ...* and *He/she doesn't have to ...*
- Students fill the gaps. Then go through the answers:

  a I don't have to get up ... he often has to work ...
  b I have to clean ...
  c He has to go ... but he doesn't have to do ....
  d ... you don't have to go.

How to say it

1 The sound of 'must' and 'mustn't' in sentences

- ▭ Play the recording, pausing and getting students to repeat the sentences. Focus on:
  - the consonant clusters in /mʌst_teɪk/, /mʌst_tel/, /mʌsnt_teɪk/, /mʌsnt_fiːd/, /mʌsnt_seɪ/
  - the rhythm of the sentences, with both verbs (e.g. *must* and *take*) stressed.

2 The sound of 'can' and 'can't' in sentences

- ▭ Play the recording. Ask students to repeat the sentences. Point out:
  - *can* = /kæn/ when it's stressed (/kæn aɪ/), but /kən/ when it's unstressed (/juː kən/)
  - the difference between /kæn/ and /kɑːnt/.

▭ Tapescript for Exercise 3: *All in a day's work*

1 I work as a cleaner in a big hotel. It's not a very nice job. I have to get up very early – I get up at about 5 o'clock, and I start work at 6. And some of the people are friendly, but not all of them – of course I always have to be polite, and that's quite difficult sometimes. One good thing is, I don't have to work long hours – I finish at about 10 in the morning, and then I can go home.

2 Well, I work on a fishing boat. It's a hard job, and it's quite dangerous too. You have to be very careful when the weather's bad. We go out to sea for about three or four weeks usually, so I have to be away from home a lot. The good thing about it – about the only good thing – the money's very good, so I don't have to work all year – I work about six months, usually, and that's good enough to live on.

3 I work in an Italian restaurant in London – I'm a waitress. And it's quite a nice job, I like it. I have to be nice to everyone and smile a lot, of course, but people are usually friendly anyway, so that's not a problem. I have to work late in the evening, usually till about 11 or 12 at night. But then I don't have to get up early because I don't work in the morning.

20

This unit is about various aspects of the body and physical activity:
– parts of the body (e.g. *head, eye, finger*)
– adjectives for describing the body (e.g. *long, short, thin*)
– action verbs (e.g. *run, jump, kick*) in the Present and Past tense.
The Reading and Listening activity is about bungee jumping.

1 Aliens

This exercise uses the idea of recognising an alien as a way of introducing parts of the body and descriptive adjectives, and recycling colours. Students match descriptions to the pictures, and then write a description themselves.

➤ Workbook: Exercise A, Listening

Parts of the body: head, eye, nose, mouth, ear, body, neck, arm, hand, finger, leg, foot.   *Adjectives:* long, thin, short, large, small.   *Recycled language:* colours. *Other new words:* alien, friendly, careful, mistake, human, at the top.

1 Reading & matching; presentation of parts of the body

- Look at the picture and establish the situation: this is a bar somewhere in the galaxy, it is full of aliens (= people from other places in the galaxy). You want to know which aliens are friendly and which are not.

- Read through the texts with the class, presenting new vocabulary as you go. Present parts of the body simply by pointing to yourself. After each paragraph, ask students if they can see the alien in the picture.

- After reading the whole text, establish which are the friendly aliens. Answers:
  (left – right) 1 a Bolonid   2 a Gnerg   3 an Ogon   4 unknown   5 a Zap
  6 unknown   7 a Bzerk   8 unknown

2 Vocabulary task: labelling a diagram

- Ask students to look at the texts again and identify the parts of the body in the diagram. Build up a list on the board. Answers:
  1 head   2 eye   3 nose   4 mouth   5 neck   6 leg   7 foot   8 body
  9 arm   10 hand   11 finger   12 ear

3 Activation: describing an alien

- Choose one of the unfriendly aliens in the bar. Ask students to suggest a name, and build up a description on the board, getting students to help you.

Note
The picture is similar to a scene in one of the *Star Wars* films. As a lead-in, you could ask students if they have seen these films.

Pairwork option
Present key vocabulary for parts of the body, using the diagram in Part 2. Then students work in pairs, reading through the text and identifying the aliens.

Alternative: writing
Alone or in pairs, students choose one of the unfriendly aliens and write a description. Then ask a few students to read out their descriptions to the class.
Students could do Part 4 as homework.

Homework option
Students invent an alien of their own and write a description of it. They could also illustrate it with a picture.

📼 Tapescript for Exercise 2: *Are you an athlete?*

'Can you run 100 metres?' Yes, I can do that. And run five kilometres ... no. 'Can you swim 100 metres?' Yes, I can swim 100 metres, but I can't swim one kilometre. Can I ride a bike? Yes. Can I ride a bike with no hands? No, I don't think so. Climb up a ladder, yes. Climb up a rope? Yes, I can do that. Jump over a stream one metre wide? I can, that's easy. Jump over a wall one metre high? No, I can't do that. Catch a tennis ball in one hand is easy. Throw a tennis ball 50 metres? No, I can't do that. 'Can you kick a football 100 metres?' No, I can't do that. 'Can you stand on your head?' No! And 'Can you walk on your hands?' No.

20 The body

1 Aliens

1 Imagine you're a human space traveller in this bar. Which aliens are friendly? Which are unfriendly?

2 Find words in the text to label the diagram.

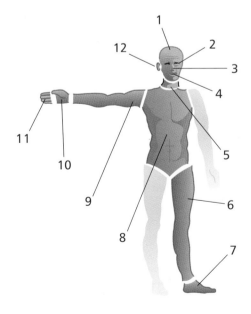

Friendly aliens

Before you talk to an alien, be sure that it's friendly. Be very careful – there are millions of different types of alien, and it's easy to make a mistake.

These aliens are friendly to humans:

Gnergs are yellow or green. They have three long thin legs, three arms, and three fingers on each hand. They have one eye in the middle of their head, and a long thin nose.

Zaps can be any colour. They have a long thin body and eight legs. They have two heads. Each head has a large mouth and two eyes on long stalks.

Bolonids look a bit like humans, but they have a small body and small arms and legs. They are light green, and have large black eyes and no ears.

Bzerks have one long leg, two arms and no head. They have one big eye at the top of their body. They are usually red or purple.

Ogons also look a bit like people, but they have a small head on the end of a very long neck. They are green with short legs and large white hands and feet.

3 Choose one of the unfriendly aliens in the bar. How could you describe it?

2 Are you an athlete?

1 Match the verbs with the pictures.

2 🔲 A woman does this quiz. Listen and give her a score out of 50.

catch	run
climb	stand
jump	swim
kick	throw
ride	walk

A B C D E

F G H I J

Can you ...

1 ... **run 100 metres?** (1 point)
... **run 5 kilometres?** (5 points)

2 ... **swim 100 metres?** (2 points)
... **swim 1 kilometre?** (5 points)

3 ... **ride a bike?** (1 point)
... **ride a bike with no hands?** (3 points)

4 ... **climb up a ladder?** (1 point)
... **climb up a rope?** (6 points)

5 ... **jump over a stream 1 metre
wide?** (1 point)
... **jump over a wall 1 metre high?**
(4 points)

6 ... **catch a tennis ball in one hand?**
(1 point)
... **throw a tennis ball 50 metres?**
(3 points)
... **kick a football 100 metres?**
(3 points)

7 ... **stand on your head?** (4 points)
... **walk on your hands?** (10 points)

3 Ask your partner the questions. How many points does he/she score?

3 Action!

1 Here are some scenes from a TV advertisement for a chocolate bar. What is the man doing in scenes 2–8? Use these verbs.

climb drive fly jump ride run swim

What's happening in scenes 1 and 9?

2 Look at these past forms. What are the past forms of the other verbs in the box?

climbed   drove

3 Now read the story on page 108.
Tell the story, using verbs in the box instead of *went*.

4 Look at the pictures again. Can you tell the story in your own words?

2 Are you an athlete?

*This exercise is in the form of a questionnaire about physical activities.
It introduces a range of action verbs.*

> *Action verbs:* catch, climb, jump, kick, ride, run, stand, swim, throw, walk.
> *Other new words:* metre, kilometre, stream.   *Recycled language:* can.

1 Matching task; presentation of action verbs

● Look at the pictures and ask students to match them with the verbs. Ask
students to make simple sentences using the verbs, e.g. *What's he doing? He's
kicking a ball.* Answers:

A walk   B kick   C jump   D run   E swim   F ride   G catch   H climb
I throw   J stand

2 Listening & giving a score

● Read the questionnaire and make sure students understand all the questions.

● ▭ Play the recording. Students listen and note down a score.

● See if students agree about the score. (Probable score: 13 points.)

3 Activation: doing the questionnaire

● Pairwork. Students ask each other the questions and note down a score for each
other. As a round-up, find out who had the highest (and lowest) scores.

3 Action!

*This exercise is based on a TV advertisement in which a man performs a series of
tasks in order to bring his partner a chocolate bar. This builds on the action verbs
introduced in the previous exercise, and practises their Past tense forms.*

> *New verbs:* fly.   *Irregular past forms:* drove, flew, rode, ran, swam.
> *Other new words:* advertisement, good-looking, helicopter, horse, rock, chocolate bar.
> *Recycled language:* direction prepositions.

1 Introduction: describing pictures

● Look at pictures 2–8 and ask students what is happening in them. They should
use action verbs and direction prepositions. Try to elicit these answers:

  2 He's running out of the house.   3 He's driving along the road, to an airport.
  4 He's flying in a helicopter across the sea/to an island.
  5 He's riding a horse through the trees.   6 He's jumping off a bridge into a river.
  7 He's swimming across the river to a rock.   8 He's climbing up the rock.

● Establish what is happening in Pictures 1 and 9. Suggested answers:

  1 He's going out of the room.
  9 She's eating the chocolate bar.

2 Presentation of past forms

● Write the past forms of the verbs on the board:

> climbed   jumped   ran
> drove   rode   swam
> flew

3 Reading & vocabulary task

● Either read through the story with the class, presenting new words as you go, or
give time for students to read the story quietly to themselves.

● Go through the story together, and ask students to change *went* to a more
appropriate verb. Expected answers:

  … he *ran* out of the house … he *drove* to a small airport … he *flew* across the sea …
  he *rode* across the island … he *jumped* off the bridge … he *swam* to the rock … he
  climbed up the rock …

4 Activation: telling the story

● Ask students to look only at the pictures, not the story. Students try to tell the
story round the class, each taking a sentence or two in turn. They should try to
use the action verbs they have practised.

➤ Workbook: Exercise B

> *Language note*
> You can *ride* a bicycle or a horse.

> ▭ The tapescript is on page T83.

> *Presentation option*
> Write some of the expressions the
> woman uses on the board:
>
> > **I can do that.**
> > **I can't do that.**
> > **That's easy**
> > **I (don't) think so.**

> *Homework idea*
> Students try out the questionnaire
> on members of their family or
> friends. They tell the class the
> results in the next lesson.

➤ Workbook: Exercise C

> *Language note*
> *Fly, ride* and *drive* can be transitive
> or intransitive. We can say:
>
> He flew to the island.
> *or* He flew a plane to the island.
> He rode along the road.
> *or* He rode his horse along the road.
> He drove to the airport.
> *or* He drove his car to the airport.

> *Review option*
> Leave this stage until the next
> lesson. Then ask students how
> much they can remember of the
> story.

4 I did it!

This combined Reading and Listening activity is about bungee jumping. The reading consists of a series of sentences, which students have to put in the right order. In the listening someone explains what happens when you bungee jump. The description includes a few technical words (e.g. elastic, crane, harness), *but all these are labelled in the photos.*

Reading skills: *understanding the sequence of events.*
Listening skills: *listening to understand a process; listening to confirm predictions.*

> *New words (reading):* cage, certificate, take off, put on, pay, fix, harness, elastic, slowly. *New words (listening):* count, crazy, thick. *Recycled language:* descriptive adjectives.

1 Presentation of vocabulary; reading & sequencing task

- Look at the pictures, and establish very simply what happens when you go bungee jumping: you jump from a crane, tied to a long piece of elastic. Do not go into details at this point.

  If you like, use this stage to present some of the key vocabulary used in the sentences, e.g. *crane, harness, elastic, cage, put on, take off.*

- Give time for students to look at the sentences, either alone or in pairs, and decide what order they should be in.

- Discuss the answers together. Try to reach agreement about the order (the answer will become clear when they hear the recording).

2 Prediction task; listening to answer questions

- Read through the questions, and ask students to guess the answers.

- 🔲 Play the recording and check the order of the stages. Answers:

  1 You pay.
  2 You put on a harness.
  3 They fix the elastic to the harness.
  4 You get in the cage and they close the door.
  5 You go up in the cage.
  6 They open the door of the cage.
  7 You jump.
  8 The cage comes down slowly.
  9 You take off the harness.
  10 They give you a certificate.

- 🔲 Play the recording again, pausing from time to time and checking answers to the questions. Answers:

  a It's expensive to jump. The cage is big. The elastic is long, thick, and strong. The top of the crane is very high. People look very small.
  b One end to the cage, the other end to your harness.
  c Around 60 metres.
  d The man counts to three.
  e The cage comes down slowly to the ground.

3 Extension: feelings about bungee jumping

- Ask the class to imagine they have a chance to bungee jump. Ask who would do it and who wouldn't. Ask one or two students to say why/why not.

🔲 Tapescript for Exercise 4: *I did it!*

Well, first you have to pay, and it's quite expensive – I paid £40 for just one jump. And then you put on a harness. And the harness goes round your body, and down your legs to your feet. And then you walk up to the cage. The cage is quite big – big enough for five or six people – and there's this very long piece of elastic. The elastic is very thick, very strong, and one end of the elastic is fixed under the cage, and they fix the other end of the elastic to your harness.

OK, then you get in the cage, and it starts to go up. And it goes up really high – about 60 metres. And when you look down, everything's very small down there, all the people are very small.

And then the man opens the door of the cage. And you think 'I don't want to do this. This is crazy.' But the man says 'OK, you go when I count to three.' And he counts to three – one, two, three – and you jump.

And it's all very quick – you fall very quickly, then the elastic pulls you up again, and you go up and down, up and down, and then you stop, and you just hang there. And then the cage comes down slowly, slowly brings you down to the ground, and that's it – you take off your harness. And they give you a certificate, and the certificate says 'I did it!'

4 I did it!

1 Look at the pictures. What do you think happens when you do a bungee jump? Put the sentences in the right order.

| | The cage comes down slowly. |

| | You jump. |

| | You get in the cage and they close the door. |

| | They give you a certificate. |

| | You pay. |

| | You take off the harness. |

| | You put on a harness. |

| | You go up in the cage. |

| | They open the door of the cage. |

| | They fix the elastic to the harness. |

2 You will hear someone describing his first bungee jump. Before you listen, look at these questions.

a The speaker uses these adjectives. What is he talking about?

expensive	long	strong
high	big	thick	small

b Where do they fix the two ends of the elastic?

c How high are you when you jump?

d How do you know when you have to jump?

e How do you get down?

📼 Now listen and answer the questions.

3 Imagine bungee jumping comes to your town. Would you jump?

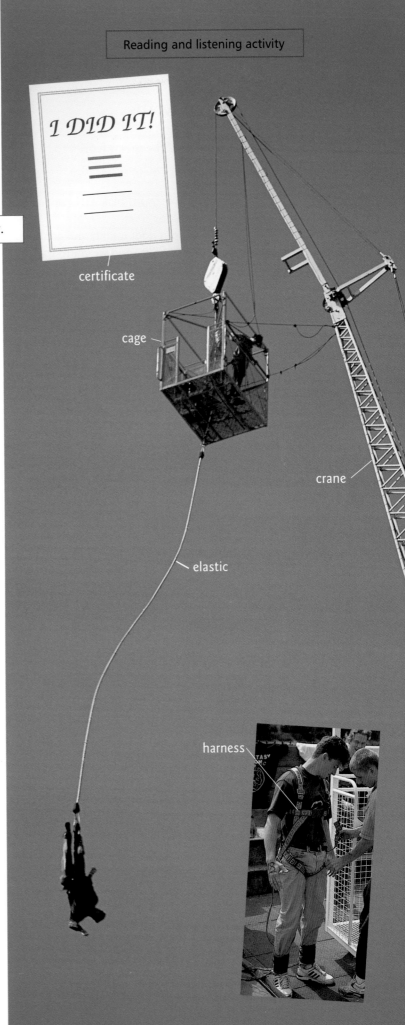

I DID IT!

certificate

cage

crane

elastic

harness

Unit 20 The body   85

Focus on ... Adverbs

Here is part of a story. The green words are all *adverbs*.

I woke suddenly at 6 o'clock. Marie was by my bed. 'Get dressed quickly,' she said, 'or we'll be late.'

When I was ready, we closed the front door quietly and got in the car. Marie drove well – fast but carefully – and we got to the harbour by 7 o'clock. The boat was there, and we jumped in.

As we moved slowly out of the harbour, a black car came round the corner. It was Carlos.

'Marie! Come back!' he shouted angrily. But he was too late.

1 Read the story and complete the table.

2 Complete this rule.

To form an adverb, we usually add .... to the adjective.

Adjective	Adverb
quiet	quietly
slow	
quick	
sudden	
careful	
angry	
fast	
good	

3 Add adverbs to these sentences.

He learns languages.

We drove into town.

I opened the door and went out.

'What do you want?' she asked.

She wrote her name on a piece of paper.

4 Write a true sentence about yourself. Use one of the adverbs in the table.

Sounds: A room in Australia

1 📼 Listen to the sound 'r' in English.

/r/ I can read Arabic, but I can't write it very well.

Listen to these sounds: /br/, /fr/, /tr/, /dr/, /θr/.

We drove through France.

She worked as a waitress in Australia.

For three days, I had only bread and fruit.

2 📼 Listen and practise.

room friend Britain country drive
tourists France bring trousers bedroom
wearing from bread dry

3 Write a sentence. Use words from the box.

4 Read out your sentence.

Phrasebook: Could you ...?

This person is ill in bed. He mustn't eat fat, drink alcohol or smoke.

📼 Listen to the conversation and fill the gaps.

– Could you bring me .... ?
– Yes, of course.
– And could you buy me .... ?
– No, sorry.

Imagine you are the person in bed. Ask for these things.

Study pages J

Focus on ... *Adverbs*

This exercise focuses on adverbs and shows how they are different from adjectives.

> *Key language:* adverbs.
> *New adjectives:* quick, sudden, careful, angry.
> *Recycled language:* good, quiet, fast, slow; action verbs

1 ● To establish what an adverb is, write these examples on the board:

> **She's a quiet girl.**
> **She's very quiet.**
> **She speaks quietly.**

Point out that:

  – *quiet* is an adjective (it describes the girl).
  – *quietly* is an adverb (it describes how she speaks).

● Read through the story, presenting new words as you go. Demonstrate the meaning of e.g. *quickly, slowly, angrily* by miming, and give other examples if necessary.

● Students complete the table. Then write it on the board:

Adjective	Adverb
quiet	quietly
slow	slowly
quick	quickly
sudden	suddenly
careful	carefully
angry	angrily
fast	fast
good	well

2 ● Establish the rule:

To form an adverb, we usually add *-ly* to an adjective.

3 ● Look at each sentence in turn, and ask students to add suitable adverbs. Possible answers:

He learns languages well/quickly/fast/slowly.
We drove fast/quickly/slowly/carefully ...
I opened the door carefully/slowly/quietly/quickly ...
... she asked angrily/quietly/suddenly/quickly/slowly.
She wrote her name carefully/quickly/slowly ...

4 ● To demonstrate, write a true sentence about yourself on the board.

● Students write a sentence, using one of the adverbs.

● Ask students to read out their sentences.

> *Idea for further practice: the adverb game*
> A student chooses an adverb (e.g. *carefully*). Other students ask him/her in turn to mime actions, e.g. *cook a meal, smoke a cigarette*. The student mimes the actions according to the adverb, e.g. mimes cooking a meal carefully, smoking a cigarette carefully, and so on. The other students try to guess the adverb.

Sounds: *A room in Australia*

> The sound /r/ on its own; the sound /r/ in combinations: /br/, /fr/, /tr/, /dr/, /θr/.

1, 2 ▭ The important thing here is not for students to produce the sounds precisely (which may be quite difficult), but to recognise them and produce them approximately.

If students have problems, focus on these features:

  – /r/ is pronounced at the front of the mouth, with the lips rounded.
  – /br/ can be practised by saying the sounds /b/ and /r/ separately, and then bringing them together. The same applies to /fr/, /dr/, /tr/ and /θr/.

3 Students write a sentence using words from the box, and including any other words they like, e.g.

  – There are some dry trousers in the bedroom.
  – Please bring me some bread from the kitchen.

4 Students read out their sentences in turn. Focus on the pronunciation of the /r/ sounds.

Alternative: Dictation. Students dictate their sentence to the person next to them. As a check, ask students to read out the sentence they wrote down.

Phrasebook: *Could you ...?*

This exercise teaches requests using Could you ...?

> *Key language:* Could you ...?, bring me, buy me.
> *Recycled language:* everyday objects.

● To establish the situation, say a number of items and ask the class if they think the man can have them or not, e.g. *water, bread, cheese, wine, cigars, meat, fish, fruit.*

● ▭ Play the recording. Students fill the gaps. Answers:

Could you bring me *some fruit*?
Could you buy me *a bottle of beer*?

If you like, ask students to practise the dialogue in pairs.

● Look at the pictures. Establish what the items are and what the man will ask. Possible answers:

Could you buy me some cigarettes?
Could you bring me some flowers?
Could you buy me a magazine?
Could you buy me a bottle of Coca-Cola?
Could you bring me a TV?
Could you buy me an ice-cream?

● *Either:* Students take it in turns to be the person in bed. They choose one item and ask another student for it.
Or: Students have conversations in pairs, with one student taking the role of the person in bed.

> ▭ Tapescript for Phrasebook: *Could you ...?*
>
> A Could you bring me some fruit?
> B Yes, of course.
> A And could you buy me a bottle of beer?
> B No, sorry, I can't do that.

Consolidation

Verbs with to, at and about

This exercise focuses on common verb + preposition pairs. This recycles verbs which have appeared in earlier units.

1 Look at the pictures and present any expressions that students are not familiar with. Emphasise that we must say e.g. *listen to the radio, arrive at the station* (not ~~listen the radio, arrive to the station~~).

2 Ask students to complete the sentences. Then go through the answers. Expected answers:

    a stay at   *b* listen to   *c* arrive at   *d* think about
    e go to   *f* talk to

Review

Words

Review of time expressions (various units), places in towns (Units 5, 10), jobs (Units 2, 12), transport (Unit 18), rooms (Unit 6).

- Working alone or in pairs, students think of words to add to the lists and write them down.
- Go through the answers together, and write the words on the board. If you like, ask students to spell them. Expected answers:

    a hour, month, year
    b restaurant, café, hotel, school, petrol station, post office, airport, bus station
    c doctor, taxi driver, police officer, singer, secretary, student, waiter, waitress, cleaner
    d train, bus, bicycle (bike), taxi, boat, ferry
    e bathroom, kitchen, living room, balcony, toilet

Verbs in the past

Review of Past simple tense (Unit 15).

Do Part *a* with the whole class. Let students do the other parts alone or in pairs, and then go through the answers together. Answers:

a A tall woman *opened* the door. She *was* about 60 years old, and she *had* long grey hair … she *asked* me. 'I'm Tom,' I *said* …

b Yesterday *was* my sister's birthday, so I *went* to the shops … She *wanted* a new jacket, but the jackets *were* very expensive. So I *bought* her a pair of jeans.

c When we *were* children, we *played* football … and we *watched* it on TV …

Who died when?

Review of dates (Study Pages H Focus).

- Look at the dates, and ask students to say them.
- Give time for students to match the sentences. Then go through the answers together. Answers:

Queen Victoria died on 22nd January 1901.
Abraham Lincoln died on 14th April 1865.
Charlie Chaplin died on 25th December 1977.
Joan of Arc died on 30th May 1431.
William Shakespeare died on 23rd April 1616.

Consolidation

Verbs with *to*, *at* and *about*

1 Look at these examples.

to

listen to the radio   go to the cinema   talk to a friend

at

look at someone   arrive at the station   stay at a hotel

about

think about a problem   talk about the weather   read about dinosaurs

2 Fill the gaps with one of the red verbs.

a Why don't you .... my flat? You can sleep on the sofa.

b Shall we .... the news on the radio?

c What time does the plane .... Heathrow?

d I never .... work when I'm at home in the evening.

e I usually .... the shops on Saturday.

f I never .... her, because she never listens.

Review

Words

Add words to these lists.

a week, minute, day, ...

b cinema, station, library, ...

c engineer, teacher, shop assistant, ...

d car, plane, ...

e hall, bedroom, ...

Verbs in the past

What are the past forms of the verbs in the boxes? Use them to fill the gaps.

a A tall woman ▢ the door. She ▢ about 60 years old, and she ▢ long grey hair. 'Who are you?' she ▢ me. 'I'm Tom,' I ▢. 'I'm your son.'

be
say
ask
open
have

b Yesterday ▢ my sister's birthday, so I ▢ to the shops to buy her a present. She ▢ a new jacket, but the jackets ▢ very expensive. So I ▢ her a pair of jeans.

be
be
buy
want
go

c When we ▢ children, we ▢ football every day after school, and we ▢ it on TV every weekend.

be
watch
play

Who died when?

How do you say these dates? Make true sentences.

Queen Victoria		30th May 1431.
Abraham Lincoln		23rd April 1616.
Charlie Chaplin	died on	14th April 1865.
Joan of Arc		22nd January 1901.
William Shakespeare		25th December 1977.

21 Good, better, best

1 A better place to live

Comparison of adjectives

1 Look at these sentences. Which are true of your country?

☐ It has a warm climate.   ☐ It's a safe place to live.   ☐ It's an expensive place to live.

☐ It's a rich country.   ☐ The people are friendly.   ☐ The roads are dangerous.

☐ The cities are clean.   ☐ The food is good.   ☐ It's a beautiful country.

Does your partner have the same answers?

2 Choose one other country, and compare it with your own country.
Which do you think

– is warmer?   – is safer?   – is more expensive?

– is richer?   – has friendlier people?   – has more dangerous roads?

– is cleaner?   – has better food?   – is more beautiful?

Are there any other differences?

3 Which country do you think is a better place to live? Why?
Write one or two sentences.

> I think .... is a better place to
> live than .... because ...

21

This unit introduces comparative and superlative forms of adjectives. It focuses on:
– comparative adjectives
– superlative adjectives
– comparative sentences with *than ...*
– comparative questions with *Which?*

1 A better place to live

In this exercise students make comparisons between their own and other countries. The exercise introduces comparative adjectives with -er and with more.

➤ Focus on Form: Exercises 1 & 2
➤ Workbook: Exercise A

> *Key structures:* Comparative forms. *New adjectives:* clean, safe, dangerous.
> *Recycled language:* adjectives.

1 Introduction; presentation of new adjectives

● As a way of focusing on the exercise, write these adjectives on the board:

> **cold**
> **friendly**
> **expensive**

Ask students which adjectives describe the first picture and which describe the second.

● Read the sentences and check that students understand all the adjectives. If you like, discuss which sentences might apply to the country in the first picture, which to the second, and which to both.

● Give students time to look at the sentences and decide which are true of their own country. They mark each box with a tick or a cross.

● Students form pairs and compare their answers.

● Discuss the answers together, and see if there are any sentences that the class disagrees about.

> *Note*
> The pictures show Milan, Italy, and Mérida in Yucatán, Mexico.

> *Mixed nationality classes*
> Students simply tell each other about their own country, rather than finding out if they agree.
> Alternatively, make sure pairs of students come from the same country.

2 Presentation of comparative forms; activation: comparing countries

● To introduce comparative forms, look at the two places in the pictures again. Ask *Which is colder? Which is friendlier? Which is more expensive?* Add these forms on the board:

> **cold**   **colder**
> **friendly**   **friendlier**
> **expensive** **more expensive**

● Read through the questions. Then divide the class into pairs or small groups (if possible, everyone in each group should be from the same country). Ask them to choose another country and compare it with their own country.

● Ask different pairs or groups to 'report back', saying which country they chose and what comparisons they made.

> *Language note*
> Short adjectives (1 or 2 syllables) form the comparative by adding *-er*. Longer adjectives form the comparative by adding *more*. *Good – better* is irregular.

> *Whole class option*
> Together, choose one other country. Go through each question in turn and ask students what they think. To give more practice, choose a second country and repeat the activity.

3 Extension: writing sentences

● To introduce this part, choose a country yourself, and write a sentence on the board following the model given, e.g. *I think Italy is a better place to live than Britain because it is warmer and it has better food.*

● Students write a sentence of their own, summarising what they talked about in their pairs or groups.

2 Which is better?

This exercise is based on a conversation in a camera shop. It introduces questions used when choosing between two things to buy.

> Key language: Which is better? Which is cheaper?

➤ Focus on Form: Exercise 3
➤ Workbook: Exercise B, Listening

1 Listening for general idea

- As a lead-in, look at the two cameras in the picture. Ask students which one they think is better, and which is cheaper.

- [cassette] Play the conversation once through. Establish which camera the man buys and why. Answer:

  He buys the Yashica, because it's cheaper and it's better for a child.

> *Alternative*
> Pause after each exchange and establish what the people said.

> [cassette] The tapescript is on page T90.

2 Listening & completing notes; presentation of questions

- [cassette] Play the conversation again. Then ask students to complete the notes orally (they don't have to be exactly the same as the dialogue, but should convey the same meaning). Possible answers:

  I'd like a small camera for a child.
  This is a Yashica. And this is a Canon.
  Which is better?
  The Canon is a better camera. But the Yashica is better for a child.
  Which is cheaper?
  The Yashica is cheaper. It's £40. The Canon is £70.
  OK. I'll have the Yashica, please.

3 Practice: role-play

- Have the conversation with one or two students. Then divide the class into pairs to practise it.

3 Do you agree?

This exercise is about the best, the highest, the most beautiful, etc. It introduces superlative forms of adjectives.

> Key structures: the ...-est, the most ...
> New words: agree, disagree, difficult, famous, actor.

➤ Focus on Form: Exercise 2
➤ Workbook: Exercise C

1 Presentation of superlatives; reading & completing a table

- To introduce the idea of superlatives, do a simple drawing on the board of three mountains of different sizes. Write beside the highest one:

  The highest mountain

  Explain the meaning of *agree* (= 'say yes') and *disagree* (= 'say no'). Then give time for students to read the text and find words to complete the table.

- Go through the answers together. Answers:

  the biggest, the most beautiful, the best.

2 Discussion

- Look at the text together. Ask students what their answers to the questions are. Try to get several different opinions about each one.

3 Activation: asking & answering questions

- Working alone or in pairs, students think of a question and write it down. If you like, write an outline structure on the board to help them:

Who		the ...-est	
What	is	the most ...	...?

- Ask students to read out their question. Other students give an answer.

> *Alternative*
> Students move freely round the class, asking other students their question and answering other students' questions.

2 Which is better?

Comparison of adjectives • than

1 A man buys a camera in a shop. Listen to the conversation. Which camera does he buy? Why?

I'd like ...

... a Yashica   ... a Canon

Which ... ?

The Canon ... The Yashica ...

Which ... ?

The Yashica ... The Canon ...

OK ...

2 Listen again and complete these notes.

3 Practise the conversation, using the notes.

3 Do you agree?

Superlatives

AGREE OR DISAGREE?

It's easy to agree about some things. Everyone agrees, for example, that Mount Everest is the highest mountain in the world, that Russia is the biggest country in the world, and that the Eiffel Tower is the tallest building in Paris.

Other questions are more difficult. For example, what's the most beautiful city in the world? Is it Paris? Rio de Janeiro? Rome? Istanbul? Cape Town? Hong Kong? Prague ...?

And what about these questions?
• What's the most beautiful building in your country?
• Who's the most famous person in the world?
• Who's the most dangerous person in the world?
• Who's the best actor in your country?
• What's the best programme on TV?

Ask ten people these questions, and you'll probably get ten different answers.

1 Read the text and find words to complete the table.

high	higher	the highest
big	bigger	
beautiful	more beautiful	
good	better	

2 What are your answers to the questions in the text? Do you all agree or not?

3 Think of a question yourself. You can ask about your town, your country or the world.

Ask other people your question. Do they all agree?

Focus on Form

1 Adjectives

Write in the missing forms.

cheap	cheaper	the cheapest
tall	taller	
young		
friendly	friendlier	the friendliest
easy	easier	
happy		
big	bigger	the biggest
hot	hotter	
expensive	more expensive	the most expensive
dangerous	more dangerous	
interesting		
good		the best

2 Comparing

Which of these sentences is true?

Cars are safer than planes.
Cars are more dangerous than planes.

Correct these sentences.

a Mexico is bigger than Brazil.
b Ronaldo is older than Prince Charles.
c Taxis are cheaper than buses.
d Britain is hotter than California.
e   Chess is easier than noughts and crosses.

3 The biggest mouth

> Koko has the biggest mouth.
> Albie has the shortest hair.

Talk about each of the clowns.

big	small	hair	eyes
long	short	ears	mouth
fair	dark		nose

How to say it

1 🔲 Listen to *than* in these sentences. Practise saying them.

This is better than my old flat.

New York's more interesting than Washington.

He's friendlier than his brother.

Germany's colder than Italy.

2 🔲 Listen to the sounds *-est* and *most*. Practise saying the sentences.

It's the biggest in the world.

It's the best place in the world.

It's the most beautiful building.

Which hotel is the most expensive?

Focus on Form

1 Adjectives

- Students complete the table. Answers:

tall	taller	the tallest
young	younger	the youngest
easy	easier	the easiest
happy	happier	the happiest
hot	hotter	the hottest
dangerous	more dangerous	the most dangerous
interesting	more interesting	the most interesting
good	better	the best

- Point out that:
  - short adjectives add -er, -est. With longer adjectives we say *more ...*, *the most ...*
  - before -er and -est, -y changes to -i. With some adjectives (*big*, *hot*) we double the last letter.

2 Comparing

- Ask students which of the sentences is true. (Answer: Cars are more dangerous than planes.)
- Students correct the sentences, giving two possible answers for each. Answers:

  a Mexico is smaller than Brazil.
  Brazil is bigger than Mexico.

  b Ronaldo is younger than Prince Charles.
  Prince Charles is older than Ronaldo.

  c Taxis are more expensive than buses.
  Buses are cheaper than taxis.

  d Britain is colder than California.
  California is hotter than Britain.

  e Chess is more difficult than noughts and crosses.
  Noughts and crosses is easier than chess.

3 The biggest mouth

- Look at the examples. Students make sentences using the other adjectives and nouns.

  Possible answers:

  Koko has the biggest mouth. Joe has the smallest mouth.
  Sam has the longest hair. Albie has the shortest hair.
  Babe has the biggest eyes. Albie has the smallest eyes.
  Albie has the biggest nose. Babe has the smallest nose.
  Joe has the darkest hair. Babe has the fairest hair.
  Sam has the biggest ears. Koko has the smallest ears.

How to say it

1 Pronunciation of 'than' in sentences

- ▣ Play the recording, pausing and getting students to repeat the sentences. Focus on:
  - the stress pattern in the comparison structures:
    <u>bet</u>ter than my <u>old</u> <u>flat</u>
    more <u>in</u>teresting than <u>Wa</u>shington
    <u>friend</u>lier than his <u>bro</u>ther
    <u>col</u>der than <u>I</u>taly
  - the reduced /ə/ sound in /ðən/.

2 Pronunciation of '-est' and 'most'

- ▣ Play the sentences and get students to repeat them. Focus on:
  - the consonant clusters in /best‿pleɪs/, /məʊst‿ˈbjuːtɪfʊl/;
  - the way *most* and *-est* link with the following vowel: /ˈbɪgɪst‿ɪn/, /məʊst‿ɪkˈspensɪv/;
  - the reduced /ɪ/ sound in /ˈbɪgɪst/.

▣ Tapescript for Exercise 2: *Which is better?*

1 A I'd like a small camera for a child. It's my daughter. She's 10.
  B OK. We've got this one. This is a Yashica. Or there's this one – a Canon.
  A Which is better?

  B Well, the Canon is a better camera, really. But maybe the Yashica is better for a child – it's very easy to use.
  A Which is cheaper?
  B The Yashica's cheaper – it's £40. And the Canon's £70.
  A OK. I'll have the Yashica, please.

This unit is about leisure activities and sports, and focuses on the following vocabulary areas:
– activities which use the verb *go* (e.g. *go swimming, go for a walk, go to the cinema*)
– names of sports (e.g. *football, running*)
– the verbs *like* and *enjoy* (+ noun or *-ing*).
The Reading and Listening activity is a mysterious story about a football club.

1 Going out

This exercise is about people's favourite activities when they go out, and is based on a survey of people in Britain. Students read the survey and then talk about what they do themselves.

➤ Workbook: Exercise A

> *Key expressions:* go to, go (out) for, go + -ing. *New words:* relatives, a bike ride, for fun, sports event, outdoor, indoor, hobby, picnic, go swimming.

1 Reading & interpreting pictures; presentation of expressions with 'go'

- Look at the list of Top 10 activities. Explain that these are what most people in Britain do if they go out at the weekend. Read through the list and give examples to explain the more general categories:

  – *go to a sports event:* e.g. a football match
  – *do an outdoor sport:* e.g. play football, go running
  – *do an indoor sport:* e.g. play table tennis, basketball
  – *follow an interest or hobby:* e.g. paint a picture, play music, go dancing

- Show these structures with go on the board:

go for	a walk / a meal	go to	the cinema / a concert	go	swimming / shopping

- Read the text and look at the pictures. Ask students where they think the people are going. Expected answers:

  A She's going swimming.
  B They're going to a football match.
  C They're going to play tennis.
  D They're going for a drive and a picnic.
  E He's going for a walk.
  F They're going to visit relatives.

> *Optional lead-in*
> As a focus for the exercise, write *At the weekend* on the board. Ask students what they do, and brainstorm ideas.

> *Note*
> The use of *going to* to talk about the future is practised in Unit 23.

2 Listening

- 🔲 Play the recording. Students listen and mark the activities he mentions on the list.

- Discuss which are the man's top five activities. Expected answers:

  1 visit friends and relatives   2 go out for a drink   3 go to the cinema
  4 go swimming   5 follow an interest (go fishing)

3 Activation: listing favourite activities

- Working alone, students write a list of things they do when they go out, starting with the one they do *most often*.

- Pairwork. Students use their list to help them tell their partner what they do most often when they go out.

> *Whole class option*
> Ask a few students in turn to tell the class what they do most often. Encourage other students to ask them questions.

🔲 Tapescript for Exercise 1: *Going out*

Yes, I visit my friends a lot at the weekend, and relatives – I see my brother quite often, and his family. And I often go out for a drink, almost every Saturday, in fact. I don't go out for meals so much. And I don't go for a walk usually, no. I never go for a bike ride. And I don't go shopping, not for fun, anyway – I don't like shopping. But

I go to the cinema a lot – not concerts, not sports events, but the cinema, certainly. I don't do much sport, really – I go swimming sometimes, but not very often. And I don't drive, haven't got a car. But most weekends I go fishing, usually on Sunday if the weather's nice.

1 Going out

Friends *and* Family *are* No 1!

It's the weekend. There's no work and there's no school. Millions of people all over Britain are spending the day at home. Millions of others are going out. **But where are they going?**

Well, now we know. A new report from Edinburgh University lists the Top 10 things that people do when they go out at the weekend.

The *Top* **10** Activities

1. visit friends or relatives
2. go out for a drink or a meal
3. go for a walk or a bike ride
4. go shopping for fun
5. go to a cinema, concert or sports event
6. do an outdoor sport
7. do an indoor sport
8. follow an interest or hobby
9. go for a drive or a picnic
10. go swimming

1 Read the article, then look at the people. Where do you think they're going? Choose from *The Top 10 Activities*.

2 🔲 A man talks about the activities in the list. What are his top *five* activities?

3 What do you do when you go out? Write a list of your top five activities.

Show your list to another student. Say where you go and what you do.

---

2 I like spending money

1 Read about person A. What do the other three people like doing?

A I like doing quiet things. I like reading and painting pictures, and I enjoy walking in the country.

B I enjoy doing physical exercise. I like 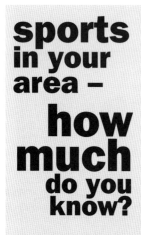, and I enjoy , and I also like .

C I like having a good time and spending lots of money. I like and , and I also enjoy .

D I like meeting new people. I enjoy , and I like . And if I'm on a bus or train, I really enjoy .

2 Which of the four people would you like to spend the day with? Why?

3 Write down two things you *like* doing, and two things you *don't like* doing.

Does your partner agree?

I like watching TV in bed.
I like looking in shop windows.
I don't like getting up early in the morning.
I don't like cooking.

3 Sports

1 Work with a partner. Answer the questions together.

sports in your area – how much do you know?

1 What's the name of your local football team? Where do they play?

What other sports can you go and watch?

2 Can you do these sports in your area? If so, where?
tennis volleyball golf

3 Where can you go swimming
– indoors? – out of doors?

4 Where is the *nearest* place to go
skiing? windsurfing? climbing?

5 Can you answer these questions?

I need to lose some weight. Are there any exercise classes?

Where's the best place to go running?

2 Discuss the answers together. How well did you do?

3 Role-play

Student A: You are a visitor to the area, and you want to know about sports. Ask B some questions.
Student B: Try to answer A's questions.

2 I like spending money

This exercise is about things that people like or don't like doing in their free time. It introduces the verbs like *and* enjoy + *-ing.*

➤ Workbook: Exercise B, Listening

> *Key language:* like/enjoy + -ing, don't like/enjoy + -ing. *New words:* ski, shop (v.), do physical exercise, spend money. *Recycled language:* activity verbs.

1 Presentation of 'like/enjoy' + -ing; reading & gap-filling task

- Read the sentences about person A. Use this to present structures with *like/enjoy* + *-ing*:

I	like enjoy	reading

- Look at the sentences about B, C and D, and establish what they like/enjoy doing. As you do so, build up new vocabulary on the board. Possible answers:

  B I like *climbing (mountains)*, and I enjoy *running*, and I also like *skiing*.
  C I like *shopping (buying things in shops)* and *eating in restaurants (going to restaurants)*, and I also enjoy *driving my car (driving fast cars)*.
  D I enjoy *dancing (going to parties)* and I like *sitting in cafés (going to cafés)* … I really enjoy *talking to other people*.

> *Language note*
> *Like* and *enjoy* can be followed by a noun or by an *-ing* form. We can say:
> I like books.
> I like reading.
> I like reading books.

2 Discussion

- Ask students to 'vote' on the person they'd most like to spend the day with.

3 Activation: writing sentences

- Working alone, students write down two things they like doing and two things they don't like doing.
- Pairwork. Students read out their sentences and find out if their partner likes the same things.
- As a round-up, ask pairs of students how much they like the same things.

3 Sports

This exercise is a questionnaire about sports in the students' own area. It is used as a test of students' own knowledge, then as a basis for role-play.

➤ Workbook: Exercise C

> *Sports and activities:* football, tennis, volleyball, golf; swimming, skiing, windsurfing, climbing, running.
> *Other new words:* lose weight, exercise classes, football team, area, local, indoors, out of doors.

1 Presentation of vocabulary; reading & answering questions

- Read through the questions, presenting any new words (most of them should be obvious from the pictures), but without discussing the answers.
- Divide the class into pairs. Students work through the questions and see how many they can answer.

2 Discussion

- Discuss the answers with the whole class. See how many of the questions someone in the class knows the answer to, and to what extent students agree about the answers. By the end of this stage all the students should be able to answer most of the questions.

> *Mixed nationality classes*
> The questions should of course refer to sports in the area where students are studying, not where they come from. This may be an opportunity for them to find out about sporting facilities, and it may be necessary for you to provide information.

3 Role-play: asking about sports

- To demonstrate the role-play, choose a good student, and pretend you are the visitor. Ask the student questions based on the questionnaire, then add one or two of your own.
- Divide the class into pairs, and give each student a role, A or B. The student who is A pretends to be a visitor to the area, and asks questions.

> *Whole class option*
> Choose three students to come to the front to represent the Information Centre. Other students in the class ask them questions about sports in the area.

4 The curse of the new ground

This combined Reading and Listening activity is the story of a curse put on a football ground. The reading tells the story in a series of episodes, which students have to put in the correct order. The listening tells the story in the correct order, and adds an ending.

Reading skills: *understanding the sequence of events.*
Listening skills: *listening to check; listening to confirm predictions.*

> *New words*: curse, football ground, strange, supporters, edge, except for, stadium, moved, shouted, build, fell down, accident, lost, manager, on the edge of, cottage, season, home match.

1 Presentation of vocabulary

- Begin by telling students that they will read about a *curse*. Make it clear what this means, either by using the students' own language or by giving an example.

- Check that students understand the meaning of the words in the list. To help you do this, talk about football and refer back to Question 1 in Exercise 3. Ask e.g. *Which is our football team? Where is their football ground? Do they have a stadium? Do they usually win or lose their matches?*

2 Reading & sequencing task

- Read Paragraph 1 together. Give time for students to read through the other paragraphs, either working alone or in pairs. They should do this fairly quickly, using the pictures to help them. They decide what order the paragraphs should be in and number them.

- Read the first paragraph again, then ask students which paragraph they think should come next. (Answer: *They wanted to move to a bigger ground …*) Read through it together, presenting new words (*land, on the edge, except for*) as you go.

  Then ask students to identify the next paragraph, and so on, reading through each paragraph in turn. The correct order is:

  2 They wanted to move to a bigger ground …
  3 An old woman lived in this cottage …
  4 The woman said no …
  5 They started to build the new stadium …
  6 In the end, they finished the stadium …
  7 That season, United won …
  8 The next year, the same thing happened …

3 Listening to check

- 🔊 Play the recording and establish how the story ends. (Answer: see tapescript.)

> *Option*
> Before you play the recording, ask students to guess an ending to the story. If you like, write possible endings on the board.

4 Extension: discussion

- Read the three statements, and get a class 'vote' on which statement students agree with most.

🔊 Tapescript for Exercise 4: *The curse of the new ground*

United were one of the best football teams in the country. They had a lot of supporters, but their ground wasn't very big. They wanted to move to a bigger ground. So they bought some land on the edge of the city. There was nothing on this land except for one small cottage. An old woman lived in this cottage. 'We're sorry,' the club told her, 'but you have to go. We want to build a new stadium on this land.' The woman said no, so the police came and moved her. But as she left, she shouted, 'United will never win a match on this land! Remember my words!'

They started to build the new stadium, but they had lots of problems. One of the walls fell down, and two workers died in strange accidents. In the end, they finished the stadium, and 40,000 supporters came to watch the first match. United lost the match 5–0. That season, United won lots of matches in other football grounds. But they lost all the matches they played at home. The next year, the same thing happened. The team's manager left, and a new one came – but it made no difference. United lost all their home matches.

So now, United Football Club want to sell the ground and find a new one. But there's one big problem: who wants to buy a football ground with a curse on it?

4 The curse of the new ground

1 Before you read, find out what a *curse* is.
Then check that you know the meaning of:

– a football ground   – supporters   – a stadium   – win a match
– a football team   – a manager   – an accident   – lose a match

2 Read the story. Can you put Parts 2–8 in the right order?

strange stories

There are many strange stories about football, but this is the strangest of them all

The curse of the new ground

1 United were one of the best football teams in the country. They had a lot of supporters, but their ground wasn't very big.

[ ] The woman said no, so the police came and moved her. But as she left, she shouted, 'United will never win a match on this land! Remember my words!'

[ ] In the end, they finished the stadium, and 40,000 supporters came to watch the first match. United lost the match 5–0.

[ ] They started to build the new stadium, but they had lots of problems. One of the walls fell down, and two workers died in strange accidents.

[ ] They wanted to move to a bigger ground. So they bought some land on the edge of the city. There was nothing on this land except for one small cottage.

[ ] The next year, the same thing happened. The team's manager left, and a new one came – but it made no difference. United lost all their home matches.

[ ] An old woman lived in this cottage. 'We're sorry,' the club told her, 'but you have to go. We want to build a new stadium on this land.'

[ ] That season, United won lots of matches in other football grounds. But they lost all the matches they played at home.

9 So now, United Football Club want ....
But there's one big problem:
....

3 [cassette] Now listen to someone telling the story.
Were you right? How does the story end?

4 What do you think of the story? Do you agree with any of these statements?

> I think it's true. Things like that happen all the time.

> I don't really believe the story. Maybe United just aren't a very good team.

> I think the whole story is untrue. Things like that are impossible.

Focus on ... Verb + to

1 Look at these examples.

I want an ice-cream.
I want to have a shower.
Do you want to go out?

I'd like a glass of orange juice.
I'd like to watch a video.
Would you like to see my photos?

I need some new shoes.
I need to phone my mother.

I have to get up early in the morning.

2 ⬚ Listen to the conversations, and fill the gaps.

1 – .... come to the
cinema this evening?
– No, sorry. ....
come, but ....
do my homework.

2 – .... go and see
a film this evening?
– No, thanks. There's a
football match on, and
.... watch it.

3 – .... go to the
cinema tonight?
– Yes, fine.
– .... go for
a drink first?
– OK. .... wash
my hair. But I can meet
you at about 6.30.

3 Write a sentence about

– something you have to do this week.
– something you need to buy.
– something you want to do this evening.
– something you'd like to do this year.

Sounds: Girls, cars, sport and computers

1 ⬚ The letter *r* is often silent, but only in British English. Listen to these sentences in British and American English.

/ɑː/ You can bring your car into the car-park.

/ɔː/ You must do more sport.

/ɜː/ She's a German girl.

/ə/ Put the letters by the computer.

2 ⬚ Listen and practise.

car	carpet	cards	market
door	floor	short	fork
girl	dirty	church	worse
exercise	mirror	centre	better

3 Write a sentence. Use words from the box.

4 Read out your sentence.

Phrasebook: What did you say?

⬚ Listen to the conversations. What do the other people say?

▼✳□✳ ✳● ✳?

Sorry, what did you say?

□✳▯□✳ ✳✳✳✳.

Sorry, could you say that again?

✿●● ●
❀☆✳?

Sorry, I don't understand.

Listen to the teacher. Tell him/her if you don't understand!

Study pages K

Focus on ... *Verb + to*

This exercise focuses on three verbs (want, would like *and* need) *which can be followed either by a noun or by* to + *infinitive. Some of these structures have already appeared in the book as set phrases: in Exercise 8.3* (I'd like), *Study Pages E Consolidation* (I'd like), *Exercise 13.2* (need), *Study Pages G Phrasebook* (Would you like ...?), *Exercise 15.1* (want to).

> *Key language:* want, need, would like + noun or to.
> *Recycled language:* have to.

1 ● Look at the examples. Show how we use *want*, *need* and *would like* with a noun or with *to* + verb:

| I want I need I'd like | a sandwich. | I want I need I'd like | to have a shower. |

● Make sure students understand the meaning of *I need* (= I must have).

2 🔲 Play the recording. Pause after each dialogue and ask students to complete the gaps. Answers:
1 Do you want to come ...? I'd like to come ... I have to do ...
2 Would you like to go ... I want to watch ...
3 Do you want to go ... Would you like to go ... I need to wash ...

3 ● To prepare for the activity, tell students about something you have to do, need to buy, etc. If you like, write sentences on the board.
● Give time for students to write sentences.
● Ask students to read out their sentences.

> 🔲 Tapescript for Focus on ... *Verb + to*
>
> 1 A Do you want to come to the cinema this evening?
>   B No, sorry. I'd like to come, but I have to do my homework.
>
> 2 A Would you like to go and see a film this evening?
>   C Oh no, thanks. There's a football match on, and I want to watch it.
>
> 3 A Do you want to go to the cinema tonight?
>   D Yes, fine.
>   A Would you like to go for a drink first?
>   D OK. I need to wash my hair. But I can meet you at about 6.30.

Sounds: *girls, cars, sport and computers*

> Vowel + 'r' combinations: /ɑː/, /ɔː/, /ɜː/ and /ə/.

1, 2 🔲 If students have problems, focus on these features:
– In standard British English, the /r/ sound isn't heard at all. In American English the /r/ is produced by rounding the lips slightly and moving the tongue forward after the vowel.
– /ɜː/ and /ə/ have the same sound quality, but /ɜː/ is long whereas /ə/ is short.

Note: There is quite a lot of variation in the way native speakers of English pronounce these sounds. The important thing is for students to recognise the sounds and be able to produce something similar to either the British or American versions of them.

3 Students write a sentence using words from the box, and including any other words they like, e.g.
– Don't sit on the floor of the car – it's dirty.
– They sell carpets at the market.

4 Students read out their sentences in turn. Focus on the pronunciation of the /ɑː/, /ɔː/, /ɜː/ and /ə/ sounds.

Alternative: Dictation. Students dictate their sentence to the person next to them. As a check, ask students to read out the sentence they wrote down.

Phrasebook: *What did you say?*

This exercise teaches ways of asking for a repetition.

> *Key language:* What did you say? Could you say that again? I don't understand. *Recycled language:* Sorry.

● Look at the three replies, and establish that they are all things you can say if you don't understand what someone says in English.

● 🔲 Play the recording. Pause after each conversation and establish what the other person said. (Answers: see tapescript on page T95.)

● To practise these expressions, ask students questions, speaking quickly or indistinctly so that they don't understand. Get them to use one of the expressions, and then repeat what you said more slowly and clearly. Possible questions:
– What colour socks are you wearing?
– How much does a box of matches cost?
– I need to buy a newspaper. Could you give some money?
– What did you have for breakfast this morning?
– Do you know where I can buy some aspirin near here?
– Did you see that film on TV last night? It was really interesting.

Consolidation

go

This exercise focuses on expressions using the verb go. *This consolidates language from Exercises 22.1 and 22.3.*

1 Look at the examples, and make sure students understand what they mean. Point out that *go* is often followed by *to*, *for* or verb + *-ing*.

2 ● Ask students to fill the gaps. Then go through the answers. Answers:

   a to   *b* for   *c* –   *d* to   *e* for   *f* to   *g* to   *h* to
   i for   *j* to

   ● If you like, build up lists on the board to show the different groups:

| go to | a concert
the shops
a football match
the cinema
the toilet
a party | go for | a walk
a drink
a meal
a drive
a picnic |

| go to | school
bed
work
church | go | swimming
shopping
jogging |

3 ● Make a few sentences about yourself, using the expressions in the exercise, e.g. *Last week, I didn't go to a concert. I went to the shops. I went swimming. I went to work, of course, and I went to bed. I didn't go for a walk, and I didn't go for a picnic.*

   ● Ask students to make similar sentences, either in pairs or round the class.

┌───┐

🔲 Tapescript for Phrasebook: *What did you say?*

1 A So where are you living at the moment, then?
  B Sorry, what did you say?
  A I said, where are you living?
  B Oh – in London.

2 A That's a lovely dress you're wearing there.
  B Sorry, could you say that again?
  A I said, that's a lovely dress. Your dress is lovely.
  B Oh, thank you.

3 A So are you a student here, then, or what?
  B Sorry, I don't understand.
  A Are you a student?
  B Yes. Yes, I'm a student.

└───┘

Review

Where is it?

Review of geographical features and place prepositions (Exercise 16.1).

● Look at the compass, and ask students to add the missing directions. Answers:

   north, west, south

● Look at the map and ask students to describe the places. Expected answers:

   Porto is in the south, on the coast, on the sea.
   Belleville is near the west coast, on a river.
   Candida is in the north, in the mountains, on a lake.

Positive and negative

Review of negative forms of various verb tenses (Units 3, 5, 7, 13, 17, 19).

Ask students to complete the sentences. Several answers are possible for each item – try to get a number of different suggestions. If students have problems with negative forms, refer back to the units where they were taught, or turn to the Reference page for that unit (pages 115–127). Possible answers:

a … he isn't very happy, he isn't a very nice man.
b … there isn't a TV.
c … there weren't many women.
d … we haven't got any cheese.
e … it hasn't got a swimming pool.
f … I can't play the piano.
g … I don't like chocolate ice-cream.
h … she doesn't drink alcohol.
i … I don't have to wear a tie.
j … they didn't give me a birthday present.

Time words

Review of at, in *and* on *with time expressions (revising language from various units, especially Study Pages C Focus, Study Pages E Focus, Unit 14, Study Pages I Consolidation).*

● Working alone or in pairs, students fill the gaps with *at*, *in* or *on*.

● Go through the answers together. Answers:

   a In   *b* on   *c* at, at   *d* in   *e* in   *f* at   *g* in
   h on   *i* in

● If you like, write the answers in groups on the board:

in	the morning April the summer 1989	on	Sunday New Year's Eve
		at	nine o'clock the weekend

Consolidation

go

1 Look at these examples.

go to | a concert
the shops

go to | school
bed

go | out
home

go | swimming
shopping

go for | a walk
a drink

2 What about these? Add *to*, *in* or – (= nothing).

a	go .... work	*f*	go .... a football match
b	go .... a meal	*g*	go .... the cinema
c	go .... running	*h*	go .... the toilet
d	go .... church	*i*	go .... a picnic
e	go .... a drive	*j*	go .... a party

3 Think about last week. What did you do? Make sentences.

I went ...   I didn't go ...

Review

Where is it?

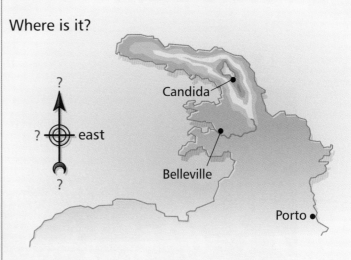

What are the missing directions?

Where are Porto, Belleville and Candida?

Positive and negative

Finish these sentences using a negative form.

Chips are very nice, but ...
... they aren't very healthy.

a He's very rich, but ...

b There's a radio in my room, but ...

c There were lots of men at the party, but ...

d We've got some bread, but ...

e The hotel has got a restaurant, but ...

f I can play the guitar, but ...

Now finish these sentences.

g I like chocolate, but ...

h She smokes, but ...

i I have to wear a jacket at work, but ...

j They gave me a birthday card, but ...

Time words

Here are some sentences from earlier pages. Fill the gaps with *at*, *in* or *on*.

a .... the summer, Istanbul is quite hot.

b We go to church .... Sunday.

c It starts .... ten past eight, and finishes .... nine o'clock.

d Spring comes late in Moscow, usually .... April or May.

e I don't have a shower .... the morning.

f I played football .... the weekend.

g I bought a new coat .... October.

h What do you do .... New Year's Eve?

i I wrote a novel .... 1989.

23 Future plans

1 I ♥ Paris

(I'm) going to

1 Read about the people at the airport. When do we use *going to*?

These people are just arriving at Charles de Gaulle Airport. They're going to spend a few days in Paris.

Joanna is going to stay with her uncle, who works for Air France.

Alfonso is in Paris on business, but he's going to have some free time in the evenings.

Mike and Lisa are going to spend two or three days in Paris and then they're going to drive down to the south of France.

2 🔲 They say what they're going to do in Paris. Listen and complete the sentences.

 Joanna is going to buy ...

She's going to visit ...

In the evening, she's going to ...

 Alfonso is going to stay ...

He's going to visit ...

In the evening, he's going to ...

 Mike and Lisa are going to stay ...

They're going to sit ...

They're going to drink ...

In the evening, they're going to ...

Imagine you can go to Paris too. Who would you like to go with?

3 Choose a place to visit, and write down three things you're going to do.

Read out your sentences. Can other students guess the place?

I'm going to climb Mount Fuji.
I'm going to eat sushi.
I'm going to

23

This unit introduces ways of talking about the future. It focuses on:
– *going to*
– questions with *going to*
– the Present continuous with future meaning.

1 I love Paris

This exercise is about people arriving in Paris and making plans for their visit. It introduces basic sentences with going to.

➤ Focus on Form: Exercise 1
➤ Workbook: Exercise A

> *Key structures:* forms of *going to*.   *New words:* on business, museum,
> art gallery, club.

1 Introduction. Presentation of 'going to'

● Look at the picture and establish the situation: these people are just arriving in Paris, and they're talking about things they're *going to do*. Present the meaning of *going to* for talking about the future, and write these structures on the board:

I'm		
He's	going to	spend a few days in Paris.
They're		

> *Optional lead-in*
> Talk with the class about what you can do in a city like Paris. Even if they don't know Paris, they can probably imagine what there is to do. Build up a list of ideas on the board.

2 Listening & completing sentences; discussion

● 🔲 Play the recording. Pause after each speaker and ask students to complete the sentences. Answers:

1 Joanna is going to buy clothes and shoes.
   She's going to visit the Louvre.
   In the evening, she's going to meet some friends and have dinner in a restaurant.

2 Alfonso is going to stay in a hotel.
   He's going to visit art galleries and museums.
   In the evening, he's going to go to the theatre.

3 Mike and Lisa are going to stay with friends.
   They're going to sit in cafés.
   They're going to drink coffee.
   In the evening, they're going to go to a café or a club, and they're going to listen to music.

● Ask students which of the people they would like to spend time with in Paris, and why. If you like, ask for a class 'vote' on this.

3 Activation: making sentences

● Students choose a place: either somewhere in their own country or region, or a well-known city or region of the world (e.g. New York, Japan). They write sentences beginning *I'm going to …*

● Students read out their sentences. The rest of the class guess what place they're going visit.

> *Pairwork option*
> In pairs, students choose a place together, and write sentences beginning *We're going to …*

🔲 Tapescript for Exercise 1: *I love Paris*

1 I'm going to go shopping. I'm going to buy clothes and shoes, probably, and I'm also going to visit the Louvre. And in the evening I'm going to meet some friends, and we're going to have dinner together in a nice restaurant.

2 Well, I'm on business here, and I'm going to stay in a hotel in the centre of Paris. But I've got some free time too, so if I have time I'm going to visit some art galleries, maybe some museums. And in the evening I'm going to go to the theatre.

3 Well, we're going to stay with friends here, and we're just going to relax, really. We're going to walk around the streets, sit in cafés, you know, drink coffee … And in the evening we're going to go to a café or a club, probably, and listen to music.

2 Do you plan ahead?

In this exercise, students ask each other questions about their plans for the weekend; their answers reveal how much they plan ahead. This exercise practises questions with going to.

> ➤ Focus on Form: Exercise 2
> ➤ Workbook: Exercise B

> *Key structures:* questions with *going to*; short answers.   *New words:* late, housework, anyone, plan (v.), exactly.   *Recycled language:* leisure activities.

1 *Presentation of questions with 'going to'; pairwork interviews*

- As a lead-in, ask students to think about next weekend and ask the first two questions (*Are you going to get up late? Are you going to do any housework?*) round the class. Get students to answer *Yes, I am, No, I'm not* or *I'm not sure*. Then ask what your questions were, and write them on the board:

> **Are you going to** | **get up late?**
> | **do any housework?**

- Explain the point of the activity: to find out if students plan ahead (= plan what they are going to do). Read through the boxes at the two ends of the scale, and make sure students understand them.
- In pairs, students ask the questions and mark their partner's answers.

Optional lead-in
Get students to ask you the questions, and to give you a 'score' to find out how much you plan ahead.

2 *Interpreting the data*

- Students add up their partner's score, and mark their place on the scale.
- As a round-up, find out which people in class plan ahead most and least.

3 *Activation: making questions*

- Either alone or in pairs, students make up a question of their own about next weekend, beginning *Are you going to …?*.
- In turn students ask their question and choose other students to answer it.

Alternative
Students move freely round the class, asking their question and answering other people's questions.
As a round-up, ask students how most people answered their question.

3 Help!

This exercise introduces the use of the Present continuous for talking about things that are arranged for the future.

> ➤ Focus on Form: Exercise 3
> ➤ Workbook: Exercise C, Listening

> *Key structures:* Present continuous tense.   *New words:* move, look after.
> *Recycled language:* Could you …?

1 *Presentation of Present continuous; listening & completing a table*

- Give examples about yourself to show how we can use the Present continuous tense to talk about the near future, e.g. *I'm having fish for supper tonight. My brother's visiting me at the weekend. We're going to the cinema together.*
- 🔲 Play the recording, and establish the answers to *a* and *b*. Answers:

  a He's painting his living room.   *b* Could you help me?

- Play the recording again. Students listen and make notes in the table.
- Go through the answers to *c*. Answers:

  1 *Saturday:* She's working. *Sunday:* She's seeing friends.
  2 *Saturday:* He's playing football. *Sunday:* He's going swimming.

Language note
We use the Present continuous for talking about things in the future that have already been arranged.

🔲 The tapescript is on page T98.

2 *Activation: answering questions*

- Take the part of Bob, and ask students round the class: *I'm painting my flat this weekend. Could you help me?* Get them to give suitable replies.

3 *Role-play: asking people to help*

- Look at the pictures, and establish what the questions should be, e.g.

  I'm painting my kitchen at the weekend. Could you help me?
  I'm moving my piano on Saturday. Could you help me?
  I'm cleaning my flat this weekend. Could you help me?
  I'm looking after my sister's children on Sunday. Could you help me?

- Role-play. Students choose an activity and ask other people to help them.

Alternative
Students move freely round the class, trying to find someone to help them.

2 Do you plan ahead?

1 Ask you partner questions about next weekend.

If your partner is *sure* of the answer, write
✓ (= Yes) or ✗ (= No) beside the question.

If your partner *isn't sure*, write **?** .

> Are you going to get up late?

Yes, I am.   No, I'm not.   I'm not sure.
  ✓   ✗   ?

2 Count the number of times you wrote **?**.

Mark your partner's place on this scale.

Questions with 'going to'

Next weekend, are you going to …

☐ … get up late?
☐ … do any housework?
☐ … go out for a meal?
☐ … write to anyone?
☐ … visit anyone?
☐ … do any sport?
☐ … go for a walk?
☐ … watch TV?
☐ … read a book?
☐ … buy any clothes?

You plan things carefully and know exactly what you're going to do.	0	1	2	3	4	5	6	7	8	9	10	You don't like planning. You just wait and see what happens.

3 Think of a question of your own. Ask other students your question.

How many say *Yes*? How many say *No*? How many aren't sure?

3 Help!

Present continuous

1 🔲 You will hear two short conversations. Listen and answer the questions.

a What is Paul doing at the weekend?
b What does he ask?
c What are the other people doing? Complete the table.

	Saturday	Sunday
1	She's …	
2	He's …	

2 Imagine that Paul wants your help. What do you say?

3 Imagine you want to do one of these things this weekend.

paint your kitchen

move a piano

clean your flat

look after four small children

Try to find someone to help you!

Focus on Form

| Mike | Sheila | Carole | George | Anna |

1 going to

am / is / are + going to + verb

These five people are coming back from the shops. Look at their shopping, and match the bubbles with the people.

a I'm going to paint the kitchen.

b I'm going to have a pizza.

c I'm going to take some photos.

d I'm going to wash some clothes.

e I'm going to play a computer game.

What other things are they going to do?

Mike's going to watch a video.
Sheila's going to ...

2 Are you going to ... ?

Student A: Imagine you are one of the people.
Student B: Ask questions. Who is A?

Are you going to read a book?

No, I'm not Anna.

Are you going to ...

3 Present continuous

These sentences are about the future.

This evening, I'm having a driving lesson.
On Friday, some friends are coming to stay.
On 15th June, my brother's getting married.
In the summer, we're all going to France.

What about you? Write sentences about yourself and your family.

How to say it

1 🔊 Listen to *going to* in these sentences. Practise saying the sentences.

I'm going to clean my room.

He's going to buy a new suit.

We're going to visit some friends.

She's going to stay with her uncle.

2 🔊 Listen to the rhythm of these sentences. Practise saying them.

■ ▪ ▪ ■ ▪ ▪ ■
I'm going to buy her a present.

▪ ▪ ▪ ▪ ■ ▪ ■
Are you going to change some money?

▪ ▪ ▪ ■ ▪ ▪
Is she going to write to us?

▪ ▪ ▪ ▪ ▪ ■ ▪ ■ ▪
Are they going to stay at our house?

Focus on Form

1 *going to*

- Ask students to match the bubbles with the people.
  Answers:

  a Anna *b* George *c* Carole *d* Mike *e* Sheila

- Ask students what else each person is going to do.
  Expected answers:

  Mike is going to watch a video, eat chicken and chips.
  Sheila is going to read a newspaper/magazine, wash her hair /
  have a shower.
  Carole is going to learn Spanish, play the piano.
  George is going to write a letter, make a cake.
  Anna is going to listen to music, read a book.

2 *Are you going to …?*

- To demonstrate the activity, choose one of the people in
  Exercise 1 yourself. Students try to guess who you are by
  asking questions with *Are you going to …?*, e.g.

  – Are you going to learn Spanish?
  – No, I'm not Carole.
  – Are you going to wash your hair?
  – No, I'm not Sheila.
  – Are you going to write a letter?
  – Yes. I'm George.

- Either divide the class into pairs to do the activity, or ask a
  student to choose one of the people, and the rest of the
  class ask questions.

3 *Present continuous*

- To introduce the exercise, write a few sentences on the
  board about yourself.
- Students write sentences about themselves.
- As a round-up, ask students to read out their sentences.

How to say it

1 *Pronunciation of 'going to' in sentences*

- [recording] Play the recording, pausing and getting students to
  repeat the sentences. Focus on:
  – the reduced /ə/ sound in /tə/;
  – the reduced /ɪ/ sound in /hɪz/, /ʃɪz/.

2 *Rhythm of sentences with 'going to'*

- [recording] Play the recording, pausing and getting students to
  repeat the sentences. Focus on the pattern of stressed
  and unstressed syllables, and the intonation of the
  questions.

[recording] Tapescript for Exercise 3: *Help!*

1 A Hi, look, I'm painting my living room on Saturday …
  B Oh yes …
  A Could you help me?
  B Sorry. I'm working on Saturday.
  A Oh. What about Sunday?
  B No, I'm seeing friends on Sunday. Sorry.

2 A Is that John?
  C Yes.
  A Oh John, hi, it's Paul here.
  C Oh hi, Paul.
  A Um, I'm painting my living room this weekend. Could
    you help me?
  C No, sorry. I can't. I'm playing football on Saturday …
  A What about …?
  C … and on Sunday I'm going swimming. Sorry.

24

This unit is about feelings. It covers three main vocabulary areas:
– physical feelings (e.g. *feel tired, hungry, hot*)
– emotions (e.g. *feel happy, angry, excited*)
– reactions to films, etc. (e.g. *I enjoyed it, it was boring*).
The Reading and Listening activity is about feelings and facial expressions.

1 I'm hungry!

This exercise is about physical feelings, and introduces a range of adjectives used with the expressions I'm … *and* I feel … *It also teaches ways of making suggestions.*

➤ Workbook: Exercise A

> *Expressing feelings:* I'm … I feel … *Adjectives:* hot, cold, hungry, thirsty, tired, ill.
> *Making suggestions:* Why don't you …?, Let's …, Shall I …?
> *New phrases:* lie down, have a rest, go for a swim.

1 Presentation of adjectives; matching task

- Look at the pictures in turn, and establish which words go with each one. As you do this, make the meaning of the words clear, using simple explanations (e.g. *I'm hungry = I want to eat*) and gestures. Expected answers:

  A She's/She feels ill and hot.   B They're/They feel hot, tired and thirsty.
  C They're/They feel cold, tired and hungry.   D They're/They feel hungry and thirsty.

- Show how we can use the verbs *be* or *feel* with these adjectives:

  I'm
  I feel | thirsty.

> *Language note*
> With all these adjectives, we can say *I'm …* or *I feel …*, but not *I have* (so we cannot say ~~I have hunger~~ or ~~I have hot~~).

2 Presentation of suggestions structures; practice; listening to check

- To introduce *Why don't you …?*, write this dialogue on the board:

  A: I'm hungry.
  B: Why don't you …?

  Ask students to continue what B says
  (Possible answers: *… eat something, … have some bread*, etc.). If you like, do the same with *Shall I …?* and *Let's …*

- Look at the pictures, and ask students to suggest what the people are saying. Possible answers (left – right):

  Shall I call/phone a doctor?
  Why don't you go to bed?
  Why don't you have a sandwich? Shall I make some sandwiches? Let's have a sandwich.
  Let's go swimming. Why don't you go swimming?
  Why don't you put on a jumper?
  Let's go to a café. Let's have a drink.

- 🔲 Play the recording. Pause after each dialogue and establish what the people said. (Answers: see tapescript.)

> *Practice/Role-play option*
> Students act out the conversations in pairs.

3 Activation: saying how you feel

- Pairwork. Students go through the list of adjectives, and tell each other which ones they feel.

- As a round-up, ask a few students what they found out about their partner.

🔲 Tapescript for Exercise 1: *I'm hungry!*

1 A Are you all right?
  B No. I feel really ill.
  A Oh dear. Shall I phone the doctor?

2 A Oh, I'm tired.
  B Why don't you lie down and have a rest?

3 A I'm really hungry.
  B Why don't you have a sandwich? There's some cheese in the fridge.
  A OK.

4 A I'm hot.
  B Me too. Let's have a swim.
  A Yeah. Good idea.

5 A I feel a bit cold.
  B Why don't you put on a jumper?

6 A I feel thirsty.
  B OK. Let's go to a café and have something to drink.
  A Mm.

24 Feelings

1 I'm hungry!

1 Look at these people. How do they feel? Use words from the box.

hungry	hot	tired
thirsty	cold	ill

A

B

C

D

2 Look at the pictures in the bubbles. What do you think the people are saying?

Why don't you … ?   Shall I … ?   Let's …

I really feel ill.

I'm tired.

I'm really hungry.

I'm hot.

I feel a bit cold.

I feel thirsty.

Now listen. Did the people say the same as you?

3 How do you feel at the moment? Do you feel hungry? thirsty? hot? …? Tell your partner.

2 I felt really …

1 Here are some sentences from stories. Can you find six other words which describe people's feelings? Write them in the table.

> 'We're meeting the President tomorrow,' he said. 'Aren't you excited?'
> 'No, not really,' I replied.

> 'There's a letter for you,' she said. I opened it. I was surprised to see it was from my brother in California.

> 'What's wrong with Alice?' I asked.
> 'Oh, nothing. She's upset because her best friend didn't invite her to his birthday party. That's all.'

> He didn't know if he was happy or sad. He wanted to laugh and cry at the same time.

> Her face was white. She stood there, and said nothing, but I could see that she was angry.

> He held the knife a few centimetres from my face.
> 'I mustn't show that I'm frightened,' I told myself.

excited
....
....
....
....
....
....

2 Imagine that these things happen. How would you feel?

  a You win a holiday for two in Paris.
  b Someone writes you a letter which begins 'You don't know me, but actually I'm your sister …'
  c You're in bed when someone throws a large stone through your bedroom window.
  d Your favourite film star dies.

3 Talk about something that happened to you. Include the sentence in the bubble.

> I felt really ....!

3 Did you enjoy it?

1 🔲 You will hear four people talking about these videos. Two of them watched *Titanic* and two of them watched a *Mr Bean* video.

Listen and complete the table.

	Which video did they watch?	Did they enjoy it?	What do they say about it?
Speaker 1			
Speaker 2			
Speaker 3			
Speaker 4			

2 Choose a video, film or TV programme that you saw recently. Write down what you thought of it.

> I didn't enjoy THE ENGLISH PATIENT. It was very long and boring, and it was also very sad.

3 Find other students who saw the same thing. Do they agree with you?

> HOME ALONE is a children's film, but it was very funny and I laughed a lot. I enjoyed it.

2 I felt really …

This exercise focuses on adjectives used to describe feelings. It also gives practice in talking about feelings in the past, using I felt.

➤ Workbook: Exercise B, Listening

> *Adjectives:* excited, upset, angry, surprised, happy, sad, frightened.
> *Other new words:* laugh, hold/held, feel/felt.

1 Reading & vocabulary task; presentation of adjectives

● Read the sentences, and see if students can identify the adjectives that describe feelings. Build them up on the board, and give examples/situations to make their meaning clear. Answers:

(excited) upset, angry, surprised, happy, sad, frightened

Alternative: pairwork
Students read the sentences in pairs and find the adjectives, using a dictionary to help them.

2 Practice

● Ask students how they would feel in each of the situations. Expected answers:

a excited, happy   *b* surprised   *c* frightened, angry   *d* sad, upset

Language note
You're *upset* if something bad happens that makes you want to cry (e.g. you lose a diamond ring; your boy/girlfriend leaves you). You're *excited* about something good that's going to happen in the future, (e.g. your birthday, a holiday).

3 Activation: telling a story

● Give time for students to think of something that happened to them. If you like, divide them into pairs and let them prepare with a partner, using their own language for this stage.

● Ask for volunteers to describe what happened to them and how they felt.

Homework option
Students write a few sentences for homework, based on what they said in class.

3 Did you enjoy it?

This exercise gives practice in talking about a film or a video, saying whether or not you enjoyed it and what it was like.

➤ Workbook: Exercise C

> *Key language:* interesting, boring, funny, sad; enjoy, laugh.

1 Listening & making notes

● To introduce the activity, look at the two videos and ask students if they know them. If they do, ask them whether they enjoyed them or not.

● 🔲 Play the recording, pausing from time to time if necessary. Students listen and make notes in the table.

● Play the recording again, pausing after each speaker. Answers:

1 *Titanic*; yes; exciting, sad, really good.
2 *Titanic*; no; quite exciting, too long, actors weren't good.
3 *Mr Bean*; yes and no; some parts were funny, some parts were boring.
4 *Mr Bean*; yes; really funny.

2 Activation: writing sentences

● To introduce the activity, write one or two sentences about a film, video or TV programme you saw recently. Choose something that most of the class know. Read out your sentences, and ask who agrees with you and who doesn't agree. Try to get students to express their opinion about it too.

● Give time for students to choose a film, video or TV programme and write one or two sentences about it.

3 Discussion

● Ask students to read out their sentences in turn. See if other students agree.

Alternative
Students move freely round the class, finding other students who saw the same thing as they did. They then read out their sentences, and see if the other student agrees.

As a round-up, ask a few students how many people agreed with them.

🔲 Tapescript for Exercise 3: *Did you enjoy it?*

1 Well, I saw *Titanic*, and yes, I really enjoyed it, it was really exciting. It was also quite sad, I thought, but – really good.

2 Yes, I saw *Titanic*. It wasn't very good – it was quite exciting, I suppose, but much too long, and the actors weren't very good.

3 I saw a *Mr Bean* video. It was OK, some parts were very funny, and … but some bits were quite boring, as well. I enjoyed it.

4 I saw a *Mr Bean* video. I thought it was really funny – I enjoyed it a lot.

4 Showing your feelings

This combined Reading and Listening activity is about Paul Ekman, an American scientist who investigated whether facial expressions are universal. Students look at some of Ekman's photographs and decide how the people are feeling. They then fill gaps in a reading text about Ekman, and finally listen to check their answers.

Reading skills: *understanding key points; making predictions.*
Listening skills: *listening to check; listening to confirm predictions.*

> *New words:* feelings, everywhere, scientist, take a photo, look (+ adj), face, show, conclusion, facial expressions.

1 Introduction: matching task & discussion

- Look at the first question. Either give time for students to look at the photos in pairs, then talk about them together, or simply look at them with the whole class. Try to get opinions from the whole class, to establish if they all agree or not (e.g. *Do you think she's sad? Do you all agree? Does anyone think she looks angry?*).

- Look at the second question, and again establish whether students all agree. If necessary, make the question clearer by breaking it down into concrete examples (e.g. *Look: when I feel happy, I smile, like this. Does everyone smile if they're happy? What about people in Africa? What about people in Russia? What about Americans? Are they all the same?*).

First language option
If you want to discuss this question in detail, let students talk about it in their own language. The main point of this stage is as a preparation for reading the text.

2 Presentation of vocabulary; reading & gap-filling

- To prepare for the reading, write these words on the board, and explain what they mean:

> **scientist** **conclusion**
> **take a photo**

- Give time for students to read the text and fill the gaps.
- Read through the text together, and discuss the answers. Ask students what they think Ekman's conclusion was.

3 Listening to check

- 🖵 Play the recording, pausing after each gap to check the answers. Answers:

  1 people in the USA
  2 people from 21 countries
  3 a village in Papua New Guinea
  4 the people in this village
  Conclusion: People do show feelings in the same way everywhere.

🖵 Tapescript: see text.

4 Showing your feelings

1 Try this experiment.

- Look at these photos.
  Which of the people do
  you think are

  – happy?
  – sad?
  – angry?
  – surprised?
  – frightened?

  Compare your answers
  with other students. Are
  they the same?

- Do people show feelings
  in the same way in all the
  countries of the world?
  Do we all smile when
  we're happy, and cry
  when we're sad?

  What do you think?

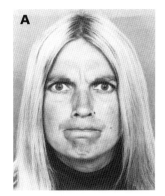

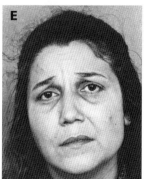

© Paul Ekman, 1975

2 Now read about Paul Ekman. Can you fill the gaps in the story?

Paul Ekman is an American scientist. He wanted to know the answer to this question: Do people show feelings in the same way everywhere in the world?

Ekman took photos of (1) .... Some people looked happy, some looked sad, some looked angry, some looked surprised, and some looked frightened. He showed the photos to (2) .... , and asked them to match the feelings with the faces. He found that everyone could do this quite easily: everyone agreed which people were happy, which were sad, which were angry, and so on.

Then Ekman went to (3) .... In this village, people had no television, they saw no films, and they never saw people from other countries. So they didn't know what people from other countries looked like. Ekman showed his photos to (4) .... , and asked them the same questions : Which people are happy? Which are sad? Which are angry? He found that even here they could answer the questions quite easily.

So Ekman's conclusion was:

the people in
this village

people from 21
countries

people in the
USA

a village in Papua
New Guinea

What do you think Ekman's conclusion was?

3 [cassette] Someone describes Paul Ekman's experiment. Listen and fill the gaps in the story.

Final review

Imagine

Choose a month, and imagine a scene with you in it.

Use these questions to help you.

Where are you?

What are you wearing?

What are you doing?

What season is it?

What time of day is it?

What's the weather like?

Are there any other people?

What are they doing?

Yesterday

Which of these things do you think your partner

– did yesterday?
– didn't do yesterday?

Write ten sentences.

eat rice

ride a bike

go shopping

climb up a ladder

play a computer game

swim

make a cup of coffee

drive a car

buy a drink

write a letter

Now ask questions and find out.
How many did you get right?

Interview

Student A: You work for a radio station in your town. You are going to interview a tourist. Here are your notes. What questions are you going to ask?

- Name
- From ... (town, country)
- ... years old
- Married? Children? How many?
- Job
- Arrived ... Is leaving ...

- Is staying at ...
- Is/isn't having a good time
- Likes/doesn't like
  – the town
  – the people
  – the food
- Is/isn't going to come again

Student B: You are a tourist. *A* is going to interview you. What are you going to say?

Now have the interview.

Final review

Imagine

Review of there is/are *(Unit 5), times (Study pages D), Present continuous tense (Unit 11), clothes (Unit 12), weather and seasons (Unit 14).*

Alternative 1: Whole class

- Ask a good (or confident) student to sit in front of the class, and to close his/her eyes.
- Ask the student to imagine a scene with him/her in it. Ask each of the questions in turn, and give time for the student to imagine the scene and give answers.
- Continue in the same way, with students coming to the front of the class in turn and other students asking the questions.

Alternative 2: Pairwork

- If you like, demonstrate the activity by calling a student to the front, as above.
- Divide the class into pairs. Students take it in turn to imagine a scene, with their partner asking the questions.
- As a round-up, ask some students to describe the scene they imagined.

Yesterday

Review of Past simple tense positive and negative (Units 15, 17), Past simple questions (Unit 17), action verbs (Unit 20).

Alternative 1: Whole class

- Choose one student and ask him/her to leave the room. Get the rest of the class to make guesses about what he/she did yesterday, and write them on the board, e.g. *She didn't eat rice. She didn't ride a bike. She went shopping …*
- Call the student back into the room. The other students ask him/her questions to find out if the guesses were correct, e.g. *Did you eat rice? Did you ride a bike? Did you go shopping?*
- If you like, repeat the procedure, choosing another student to leave the room.

Alternative 2: Pairwork

- Divide the class into pairs. Students write sentences about their partner, but without consulting each other at this stage.
- Students ask their partner questions to check if their sentences were correct.
- As a round-up, ask students what they found out about their partner.

Interview

Review of: personal details (Units 1, 2, 12), likes and dislikes (Unit 22), the future (Unit 23).

Preparation

- Look at the notes and establish what the questions should be. Expected answers:

  What's your name?
  Where are you from?
  How old are you?
  Are you married?
  Do you have any children? (Have you got any children?)
  How many children do you have? (… have you got?)
  What's your job? (What do you do?)
  When did you arrive?
  When are you leaving?
  Where are you staying?
  Are you having a good time?
  Do you like the town? the people? the food?
  Are you going to come again?

- To demonstrate the activity, take the role of the tourist yourself. Get students to ask you the questions and give suitable replies.

Role-play

Either: Call pairs of students to the front of the class to act out conversations.

Or: Divide the class into pairs, and give each student a letter, A or B. Student A in each pair then interviews Student B, who takes the role of the tourist.

Or: Give half the class Role A and the other half Role B. Students move freely round the class. Students with Role A find students with Role B and interview them. As a round-up, ask Role A students what they found out.

Can you remember?

The pictures are from earlier units:

A Unit 5	G Unit 4
B Unit 15	H Unit 12
C Unit 9	I Unit 16
D Unit 8	J Unit 18
E Unit 14	K Unit 20
F Unit 22	L Unit 6

Alternative 1: Whole class

- Choose pictures in turn, and ask students to talk about them. Prompt them by asking questions, e.g. (for picture B): *What can you see? What is the boy/man doing? What is he wearing? Do you remember the story? What happened?*

Alternative 2: Pair or individual preparation

- Working alone or in pairs, students choose a picture and prepare a few things to say about it. They can either prepare by talking to their partner or by writing notes.
- Ask students in turn to say what picture they chose and to talk briefly about it. If you like, let other students in the class ask them questions about the picture or about the topic.

Alternative 3: Fluency game

- Give students time to look at all the pictures and quickly prepare something to say about them.
- Start with any picture, and choose a student. The student talks about the picture, saying as much as he/she can. When the first student can't say any more, another student continues, and so on. When no one can say any more about the picture, choose another picture and repeat the procedure. If you like, give a point to the student who says the last thing about each picture.

Can you remember?

All of these pictures are from earlier units. Choose one of the pictures.
What can you remember about it?

A

B

C

D

E

F

G

H

I

J

Frikes
Kioni
Stavros
Kathara
Vathi

K

L

Additional material

1.2 Photos

Student A

1 one

my room – very small

2 two

my bike – new

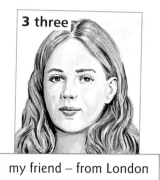

3 three

my friend – from London

4 four

?

Student B

1 one

my house – very big

2 two

my car – a Porsche

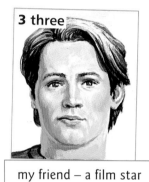

3 three

my friend – a film star

4 four

?

3.3 What's this?

Student A: Ask questions with *Who*, *What* and *Where*.
Student B: Answer the questions. (If you don't know the answer, look in the box!)

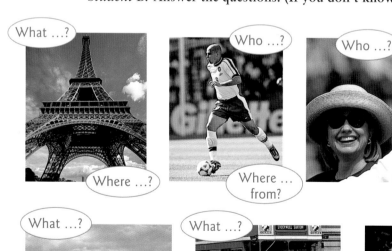

What …?
Where …?
Who …?
Where … from?
Who …?
Where … from?

What …?
Where …?
What …?
Where …?
What …?
Where … from?

> In London, the taxis are black and the buses are red.
>
> Kangaroos are from Australia.
>
> Ronaldo is a footballer. He's from Brazil.
>
> The Eiffel Tower is in Paris. It's 300 metres high.
>
> Bill and Hillary Clinton are from the USA.
>
> The Pyramids are near Cairo, in Egypt. They're 4,500 years old.

2.2 How old are they?

André

Olga

Greg

Kumiko

Caterina

4.1 Painting by numbers

red   grey

yellow   green

white   blue

black   pink

brown   orange

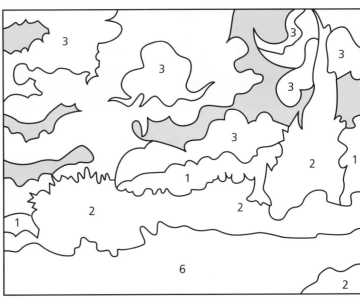

Vincent Van Gogh: Wheatfield with Cypresses

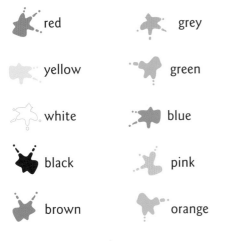

Henri Matisse: Lady in Blue

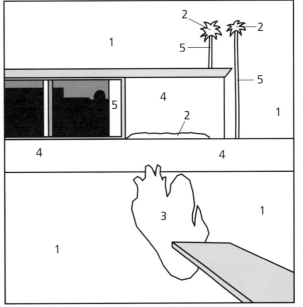

David Hockney: A bigger splash

4.3 Where's my …? *Student A*

You can't find

– your shoes
– your ball
– your glasses

Ask Student B.

Now answer
B's questions.

10.3 Is there a bank near here? *Student A*

You want to find

– a bank
– a post office
– a bookshop

Ask Student B.

Now answer
B's questions.

① = a chemist
② = a newsagent
③ = a restaurant

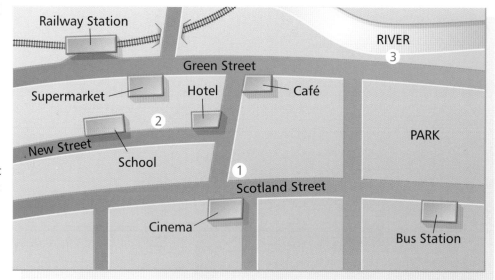

12.3 Who do you mean?

5.3 Buildings

5 Focus on Form Yes/no questions

In the Empire State Building …

… there are 102 floors.

… there are nearly 2,000 stairs between the ground floor and the top floor.

… there are 7–12 rooms on each floor.

… there are 73 lifts.

… there are five restaurants.

… there are about ten shops.

… there isn't a swimming pool.

9.2 What do you do?

Choose a role for yourself, and write it on a piece of paper.

I'm	a student. I study	music	at a college in	Cambridge.	I live in	Church Street.
	a teacher. I teach	business		Edinburgh.		King Street.
		English		Manchester.		Market Street

4.3 Where's my ...? *Student B*

Answer Student
A's questions.

Now ask A.
You can't find

– your umbrella
– your pens
– your camera

10.3 Is there a bank near here? *Student B*

Answer Student
A's questions.

① = a bank
② = a post office
③ = a bookshop

Now ask A.
You want to
find

– a chemist
– a newsagent
– a restaurant

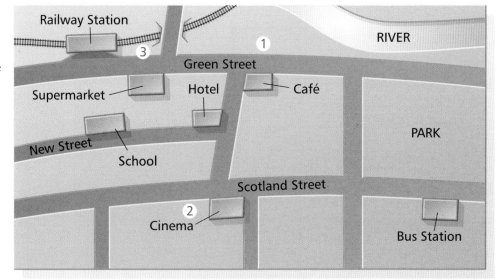

20.3 Action!

I remember I once saw an advertisement on TV for a chocolate bar. It showed a very good-looking man at home with his very beautiful wife. His wife asked him to get her a chocolate bar, so he said 'Just a moment, darling', got up and quickly put on his running shoes. Then he *went* out of the house, got into his car, and *went* to a small airport. There he got into a helicopter and *went* across the sea to an island. On the beach there was a white horse. He got on the horse, and *went* across the island until he came to a bridge over a big river. In the middle of the river there was a very high rock. He *went* off the bridge into the river, and *went* to the rock. Then he *went* up the rock, and right at the top there was a chocolate bar, in gold paper. He took the chocolate bar, and brought it back to his wife. What I never understood was – why didn't he just go round to his local supermarket and buy one?

19.2 Can I …? *Student A*

1 **You are a guest in B's flat. You want to**

- have a shower
- have a banana
- phone your mother
- play a computer game
- have a sleep

Ask questions with *Can I …?*

2 **This is your flat. B is your guest. Answer his/her questions.**

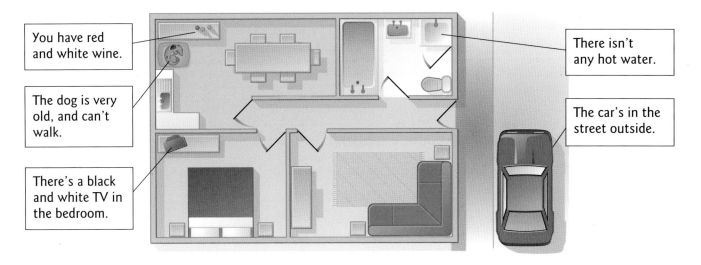

You have red and white wine.

The dog is very old, and can't walk.

There's a black and white TV in the bedroom.

There isn't any hot water.

The car's in the street outside.

19.2 Can I …? *Student B*

1 **This is your flat. A is your guest. Answer his/her questions.**

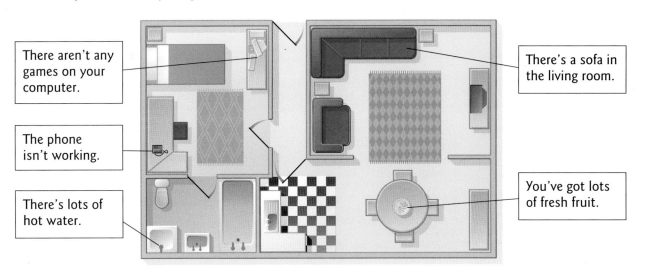

There aren't any games on your computer.

The phone isn't working.

There's lots of hot water.

There's a sofa in the living room.

You've got lots of fresh fruit.

2 **You are a guest in A's flat. You want to**

- take the dog for a walk
- have a glass of wine
- wash your hair
- watch TV
- use A's car

Ask questions with *Can I …?*

Tapescripts

1.1 Hello Goodbye

A Hello. I'm Sam.
B Oh, hello. I'm Anna.
A Where are you from, Anna?
B I'm from Berlin.

A Hello.
C Oh, hi. I'm Paul. I'm a student here.
A Oh, really? My name's Sam.

A Oh, hi, Lisa. How are you?
D I'm fine. How are you?
A Oh, I'm OK.

A Hello. My name's Sam.
E Hi. I'm John. I'm a teacher here.
A Oh, really? Where are you from?
E I'm from London.

1.2 Photos

This is my car. It's a Citröen, it's very old.
This is my flat. It's very small.
And this is my friend Nina. She's from Italy.
Oh, and this is my friend George. He's from London and he's a student.

2.2 How old are they?

1 My name's André. I'm nine years old, and I'm from Germany.
2 My name's Olga. I'm 16, and I'm from Russia.
3 Hello. My name's Greg. I'm 18 years old, and I'm from the United States.
4 This is Kumiko. She's one year old, and she's from Japan.
5 My name is Caterina. I'm 20, and I'm from Italy.

2.3 Parents and children

1 My name's Paul. I'm married and my wife is a doctor. We have two children. My daughter is 8, and my son is just 3.
2 My name's Isabelle. I'm 19 years old and I'm a student at university. I have one brother – his name's Alan. My mother's a teacher, and my father's a taxi driver.

2.4 Who's who?

A is Donna. She's a police officer, she's 20, she's from Scotland and she has a grey car. B is James. He's a student, he's 17, he's from Ireland and he has a red car. C is Alice. She's a singer, she's 19, she's from Wales and she has a white car. And D is Bob. He's a waiter, he's 18 years old, he's from England and he has a green car.

Study pages A
Phrasebook: Good morning

1 A Good morning.
  B Good morning. How are you?
  A Fine, thanks.
2 A Good afternoon.
  B Good afternoon.
3 A Good evening, sir.
  B Good evening. Room 315, please.
4 A Good night.
  B Good night. See you tomorrow.

3.1 Sorry

A A Jane – hello. How are you?
  B I'm not Jane, I'm Cathy.
  A Oh – yes, sorry. Cathy, hello. How are you?

B A Excuse me. Two coffees, please.
  B Actually, I'm not a waiter. I'm a customer.
  A Oh, I'm sorry.
C A Oh, good. A taxi. Hello. The Hilton Hotel, please.
  B Sorry. This isn't a taxi. It's my car!
  A Oh, I'm so sorry.
D A Oh, is that your baby? Isn't she lovely? What's her name?
  B He isn't a girl, actually. He's a boy.
  A Oh, of course. Isn't he lovely?
E A So where are you from? New York?
  B No, we aren't American. We're English.
  A Oh, you're English.
  C Yeah, that's right – we're from London.

3.2 Is this seat free?

A Excuse me. Is this your umbrella?
B Oh. Yes, it is. Thanks. Are you a student here?
A Yes. Yes, I am. My name's Mark.
B Hi. I'm Sonia.
A Hi, Sonia. Um, is this seat free?
B Yes, of course.

4.2 Birthday presents

1 A Here's a present for you.
  B Hmm, what is it? ... It's a football! Oh, thank you!
2 A Here you are. Happy birthday.
  B Oh, thanks ... Ooh, a CD. Flamenco music. That's nice. Thank you.
3 A A present for you.
  B Ooh ... It's a jumper! Lovely, thank you!
4 A A present for you. Happy birthday.
  B An umbrella! Thanks.
5 A A present for you. Happy birthday.
  B Mmm ... A watch! Wow! Thank you!
6 A Here you are. Happy birthday.
  B Oh, thanks. Ooh, a lamp! It's lovely! Thank you.

4.4 Precious stones

This is a gold sword, and it's from Istanbul in Turkey. And as you can see, it has lots of diamonds on it, and three very big emeralds.
Now this is a very beautiful brooch. It's from the USA. It has about 100 very small diamonds in it.
And this necklace has rubies and diamonds in it. It's very old, and it's from France.
And this is a very beautiful green bottle. It's from India, and it has red and green stones on it. The red stones are rubies and the green stones are emeralds.

Study pages B
Phrasebook: Excuse me

1 A Ooh, sorry!
  B Oh, that's all right.
  A No, no, I'm sorry – really.
  B It's OK.
2 A Excuse me.
  B Yes?
  A Mr Brown's on the phone.
  B Oh, OK ... Excuse me just a moment.
3 A Excuse me!
  B Yes, sir?
  A A glass of water, please.
  B Certainly, sir.

4 A Excuse me ... Excuse me!
  B Oh, sorry.
  A Thank you.

5.1 Favourite places

1 My favourite place is Penang, in Malaysia. It's very hot, and there are some beautiful beaches. There's a big airport, there are lots of hotels, there are lots of restaurants, and there are lots and lots of tourists.
2 My favourite place is Glenelg in Scotland. It's a very small village – there's just one small shop, there's a church, and that's all. But it's a very beautiful place. It's on the sea, and there are mountains all around.
3 My favourite place is a town called Ouro Preto in Brazil. It's not very big – there are four or five hotels, maybe. But it's a very old town, and there are lots of beautiful old buildings and some beautiful old churches.

6.1 From room to room

A Well, this is the hall – there are two cupboards here, for coats ...
B Oh yes ...
A And here's the living room.
B Oh good – there's a TV.
A Yes, there's a nice sofa too, and a table. And this is a new carpet.
B And that's the balcony?
A Yes, through here. It's a big balcony, again with a table and chairs.
B Mm. Nice place to eat.
A Yes ... Now if we go back through here ... This is the small bedroom – just a bed and a small cupboard here ... and this is the big bedroom through here.
B Oh yes, a nice big bed.
A And there are cupboards here for clothes, and a small TV.
B Great. That's lovely.
A Yeah, it's a nice room. OK, so ... This is the bathroom. Quite small, but there's a bath and a shower, as you can see.
B And the toilet's here.
A Yes, that's right ... OK ... And this is the kitchen. Again, quite small. There's a cooker here, and a fridge, and cupboards of course ... And that's it.

6.3 What's your address?

1 OK, my name's Alison Bailey, that's B-A-I-L-E-Y, OK? And the address is Flat 2, 52 Brighton Road – yes, B-R-I-G-H-T-O-N, Brighton Road, Ealing – E-A-L-I-N-G, and that's London W5 9QT – that's the post code. The phone number is 0181 746 9032.
2 Right. It's Mario Dimambro, D-I-M-A-M-B-R-O, Dimambro. 247 Via Roma – R-O-M-A, Genova – G-E-N-O-V-A, Italy. And the phone number: 656631. That's it.
3 Yes, Philip Denver. Philip – that's P-H-I-L-I-P, one L, and Denver, D-E-N-V-E-R. And it's a thousand and forty nine, 1-0-4-9 Lincoln Drive – L-I-N-C-O-L-N Drive, Boston, 342354, USA. Oh, the telephone? It's 001 – that's for the USA, then 617 584 3921.

6.4 Billionaires

1 Bill Gates's house is on a lake, so you can go there by car or by boat. It's quite big – it has six bedrooms and about 20 other rooms. There's a big dining room, which has seats for about 100 people, and there's also a beautiful library, with lots of old books. The library also has a notebook with writing by Leonardo da Vinci, and that cost more than $30 million. And what's interesting is that there are video screens everywhere – on the walls in all the rooms, even the bathrooms – and these just show pictures – so one day you can have a Picasso, and the next day you can have a Van Gogh, and so on. So it's a nice place, and the rooms have big windows, so you can see the lake and the mountains.

2 The Sultan's Palace is huge – it has nearly 1,800 rooms, 18 lifts, and about 250 toilets. It's huge – very, very big – and some of the rooms are also very big. The dining room, for example, has seats for 4,000 people – that's a big dinner party. And there's also a throne room for the Sultan, and the walls of the throne room are covered in gold, 22-carat gold. And if you want to park your car, there's an underground garage with places for about 700 cars – the Sultan himself has 150 cars, and they're all down under the palace, in the garage.

Study pages C
Phrasebook: Can I have ...?

A Can I have a glass of water, please?
B Yes, of course. Here you are.
A Thank you.

7.1 Free time

1 Well, when I'm on a bus, I usually read a magazine, or sometimes I play a computer game, or maybe listen to music.
2 In my lunchbreak? Oh, sometimes I have a burger – maybe go to the park. Sometimes I play football after lunch.
3 Well, when I'm ill in bed, usually I just read a book, maybe, or watch videos, or if a friend's there, I play cards, maybe.

7.2 Friends

John likes black coffee, I like white.
I like daytime, John likes night.
I like hot showers, he likes cold ones.
I wear new clothes, he wears old ones.

John has short hair, I have long.
I like weak tea, he likes strong.
I wear high heels, he wears low ones.
He likes fast cars, I like slow ones.

Why are we friends? Because, you see,
I like him, but he likes me.

8.1 Food ...

1 We eat a lot of rice – we eat rice every day. We eat a lot of fish, a lot of vegetables, and we eat a lot of fruit.
2 We eat quite a lot of bread, and also rice and beans. We sometimes eat meat. We eat a lot of vegetables and we eat a lot of fruit.
3 We eat a lot of bread, eggs, cheese. We eat a lot of meat, a lot of potatoes and other vegetables. And quite a lot of fruit.
4 We eat a lot of pasta, olive oil, quite a lot of salad and vegetables. But we also eat fish and cheese.

8.3 Waiter!

A Can I have a knife and fork, please?
B I'm very sorry. Yes, of course, sir.
C And I'd like some ketchup, please.
B Ketchup, yes, certainly.

8.4 Fast food

1 A Two cheeseburgers, please ...
  B Two cheeseburgers ...
  A ... and one French fries.
  B Is that small or large?
  A Large, please. And a diet Coke – small.
  B OK. Any dessert?
  A No. That's all, thanks.
  B OK. That's four eighty, please.
2 B Yes please?
  C The hot chilli burger – is that very hot?
  B It's quite hot, yes.
  C OK, I'll have the big burger bonanza then, please.
  B A big burger bonanza. OK ... anything else?
  C Just a cup of coffee, please.
  B OK, that's three twenty, please.
3 B Yes please?
  D The children's meals – what do you get?
  B They come with a small French fries and a small drink.
  D OK, so ...
  E Nuggets and Fanta!
  F Pizza slice and Coke!
  D Two children's meals, please – one chicken nuggets and Fanta, and one pizza slice and Coke.
  B Pizza slice, Coke. Anything else?
  D No, that's all, thanks.
  B OK. Five twenty, please.

Study pages D
Phrasebook: On the phone

1 A Hello. Jane Miller.
  B Hello. Can I speak to George, please?
  A Yes. Just a moment.
  C Hello.
  B Hello, George. It's Mike.
2 A Hello. 26439.
  B Hello. Is Louisa there, please?
  A No, she isn't. Sorry.
  B OK. Never mind.

9.2 What do you do?

A So ... what do you do?
B Oh, I'm a student.
A Oh, yes. What do you study?
B Music.
A Really? I'm a music teacher.
B Are you really? Where do you work, then?
A Oh, at a school, in Cambridge.
B Really? Do you live in Cambridge?
A Yes. Yes, I do. Why, where do you live?
B Cambridge. I live in Cambridge, too.
A Really? Where?
B In Bridge Street – I have a flat in Bridge Street.
A No, that's amazing ...

9.3 From morning till night

Well, I usually get up at a quarter past 7, and then I have breakfast around 8. Then I go to work at half past 8. I start work at a quarter past 9, usually, and I work till half past 12 and then I have lunch. Then I work again in the afternoon, and I always finish work at 5 o'clock. So I get home at 5.30. I have a sandwich then, when I come home, and then I usually have dinner quite late, at about 7 o'clock in the evening. And I go to bed, ooh, at around half past 11, usually.

10.1 At the market

A A Can I see that radio?
  B Yes, here you are.
  A How much is it?
  B £25.
  A Oh no, that's too expensive.
  B All right, 20 then.
B A How much are these lighters?
  B They're £1 each.
  A OK, I'll have one, please.
  B What colour do you want? Red, blue, green?
  A Blue, I think.
  B Here you are, then. That's £1, please.
C A Hello. Can I help you?
  B Yes. What size is that jacket?
  A It's size 38.
  B Oh, that's too big. Thanks anyway.

10.3 Is there a bank near here?

1 A Is there a bank near here?
  B Yes, there's one on the main road, next to the school.
2 A Excuse me, where's the post office?
  B Oh, it's just opposite the station.
3 A Excuse me, is there a supermarket near here?
  B Yes, there's one in Bridge Street, just by the river.
4 A Is there a chemist near here?
  B Yes, let's see ... Yes, there's one on the main road, between the school and the cinema.
5 A Is there a newsagent near here?
  B Yes, there's one in the next street.
6 A Excuse me, is there a good restaurant near here?
  B Yes, there's a very good one near the station – it's called Dino's.
7 A Excuse me, is there a good bookshop near here?
  B No, there isn't, but there's one in the town centre, near the bus station.

10.4 Open and closed

1 In Poland the banks are open till 7 o'clock in the evening. And in towns, supermarkets stay open all night, so you can buy bread at 3 o'clock in the morning.
2 In Greece the shops close at 2 o'clock in the afternoon and open again at 5 o'clock. But there are also lots of kiosks, and they stay open all day.
3 In many cities in Thailand there are large street markets which stay open in the evening. You can buy lots of things there: watches, cameras, books, clothes – lots of things. And they usually stay open till about 12 o'clock at night.

Study pages E
Phrasebook: What does it mean?

1 A What does 'slow' mean?
  B It means 'not fast'.
2 A What does 'millionaire' mean?
  B It's a person who has lots of money.
3 A What's 'amigo' in English?
  B Friend.
4 A What's 'vino' in English?
  B Wine.

11.2 Questions

A Is anyone sitting here?
B Er, no.
A Are you staying at this hotel?
B Yes. Yes, I am.
A What are you reading?
B Excuse me.
A Hey, where are you going?

12.2 Jobs

1 I'm a singer. I sing with a band. I always wear the same thing when I sing – I wear a red jacket and black trousers.
2 Well, I'm a doctor. I work in a large hospital. And I wear a skirt and a blouse and a white coat.
3 I'm a shop assistant. I work in a bookshop. And I usually wear just a jumper and jeans.

12.3 Who do you mean?

1 Anna? She's got blond hair, quite short, and she wears glasses. She's about 25, quite attractive.
2 You know Anna – she drives a blue Volkswagen. She's quite tall, usually wears jeans.
3 You must know Anna – she lives in the next street. She teaches maths, and she's got those two small children.

12.4 Love is all around

I feel it in my fingers, I feel it in my toes.
Well, love is all around me, and so the feeling grows.
It's written on the wind, it's everywhere I go.
So if you really love me, come on and let it show.

13.2 Shopping list

A Let me see ... We need some orange juice, and some tomatoes, and ... We haven't got any eggs ... What else?
B What about bread?
A No, we've got lots of bread ... Rice? No, we've got rice ... Ah, we haven't got many potatoes.
B Potatoes, OK. What about fruit?
A Oh, yes. Get some apples – and some bananas, maybe. What else? Ah yes, we haven't got any coffee.
B We haven't got much sugar, either.
A OK, sugar. Is that everything?
B I think so, yes.

14.3 What's the weather like?

1 Yes, it's quite warm here, but it's raining ...
2 It's nice and sunny, but it's very windy, and quite cool ...
3 It's very, very cold. And it's snowing ...
4 It's really hot here, quite humid ... No, it isn't sunny at all, it's cloudy, cloudy and very hot ...

Unit 14.4 Festivals

1 Well, we usually go to a party and then at midnight we all go out into the street and we watch fireworks.
2 Well, I usually go out to a restaurant with a lot of friends and we all have a nice meal together and we listen to music and dance and have a good time.
3 I don't do anything. Actually, I don't like New Year's Eve very much, so I go to bed early.
4 Well, we stay at home, but we stay up till midnight and we watch New Year on television.

5 We stay at home till midnight, and then we usually go and visit friends, and we have a few drinks with them.

Study pages G
Focus on ... Can

OK, I can make a cup of coffee, I can make toast, yes ... 'Can you cook rice?' Yes, I can cook rice, no problem ... I can make an omelette, not a very good omelette, but yes, I can make an omelette. Barbecue a chicken ... Yes, I can barbecue a chicken, I can do that. I can't make a cake, no, not really. But I can make my own pasta. I have a pasta machine and I often make my own pasta, yes, so I can do that. But I can't make bread, no.

Study pages G
Phrasebook: Would you like ...?

1 A Would you like an ice-cream?
  B Oh, yes please.
  A OK, what kind?
  B Chocolate.
2 A Hello! Would you like a lift?
  B Oh, yes. Thank you very much.
  A That's OK. Where are you going?
  B Just to the next village.
  A OK.
3 A Would you like another drink?
  B Ooh, yes please.
  A Orange juice, wasn't it?
  B Yes, orange juice with ice.

15.1 Bedtime story

I was about five years old. It was very late at night, and my parents were asleep. I was awake because I wanted to go to the toilet. I went to the toilet, and I saw a light under the living room door. So I opened the door and went in, and I saw a man in the living room. He was about 20 years old.

I looked at him, and he looked at me, and he smiled at me and said, 'Hi! What's your name?' And I said, 'Sam'. 'Do you want to play a game, Sam?' he asked, and I said, 'Yes.' He had a big bag in his hand, and he said, 'OK. Let's put things in this bag.'

So we played the game. I gave things to him, and he put them in his bag. I took my father's wallet out of his jacket, and I took my mother's purse out of her coat, and the man put them in his bag.

Then I went into my parents' bedroom – very quietly – and took their watches and rings, and my mother's earrings, and gave them to the man.

I gave him some other things too – the silver knives, forks and spoons, two clocks and some old books – and he put everything in his bag. It was a great game.

And in the end he said, 'OK, Sam. It's bedtime. You go back to bed now. Goodnight.' So I said goodnight and went back to bed.

15.3 Childhood places

1 Our flat was on the third floor, and it was very small – it was really just one room. It had a kitchen and a bathroom, but they were very, very small – they were like cupboards, really. The room had one big window, and outside there was a small balcony. And in the room there were two sofas, one on each side. And at night these sofas were our beds – my parents slept in one, and I slept in the other with my little sister.

2 I remember my grandmother's house, where I stayed every summer. It was in the country, and it was quite small – it only had a living room and two bedrooms – but it had a really big garden, and there were lots of trees, and it was very quiet. It was an old house, and it had lovely old wooden furniture. And I remember there was a large veranda which went all round the house, so there was always a sunny place to sit. I loved it.

16.3 Which country?

1 India – well, it's a large country, very large. It's also a very poor country, at least most people are poor. What else? It's in Asia ... The capital is New Delhi, I think, and the River Ganges flows through it. It's very hot in the summer and the winter, I think – but not in the north, of course. In the north there are mountains, very high mountains – the Himalayas.
2 What do I know about Switzerland? Well, it's in Europe, in the centre of Europe, it isn't on the sea. It has a lot of lakes, and a lot of mountains – it's very cold in the winter. It's a very rich country – a very beautiful country as well. And there are three main languages, I think – French, German and Italian.
3 Argentina is in South America, and people speak Spanish there. It's a very big country. The south of the country is very cold – I'm not sure about the north, but the south is certainly cold. And the capital is Buenos Aires.

16.4 International travel

1 B Good morning.
  A Good morning.
  B Could I see your ticket and passport, please? ... Thank you. Just one bag to check in, is it?
  A Yes, just one.
  B OK ... Would you like a smoking or a non-smoking seat?
  A Non-smoking, please, by the window.
  B A window seat, OK. There you are.
  A Thank you.
  B Thank you. Have a good flight.
2 Ladies and gentlemen, welcome to Miami, where the time is exactly 3.20 in the afternoon. We hope you had a good flight and ...
3 A Miami Beach Hotel, please.
  C Miami Beach Hotel. OK.
4 D Good afternoon.
  A Hello. You've got a room reserved for Brown.
  D Mrs Brown – just a moment ... Yes, here we are, ma'am. Three nights, is that right?
  A Yes, that's right.
  D OK ... Your room number is 926. It's on the ninth floor. Here's your key, ma'am.
  A Thank you.
5 A Hello? Richard? It's me, Karen.
  E Karen, hi. Are you in Miami? Did you have a good flight?
  A Yes, fine. Is everything OK? How are the children?
  E Oh, they're fine. They're both asleep. What's it like there? Is it hot?
  A Yes, it is. Sunny and very hot. What's it like in London?
  E Oh, still raining.

A OK, look. I'll phone again
  tomorrow. OK?
E OK. Bye.
6 F Room service. Can I help you?
  A Yes, I'd like a chicken sandwich,
    please.
  F Yes, ma'am. Anything to drink?
  A Yes, a cold beer, please.
  F OK. What's your room number?
  A 926.
  F 926. Fine. Thank you.

Study pages H
Focus on … Dates

My name's Henry. My birthday's on
1st March.
My name's André. My birthday's on
26th July.
My name's Hazel, and my birthday is
22nd April.
OK, my name's Chris, and my birthday
is 9th June.
Hello, my name's Natasha, and my
birthday's on 26th December.
My name is Gabi, and my birthday is on
20th February.

Study pages H
Phrasebook: I'm not sure

A What's the capital of India?
B I think it's Bombay.

A What is the capital of India?
C I don't know. Is it Calcutta?

A What's the capital of India?
D I have no idea. Sorry.

A What is the capital of India?
E I'm not sure, but I think it's Delhi.

17.2 Did you see …?

1 A Did you see that programme about
    hospitals last night?
  B Yes, I did.
  A Did you like it?
  B Yes, I did. It was quite interesting.
2 A Did you watch the football match
    on Sunday?
  B No, I didn't. Was it good?
  A Yes, it was. We won 2–0.
3 A Did you go to the concert yesterday?
  B No. Did you?
  A Yes, I did.
  B Did you enjoy it?
  A No, it was really boring.

17.3 Memory test

A OK, can you remember your first day
  at school?
B My first day at school …
A What did you wear?
B I wore … I don't know. Jeans and a T-
  shirt, probably, but I don't really
  remember.
A OK, and what was your teacher's name?
B Oh, I remember that. It was Mr Fish.
A Mr Fish?
B Yes.

A Can you remember your first day at
  school?
C Yes, I think so.
A OK, what did you wear?
C I wore a dress, a summer dress – it was
  a very hot day, and I wore a red and
  white dress.
A What was your teacher's name?
C My first teacher? Mrs … Mrs Grey, I
  think.

18.1 From A to B

Well, the prisoner climbs through the
window on to the balcony, and then he
climbs down the rope. Then he goes along
the path until he comes to the hut. Then
he goes into the hut, and he goes down
the ladder, and then down the second
ladder. Then he goes down the steps, and
he goes across the bridge, and he goes on
until he comes to the lake. Then he gets
into the boat and goes across the lake.
When he reaches the other side, he climbs
up the tree. Then he goes through a short
tunnel, climbs up the ladder and climbs
over the wall – and he's free.

18.3 It's on the left

1 You come out of the station and turn
  right into King Street. Then you turn
  left into this little road here, and the
  cinema's at the end, just here on the
  corner of Canal Street. OK?
2 OK. You get off the bus here, opposite
  the bridge. Then you go across the
  river and just carry straight on – you're
  in Bridge Street now, so just carry on
  along Bridge Street and you come to a
  church. Go past the church and turn
  right, and the house is just along there.

18.4 The island of Odysseus

Most people go to Greece by plane. So if
you fly into Athens, first of all you need
to get down to Patras. So you take a bus
or a train down to Patras. That takes
three or four hours. Then you can take a
ferry boat that calls in at Kefalonia and
then goes to Ithaki, and that takes maybe
four or five hours.

You can also fly in to Kefalonia, there's an
airport on Kefalonia. But there aren't any
buses at the airport, so you have to take a
taxi. You take a taxi right across the
island, and that takes maybe 45 minutes
or an hour. And then from there you can
take a ferry over to Ithaki, and that takes
about one hour.

A lot of people drive down to Greece, and
you can get a ferry across to Greece from
Italy, which takes about 24 hours, about
one day. And then you get off the ferry at
Igoumenitsa, drive down the coast for
two or three hours, and then you can get
a ferry across to Ithaki.

So that's three ways of getting to Ithaki.

Study pages I
Phrasebook: Let's …

1 A Let's get some petrol.
  B Yes, that's a good idea.
2 A Shall we dance?
  B No, I don't want to just at the
    moment.
3 A Let's ask for the bill.
  B Not yet. I'd like another drink.
4 A Shall we take a taxi?
  B No. Let's walk.

19.2 Can I …?

1 A Can I use the phone?
  B Of course. It's in the hall.
2 A Can I smoke?
  C No, sorry, you can't, not in here.
    But you can smoke on the balcony.
3 A Can I listen to the news?
  B Yes, of course you can. There's a
    radio in the kitchen.

4 A Can I have a glass of beer?
  C Sorry, we haven't got any beer. You
    can have fruit juice, or lemonade.

19.3 All in a day's work

1 I work as a cleaner in a big hotel. It's
  not a very nice job. I have to get up
  very early – I get up at about 5 o'clock,
  and I start work at 6. And some of the
  people are friendly, but not all of them
  – of course I always have to be polite,
  and that's quite difficult sometimes.
  One good thing is, I don't have to work
  long hours – I finish at about 10 in the
  morning, and then I can go home.
2 Well, I work on a fishing boat. It's a
  hard job, and it's quite dangerous too.
  You have to be very careful when the
  weather's bad. We go out to sea for
  about three or four weeks usually, so I
  have to be away from home a lot. The
  good thing about it – about the only
  good thing – the money's very good,
  so I don't have to work all year – I
  work about six months, usually, and
  that's good enough to live on.
3 I work in an Italian restaurant in
  London – I'm a waitress. And it's quite
  a nice job, I like it. I have to be nice to
  everyone and smile a lot, of course,
  but people are usually friendly anyway,
  so that's not a problem. I have to work
  late in the evening, usually till about
  11 or 12 at night. But then I don't
  have to get up early because I don't
  work in the morning.

20.2 Are you an athlete?

'Can you run 100 metres?' Yes, I can do
that. And run five kilometres … no. 'Can
you swim 100 metres?' Yes, I can swim
100 metres, but I can't swim one
kilometre. Can I ride a bike? Yes. Can I
ride a bike with no hands? No, I don't
think so. Climb up a ladder, yes. Climb
up a rope? Yes, I can do that. Jump over a
stream one metre wide? I can, that's easy.
Jump over a wall one metre high? No, I
can't do that. Catch a tennis ball in one
hand is easy. Throw a tennis ball 50
metres? No, I can't do that. 'Can you kick
a football 100 metres?' No, I can't do
that. 'Can you stand on your head?' No!
And 'Can you walk on your hands?' No.

20.4 I did it!

First you have to pay, and it's quite
expensive – I paid £40 for just one jump.
And then you put on a harness. And the
harness goes round your body, and down
your legs to your feet. And then you walk
up to the cage. The cage is quite big – big
enough for five or six people – and
there's this very long piece of elastic. The
elastic is very thick, very strong, and one
end of the elastic is fixed under the cage,
and they fix the other end of the elastic to
your harness.

OK, then you get in the cage, and it
starts to go up. And it goes up really high
– about 60 metres. And when you look
down, everything's very small down
there, all the people are very small.

And then the man opens the door of the
cage. And you think 'I don't want to do this.
This is crazy.' But the man says 'OK, you go
when I count to three.' And he counts to
three – one, two, three – and you jump.

And it's all very quick – you fall very quickly – then the elastic pulls you up again, and you go up and down, up and down, and then you stop, and you just hang there. And then the cage comes down slowly, slowly brings you down to the ground, and that's it. You take off your harness. And they give you a certificate, and the certificate says 'I did it!'.

Phrasebook: Could you ...?

A Could you bring me some fruit?
B Yes, of course.
A And could you buy me a bottle of beer?
B No, sorry, I can't do that.

21.2 Which is better?

A I'd like a small camera, for a child. It's my daughter. She's 10.
B OK. We've got this one. This is a Yashica. Or there's this one – a Canon.
A Which is better?
B Well, the Canon is a better camera, really. But maybe the Yashica is better for a child – it's very easy to use.
A Which is cheaper?
B The Yashica's cheaper – it's £40. And the Canon's £70.
A OK. I'll have the Yashica, please.

22.1 Going out

Yes, I visit my friends a lot at the weekend, and relatives – I see my brother quite often, and his family. And I often go out for a drink, almost every Saturday, in fact. I don't go out for meals so much. And I don't go for a walk usually, no. I never go for a bike ride. And I don't go shopping, not for fun, anyway – I don't like shopping. But I go to the cinema a lot – not concerts, not sports events, but the cinema, certainly. I don't do much sport, really – I go swimming sometimes, but not very often. And I don't drive, I haven't got a car. But most weekends I go fishing, usually on Sunday if the weather's nice.

22.4 The curse of the new ground

United were one of the best football teams in the country. They had a lot of supporters, but their ground wasn't very big. They wanted to move to a bigger ground. So they bought some land on the edge of the city. There was nothing on this land except for one small cottage. An old woman lived in this cottage. 'We're sorry,' the club told her, 'but you have to go. We want to build a new stadium on this land.' The woman said no, so the police came and moved her. But as she left, she shouted, 'United will never win a match on this land! Remember my words!'

They started to build the new stadium, but they had lots of problems. One of the walls fell down, and two workers died in strange accidents. In the end, they finished the stadium, and 40,000 supporters came to watch the first match. United lost the match 5–0. That season, United won lots of matches in other football grounds. But they lost all the matches they played at home. The next year, the same thing happened. The team's manager left, and a new one came – but it made no difference. United lost all their home matches.

So now United Football Club want to sell the ground and find a new one. But there's one big problem: who wants to buy a football ground with a curse on it ?

Focus on ... Verb + to

1 A Do you want to come to the cinema this evening?
  B No, sorry. I'd like to come, but I have to do my homework.
2 A Would you like to go and see a film this evening?
  C Oh no, thanks. There's a football match on, and I want to watch it.
3 A Do you want to go to the cinema tonight?
  D Yes, fine.
  A Would you like to go for a drink first?
  D OK. I need to wash my hair. But I can meet you at about 6.30.

Phrasebook: What did you say?

1 A So where are you living at the moment, then?
  B Sorry, what did you say?
  A I said, where are you living?
  B Oh – in London.
2 C That's a lovely dress you're wearing there.
  B Sorry, could you say that again?
  C I said, that's a lovely dress. Your dress is lovely.
  B Oh, thank you.
3 D So are you a student here, then, or what?
  B Sorry, I don't understand.
  D Are you a student?
  B Yes. Yes, I'm a student.

23.1 I love Paris

1 I'm going to go shopping. I'm going to buy clothes and shoes, probably, and I'm also going to visit the Louvre. And in the evening I'm going to meet some friends, and we're going to have dinner together in a nice restaurant.
2 Well, I'm on business here, and I'm going to stay in a hotel in the centre of Paris, but I've got some free time too, so if I have time I'm going to visit some art galleries, maybe some museums. And in the evening I'm going to go to the theatre.
3 Well, we're going to stay with friends here, and we're just going to relax, really. We're going to walk around the streets, sit in cafés, you know, drink coffee ... And in the evening, we're going to go to a café or a club, probably, and listen to music.

23.3 Help!

A Hi, look, I'm painting my living room on Saturday ...
B Oh yes ...
A Could you help me?
B Sorry. I'm working on Saturday.
A Oh. What about Sunday?
B No, I'm seeing friends on Sunday. Sorry.

A Is that John?
C Yes.
A Oh, John, hi, it's Paul here.
C Oh, hi, Paul.
A I'm painting my living room this weekend. Could you help me?
C No, sorry. I can't. I'm playing football on Saturday ...
A What about ...?
C ... and on Sunday I'm going swimming. Sorry.

24.1 I'm hungry!

1 A Are you all right?
  B No. I feel really ill.
  A Oh dear. Shall I phone the doctor?
2 A Oh, I'm tired.
  B Why don't you lie down and have a rest?
3 A I'm really hungry.
  B Why don't you have a sandwich? There's some cheese in the fridge.
  A OK.
4 A I'm hot.
  B Me too. Let's have a swim.
  A Yeah. Good idea.
5 A I feel a bit cold.
  B Why don't you put on a jumper?
6 A I feel thirsty.
  B OK. Let's go to a café and have something to drink
  A Mm.

24.3 Did you enjoy it?

1 Well I saw *Titanic*, and yes, I really enjoyed it, it was really exciting. It was also quite sad, I thought, but ... really good.
2 Yes, I saw *Titanic*. It wasn't very good – it was quite exciting, I suppose, but much too long, and the actors weren't very good.
3 I saw a *Mr Bean* video. It was OK, some parts were very funny and ... but some parts were quite boring as well. I enjoyed it.
4 I saw a *Mr Bean* video. I thought it was really funny – I enjoyed it a lot.

24.4 Showing your feelings

Paul Elkman is an American scientist. He wanted to know the answer to this question: Do people show feelings in the same way everywhere in the world?

Ekman took photos of people in the USA. Some people looked happy, some looked sad, some looked angry, some looked surprised, and some looked frightened. He showed the photos to people from 21 countries, and asked them to match the feelings with the faces. He found that everyone could do this quite easily: everyone agreed which people were happy, which were sad, which were angry, and so on.

Then Ekman went to a village in Papua New Guinea. In this village, people had no television, they saw no films, and they never saw people from other countries. So they didn't know what people from other countries looked like. Ekman showed his photos to the people in this village, and asked them the same questions: Which people are happy? Which are sad? Which are angry? He found that even here they could answer the questions quite easily.

So Ekman's conclusion was that people do show feelings in the same way everywhere in the world.

Reference section

1 People and places

Verb *to be*

Long form	Short form
I am	I'm
You are	You're
He/She is	He's/She's
We are	We're
They are	They're

He   My brother's a student.
He's a student.

She   My mother's a doctor.
She's a doctor.

It   This car is a Rolls Royce.
It's a Rolls Royce.

They   My friends are students.
They're students.

You can be singular or plural:

How are you? How are you?
I'm fine, thanks We're fine, thanks.

Questions *Answers*
What's your name? → (It's) Bill.
How are you? → I'm fine (thanks).
Where are you from? → (I'm from) Japan.

Countries

 Britain the USA Spain Japan

France Germany Italy Brazil

Russia Australia

Useful vocabulary

teacher	flat	small	hello
student	office	old	goodbye
friend	car	this	I don't know

2 In the family

Singular and plural

To make a plural, add -*s*:

a boy → boys   a bird → birds   a car → cars

-*y* changes to -*ies*:

a baby → babies   a family → families

Note:
child → children

Verb *to have*

I have	We have
You have	They have
He/she has	

Numbers 1–20

1	one	6	six	11	eleven	16	sixteen
2	two	7	seven	12	twelve	17	seventeen
3	three	8	eight	13	thirteen	18	eighteen
4	four	9	nine	14	fourteen	19	nineteen
5	five	10	ten	15	fifteen	20	twenty

Families

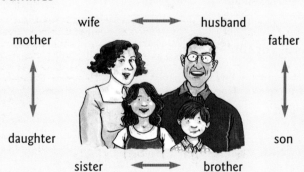

wife ↔ husband
mother   father
daughter   son
sister ↔ brother

Useful vocabulary

boy	child	dog	doctor	taxi driver
girl	children	cat	university	
baby	family	bird	married	

Study pages A

The English alphabet

> Aa Bb Cc Dd Ee Ff Gg Hh Ii Jj Kk Ll Mm
> Nn Oo Pp Qq Rr Ss Tt Uu Vv Ww Xx Yy Zz

A, E, I, O, U are *vowels*. The others are *consonants*.
Y can be either a vowel (*baby*) or a consonant (*yes*).

my, your, his, her

| I → my |
| you → your |
| he → his |
| she → her |

I'm a student. This is my flat.
How are you? What's your name?
He's English. His wife is Italian.
She's 18. Her brother's 15.

3 To be or not to be?

Verb *to be*

Negative
To make the negative, add *not* or *n't*:

They are here. They aren't here.
This is my car. This isn't my car.

Long form	Short form
I am not	I'm not
You are not	You aren't
He/She is not	He/She isn't
We are not	We aren't
You are not	You aren't
They are not	They aren't

Questions
To make a question, change the word order:

¹ ²
They are here. Are they here?
¹ ²
This is my car. Is this your car?

> Are you 18?
> Is he from the USA?
> Are they married?

Wh- questions

Where is she?	She's in Paris.
What's that?	It's my car.
Who's that?	It's my son.
How old is he?	He's seven.
How is your wife?	She's fine.

Useful vocabulary

waiter	seat	coffee
customer	free	these
England	café	thanks

4 Things around you

Colours

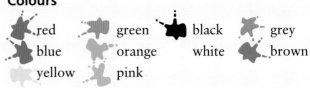

red green black grey
blue orange white brown
yellow pink

Light and dark colours
light blue light green light brown
dark blue dark green dark brown

Things in rooms

Where is it?

The lamp is *on* the table.
The picture is *behind* the lamp.
The bag is *under* the table.
The shoes are *by* the door.

Questions	*Answers*
Where's the bag?	It's under the table.
Where are my shoes?	They're by the door.

Useful vocabulary

face	tree	book	jumper
hair	watch	camera	umbrella
sky	football	shoes	glasses
mountain	ring	bag	pen

Study pages B

Numbers 20–100

20 twenty	50 fifty	80 eighty
30 thirty	60 sixty	90 ninety
40 forty	70 seventy	100 a hundred

21 twenty-one	34 thirty-four	47 forty-seven
22 twenty-two	35 thirty-five	48 forty-eight
23 twenty-three	36 thirty-six	49 forty-nine

a and *an*

We use *a* before consonants:
a table   *a* window   *a* hundred

We use *an* before vowels (*a, e, i, o, u*):
an umbrella   *an* address book

this, that, these, those

this   these   that   those

Sorry and *Excuse me*

Sorry!   Excuse me!   Excuse me!

5 There's …

There is and There are

Use:
- *There is* (or *There's*) and *There isn't* + singular
- *There are* and *There aren't* + plural

There's a café in the village.

There isn't an airport here.

There are three cafés in the village.

There aren't any good restaurants.

Questions
To make questions, change the word order:

There¹ is² a café near here.   Is¹ there² a café near here?

There¹ are² two good hotels.   Are¹ there² any good hotels?

some and any

some:	There are some good bookshops here.
any:	There aren't any good bookshops here. Are there any good bookshops here?

How many?

How many floors are there?

How many people are there?

Useful vocabulary

place	building	lift	TV
shop	floor	toilet	town
hotel	swimming pool	tourist	village
restaurant	car park	beautiful	airport
church	stairs	library	favourite
beach			

6 Where you live

Things in the home

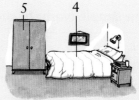

living room   bedroom

kitchen   bathroom

1	sofa	5	cupboard	9	clock
2	TV	6	cooker	10	bath
3	carpet	7	fridge	11	shower
4	single bed	8	shelf	12	mirror

Where?

There's a plant in the corner.

Where's the phone? It's by the door.

The radio is on the shelf.

There are two pictures on the wall.

Name and address

First name: *Carole*   City: *Cambridge*

Last name: *Jones*   Post code: *CB26 3JY*

Street: *55 Kings Road*   Country: *England*

Phone number: *01223 049584*

Study pages C

Possessives

I	→ my	This is my daughter.
you	→ your	Is this your bag?
he	→ his	His first name is Robert.
she	→ her	Her phone number is 260375.
we	→ our	This is our bedroom.
they	→ their	What's their address?

With nouns, add *'s*:

my father	→ my father's	This my father's car.
Maria	→ Maria's	Are you Maria's brother?

Note: *'s* has two meanings:

I'm Maria's brother (= I'm her brother).

Maria's at home (= Maria is at home).

First, second, third …

1st	first	5th	fifth	8th	eighth
2nd	second	6th	sixth	9th	ninth
3rd	third	7th	seventh	10th	tenth
4th	fourth				

What's your first name?   It's her tenth birthday

My flat is on the sixth floor.   He's their third child.

Can I have…?

Can I have	a glass of water that book	please?

Yes, (of course). Here you are.	Thank you.

7 Things people do

Present simple (verb: *to speak*)

I speak You speak We speak They speak	English.

He She	speaks English.

After *he/she/it* or a noun, add *-s*:
She listens to jazz.
Our teacher plays the guitar.

Negative
To make the negative, use *don't* or *doesn't* + verb:

I don't You don't We don't They don't	speak English.

He She	doesn't speak English.

Note: After *don't/doesn't*, the verb stays the same:
I don't wear jeans. → He doesn't wear jeans.
(*not* ~~He doesn't wears~~ …)

Verbs

go (to the shops)   like (cars, music)
have (a sandwich)   wear (jeans, glasses)
listen (to music)   smoke (cigarettes)
look (out of the window)   eat (meat, pizza)
play (cards, football)   drink (coffee)
read (a magazine)   talk (to a friend)
watch (TV)   speak (English)
live (in London)

Adjectives

high   low   new   old
hot   cold   short   long
fast   slow   strong   weak

8 Food and drink

Basic food

rice   oil   cheese   meat   fruit   beans
bread   pasta   eggs   fish   vegetables   potatoes

Drinks

water   lemonade   tea   wine   milk
fruit juice Coca-Cola   coffee   beer   milk shake

I	often sometimes never	drink tea.

I drink tea every day.

Things on the table

plate   knife   salt
glass   fork   pepper
cup   spoon   sugar

Asking for things

Can I have	a glass of water a knife	please?

I'd like	a Coca-cola a plate	please.

Study pages D

The time

What's the time?
It's …

2 o'clock   (a) quarter   half   (a) quarter
              past 7   past 9   to 7

5 past 4   20 past 11   25 to 11   10 to 3

Personal pronouns

Subject	Object	Possessive
I	me	my
you	you	your
he	him	his
she	her	her
it	it	its
we	us	our
they	them	their

Subject: I live here.   He's at home.
Object: Listen to *me*.   I don't like *him*.
Possessive: This is *my* flat.   What's *his* name?

9 Do you…?

Present simple questions

To make questions, use *do* or *does* + verb:

Do you Do they	like music?

Does he Does she	like music?

Note: After *do/does*, the main verb stays the same:

Do you go to school? → Does he go to school?
(not ~~Does he goes~~ …?)

Questions	*Short answers*
Do you eat meat?	Yes, I *do*. No, I *don't*.
Do they live here?	Yes, they *do*. No, they *don't*.
Does she have a car?	Yes, she *does*. No, she *doesn't*.
Does your father smoke?	Yes, he *does*. No, he *doesn't*.

Wh- questions

Where do they live?	(They live) in Cairo.
When do you go to school?	At 8 o'clock.
What does he do?	He's a bus driver.
What does she study?	(She studies) English.

Everyday activities

get up	start work		breakfast
go to bed	finish work	have	lunch
go to work/school	come home		dinner

Other new verbs

keep (a diary)	carry (a bag)
sleep	study (English)

10 Things people buy

Shopping

Questions		*Answers*
Can I see that camera?	→	Yes, here you are.
How much is that jumper?	→	It's £35.50.
What size are these shoes?	→	They're size 34.

Shops and things they sell

butcher	meat (beef, lamb, pork, chicken)
chemist	medicines, sun cream, toothpaste
bookshop	books
newsagent	newspapers, magazines, pens, paper
kiosk	ice-cream, cigarettes, drinks, magazines
baker	bread, cakes
greengrocer	vegetables, fruit
clothes shop	clothes

Other places in towns

supermarket	restaurant	cinema	station	bank
post office	café	school	hotel	

Place prepositions

The café is *by* the river.   It's *opposite* the school.
It's *next to* the cinema.   It's *near* the station.
It's *between* the cinema *and* the river.

Other useful vocabulary

aspirin	T-shirt	expensive	Can I help you?
sunglasses	map	too (big)	

Study pages E

Days of the week

Monday	Friday
Tuesday	Saturday
Wednesday	Sunday
Thursday	

To talk about days, use *on*:
They go to church *on* Sunday.
I go to work *on* Monday morning.
We usually go to the cinema *on* Saturday evening.

Kilos and litres

5 kg = five kilos	five kilos of apples
1 kg = a kilo	a kilo of rice
0.5 kg = half a kilo	half a kilo of sugar
100 g = a hundred grams	a hundred grams of cheese
1 l = a litre	a litre of milk
0.5 l = half a litre	half a litre of wine

I like and I'd like

I like = I think it's nice	I'd like = I want
I like ice-cream.	It's hot! *I'd like* an ice-cream.
I like dogs.	*I'd like* a dog for my birthday.
I like coffee.	*I'd like* a cup of coffee, please.

11 What's going on?

Present simple and Present continuous

There are two ways to talk about the present in English: Present simple and Present continuous.

Present simple (= usually, every day)
Philippe *works* in a bank.
He *goes* to work at 8.30
and he *comes* home at 5.00.

Present continuous (= now)
Today is a holiday. Philippe *isn't working. He's sitting* on his balcony and *he's reading* the newspaper.

Present continuous

To form the Present continuous, use *be + verb + -ing*:

I'm He's/She's They're	reading.	I'm not He/She isn't They aren't	reading.

Are you Is he/she Are they	listening?	What are you doing? Where are you staying? Where is she going?

Activity verbs

wash (the dishes)	dance	read (a book)
clean (your teeth)	cook (a meal)	write (a letter)
have (a shower)	play (the piano)	listen to (the radio)
make (coffee)	watch (TV)	

Where is he?

He's asleep. (= he's sleeping)
He's out. (= he isn't at home)
He's away for the weekend. (= he isn't in this town)
He's at home.
He's at school.
He's at a friend's flat.

Other useful vocabulary

sit	football match	do your homework
anyone	at the moment	I'm afraid

12 Describing people

Clothes

He's wearing … a jacket, jeans and a jumper.

He's wearing … a coat, a hat and trousers.

She's wearing … a skirt and a blouse.

She's wearing … shorts and a T-shirt.

He's wearing … a suit, a shirt and a tie.

She's wearing … a dress.

Some clothes are plural: *trousers, jeans, shorts.*
We can also say *a pair of trousers, a pair of jeans, a pair of shorts* (but not ~~a trouser, a shorts~~).

Names of jobs

doctor	singer	engineer	shop assistant
student	waiter	secretary	

We can also say:

I work *in*	a bank. an office.	I work *for*	a large company. Esso.

Appearance

He's/She's	tall. short.	He/She has	long short	dark fair grey	hair.

Other useful vocabulary

band	drive (a car)	insurance company
hospital	French	

Study pages F

Imperatives

To form imperatives, simply use the basic verb:

Look!	Open the window, please.
Listen!	Give me that book.
Come here!	Put it on the table.

To make the negative, add *Don't*:

Don't look!	Please don't open the window.
Don't talk so much	Don't eat sweets.

Expressions with *have*

lunch · breakfast · a bath · dinner · a shower · a sandwich · **HAVE** · a sleep · a drink · a good time · a party

13 How much?

Count and non-count nouns

Some nouns in English have a singular and a plural – these are called *count nouns* (because we can count them):

a cup   four cups   a potato   potatoes

Some nouns have only a singular form – these are called *non-count nouns*. We don't use *a* or *an* with them:

paper   water   gold

Some common non-count nouns

rice	water	paper	meat	coffee	food	bread
sugar	beer	money	fruit	tea	oil	cheese

Quantity expressions

Use *many* with count nouns, and *much* with non-count nouns. Use *some*, *lots of* and *any* with all nouns.

Count	Non-count
We've got *lots of* eggs.	We've got *lots of* tea.
We haven't got *many* eggs.	We haven't got *much* tea.
We haven't got *any* eggs.	We haven't got *any* tea.
How many eggs are there?	*How much* tea is there?

have got

I've got = I have got. He's got = He has got. They mean the same as *I have, He has.* We use this form especially in spoken English.

I've got			I haven't got	
She's got	a car.		He hasn't got	a car.
They've got			They haven't got	

Other useful vocabulary

envelope	bowl	matches	jam
key	soap	blood	light a fire

14 Around the year

Seasons

spring	summer	autumn	winter
wet season	dry season		

Adjectives

wet	hot	warm	humid
dry	cold	cool	

Temperature

40° = forty degrees
0° = zero
–10° = minus ten degrees (*or* ten degrees below zero)

Months

January	April	July	October
February	May	August	November
March	June	September	December

To talk about months and seasons, use *in*:

We usually go on holiday *in July*.
What's the weather like *in December*?
It usually snows here *in (the) winter*.

The weather

It's	It's	It's	It's	It's
raining	snowing	sunny	cloudy	windy

Talking about the weather
It's lovely weather today.
The weather isn't very nice.
What's the weather like?

Other useful vocabulary

night	Christmas	holiday

Study pages G

Can

Positive and negative forms:

I		
He/She	can	play the piano.
They	can't	

Questions

Can you	
Can he	play the piano?

Numbers over 100

100	a hundred	101	a hundred and one
200	two hundred	120	a hundred and twenty
300	three hundred	121	a hundred and twenty-one
1,000	a thousand		
2,000	two thousand		
3,000	three thousand		
100,000	a hundred thousand		
1,000,000	a million		

15 In the past 1

Past simple

Regular verbs
To make the Past simple, add *-ed* or *-d*.
play → played   want → wanted   live → lived
look → looked   listen → listened   like → liked

I played	
He/She played	football yesterday.
They played	

Irregular verbs

give	gave	have	had
take	took	say	said
put	put	read	read (/red/)
see	saw	write	wrote
go	went	buy	bought

See also the list of irregular verbs on page 127.

Verb to be

I was	
You were	
He/She was	at home yesterday.
We were	
They were	

Time expressions

on	*days*: *on* Saturday.
in	*months*: *in* September, *in* July
	seasons: *in* the winter, *in* the spring
	years: *in* 1969
at	*times*: *at* 6 o'clock, *at* the weekend

Useful vocabulary

smile	light	wallet	yesterday
want	game	purse	quiet
late	thing	silver	garden

16 Around the world

North, south, east, west

He lives *in the north* of England.
The mountains are *in the east*.
It's a large town *on the west coast*.

Kinds of town

I live in a large *town*, but my parents live in a small *village* in the country.
Cairo is the *capital* of Egypt. It is a huge *city*, with more than 15 million people.
They stayed at a ski *resort* in the Alps.
Yokohoma is in Japan. It is also a large *sea port*.

Where is it?

It's … *on* the sea   *on* a river   *in* the mountains
        on the coast   *on* a lake

Continents

Countries and languages

Country	Language	Country	Language
–	Arabic	Japan	Japanese
China	Chinese	Poland	Polish
France	French	Portugal	Portuguese
Germany	German	Russia	Russian
Greece	Greek	Spain	Spanish
Italy	Italian	Turkey	Turkish

Other useful vocabulary

island	holiday	love (v.)	ferry	visit

Study pages H

Ordinal numbers

11th eleventh	**21st** twenty-first
12th twelfth	**22nd** twenty-second
13th thirteenth	**23rd** twenty-third
14th fourteenth	**24th** twenty-fourth
15th fifteenth	**25th** twenty-fifth
20th twentieth	**30th** thirtieth

Dates

1st July = the first of July
30th September = the thirtieth of September
22nd April = the twenty-second of April
3rd May = the third of May

Verbs with indirect objects

We can say:

He	wrote sent gave	a letter to me.

He	wrote sent gave	me a letter.

Other examples:
I showed *her* my passport. (not ~~I showed to her~~ …)
They sent *us* some money.
Can you bring *me* some water, please?
She gave *him* a watch for his birthday.

17 In the past 2

Past simple

Negative
To form the Past simple negative, use *didn't* + verb:

I went She went	to the concert last night.

I didn't go She didn't go	to the concert last night.

Questions
To make Past simple questions, use *did* + verb:

Did you go Did she go	to the concert?

Note: After *did* and *didn't*, the main verb is in the infinitive form, not the past:

She *played* tennis → She didn't *play* tennis
They *saw* the film → Did they *see* the film ?

was and *were*

Negatives

He wasn't They weren't	at home.

Questions

Was he Were they	at home?

Irregular verbs

make made   wear wore   win won   eat ate
get got   cost cost   leave left

See also the list of irregular verbs, page 127.

Other useful vocabulary

paint	die	programme	interesting
start	war	football match	boring
arrive	play (n.)	concert	fireworks

18 How to get there

Direction

go *along* the road   go *across/over* the bridge   climb *over* the wall

go *into* the house   come *out of* the house   go *past* the house

go *up* the steps   go *down* the steps   climb *through* the window

Giving directions

  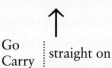

Turn left   Turn right   Go Carry | straight on

Transport

go by train   go by bus   go by taxi

drive (go by car)   cycle (go by bike)   walk (go on foot)

Other useful vocabulary

| ladder | path | bus stop | tunnel |
| hut | rope | at the end | on the corner |

Study pages I

Short answers

To give short answers, repeat the auxiliary verb (*is*, *was*, *can*, *does*, *did*, etc.).

Are you from Mexico?	Yes, I *am*.	No, I'm *not*.
Is she a teacher?	Yes, she *is*.	No, she *isn't*.
Is there a café here?	Yes, there *is*.	No, there *isn't*.
Are they working?	Yes, they *are*.	No, they *aren't*.
Was your father here?	Yes, he *was*.	No, he *wasn't*.
Can you sing?	Yes, I *can*.	No, I *can't*.
Does Carl smoke?	Yes, he *does*.	No, he *doesn't*.
Did you have a bath?	Yes, I *did*.	No, I *didn't*.

Let's ... and *Shall we* ...?

| Let's go to the cinema. Shall we go to the cinema? | That's a good idea. |
| | No, thanks. I don't want to. |

Years

We usually say years in 'pairs' of numbers:
1924 = 19 24 = nineteen twenty-four
1848 = 18 48 = eighteen forty-eight
But:
1900 = nineteen hundred   2000 = two thousand
2001 = two thousand and one

19 You mustn't do that!

must and mustn't

You must ... = Do it!

You must show your passport.
You must stay in bed.

You mustn't ... = Don't do it!

You mustn't take photographs.
You mustn't get out of bed.

can and can't

Ability	*Permission*
He *can* speak Thai ...	We *can* watch TV...
... but he *can't* speak German.	... but we *can't* play loud music.
– *Can* you swim?	– *Can* I go, please?
– Yes, I *can*.	– No, you *can't*!

Note: After *must* and *can* we do not use *to*:
You *must stay* here. (not ~~You must to stay~~ ...)
We *can't use* the phone. (not ~~We can't to use~~ ...)

have to and don't have to

I have to He has to	work hard.	I don't have to He doesn't have to	work hard.

I have to = I must do it, it's necessary:
I have to get up early during the week (because I start work at 7.30).

I don't have to = It isn't necessary:
I don't have to get up early at weekends (I can stay in bed late if I want to).

Useful vocabulary

gun	take a photo	hard	cleaner (n.)
stop (v.)	polite	dangerous	fishing boat
animals	careful		

20 The body

Parts of the body

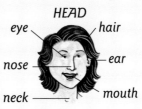

HEAD

eye, hair, nose, ear, mouth, neck

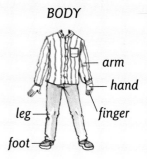

BODY

arm, hand, leg, finger, foot

Adjectives

long	thin	large *or* big	wide
short	fat	small	narrow

She has a narrow face and a long thin nose.

He has a wide face, a short nose and a small mouth.

Action verbs

stand   walk   run   jump

climb   swim   catch   throw

kick   ride   drive   fly

Other useful vocabulary

careful	friendly	in the middle	metre
stream	human	at the top	kilometre

---

21 Good, better, best

Comparative adjectives

Short adjectives (one or two syllables): add -er.
Long adjectives: use *more* + adjective.

The Pyramids are *older* than the Acropolis.

A Porsche is *more expensive* than a VW Golf.

Superlatives

Short adjectives: add -est.
Long adjectives: use the *most* + adjective.

The biggest diamond
in the world: the
'Golden Jubilee'

The most expensive
diamond in the world:
the 'D Flawless'

Comparative and superlative forms

rich	richer	richest
cheap	cheaper	cheapest
clean	cleaner	cleanest
safe	safer	safest
big	bigger	biggest
friendly	friendlier	friendliest
beautiful	more beautiful	most beautiful
dangerous	more dangerous	most dangerous
expensive	more expensive	most expensive
good	better	best

Other useful vocabulary

agree   difficult   use (v.)   disagree   actor

22 Free time

Leisure activities

go for + noun

go for	a walk a drive a bike ride

go for	a drink a meal a picnic

go to + noun

go to	the cinema a concert a party

go + -ing

go	shopping swimming skiing

Other verbs

do	an outdoor sport an indoor sport

play	football cards

visit	friends relatives

Sports and activities

football   basketball   volleyball   tennis   table tennis

walking   running   climbing   skiing   windsurfing

like, enjoy + -ing

After *like* and *enjoy*, we can use a noun or an -ing form:

I like nice clothes.   I enjoy football.
I like shopping.   I enjoy watching football.

I don't like card games.
I don't like playing cards.

Other useful vocabulary

a bike ride   lose weight   physical exercise
sports event   spend money

Study pages K

Verb + to

After *want*, *need*, *would like*, we can use a noun or
to + infinitive:

I want I need I'd like	a new bike.

I want I need I'd like	to buy a new bike. to go home now.

Questions:

Do you want	a new bike?
Do you need	to buy a new bike?
Would you like	to go home now?

Expressions with *go*

out   to work
home   to school
for a walk   to bed
GO
for a drive   to the cinema
swimming   to the shops
shopping

23   Future plans

going to

To talk about intentions or plans in the future, we use *going to*.

I'm going to He's/She's going to We're going to They're going to	stay with friends.

Questions

Are you going to write to her? Is she going to buy a flat? What are you going to do? When is he going to visit us?

Present continuous

To talk about things in the near future that are *already arranged*, we use the Present continuous:
My aunt and uncle *are staying* with us next week.
We*'re going* to the cinema this evening.
I*'m playing* tennis tomorrow afternoon.

Future time expressions

this
I'm going to watch TV *this evening*.
What are you doing *this afternoon*?

next
My brother's coming to stay *next week*
We're going to go skiing *next January*.

tomorrow
What are you doing *tomorrow*?
I'm going to work *tomorrow evening*.

Useful vocabulary

plan (v.)	move (v.)	late
exactly	housework	

24   Feelings

I'm hungry, etc.

I'm I feel	hungry. thirsty. tired. ill. hot. cold .

I'm hungry = I want to eat.
I'm thirsty = I want to drink.
I'm tired = I want to have a rest.

Feelings

happy   sad   upset   angry

excited   surprised   frightened

Present tense: I feel so happy!
                    He's very upset about it.

Past tense: I was so excited, I didn't sleep all night.
                 We felt really angry about it.

Reactions

I	enjoyed didn't enjoy	the film.

It was	interesting. boring. funny. sad.

Suggestions

Why don't you have a rest?
Shall I call a doctor?
Let's watch a video.

Other useful vocabulary

laugh	invite	hold (held)

Irregular verbs

Infinitive	Past tense
be	was/were
bring	brought
build	built
buy	bought
can	could
catch	caught
come	came
cost	cost
do	did
drink	drank
drive	drove
eat	ate
fall	fell
feel	felt
find	found
fly	flew
get	got
give	gave
go	went
have	had
keep	kept
know	knew
leave	left
lose	lost
make	made
pay	paid
put	put
read	read /red/
ride	rode
run	ran
say	said
see	saw
sell	sold
send	sent
sing	sang
sit	sat
sleep	slept
speak	spoke
spend	spent
stand	stood
swim	swam
take	took
tell	told
think	thought
throw	threw
wake	woke
wear	wore
win	won
write	wrote

Phonetic symbols

Vowels

Symbol	Example
/iː/	tree /triː/
/i/	many /'meni/
/ɪ/	six /sɪks/
/e/	bed /bed/
/æ/	black /blæk/
/ʌ/	much /mʌtʃ/
/ɑː/	car /kɑː/
/ɒ/	hot /hɒt/
/ɔː/	sport /spɔːt/
/ʊ/	look /lʊk/
/uː/	spoon /spuːn/
/ɜː/	girl /gɜːl/
/ə/	about /ə'baʊt/
	water /'wɔːtə/
/eɪ/	play /pleɪ/
/aɪ/	time /taɪm/
/ɔɪ/	boy /bɔɪ/
/əʊ/	home /həʊm/
/aʊ/	out /aʊt/
/ɪə/	here /hɪə/
/eə/	there /ðeə/

Consonants

Symbol	Example
/p/	pen /pen/
/b/	book /bʊk/
/t/	take /teɪk/
/d/	dog /dɒg/
/k/	cat /kæt/
/g/	go /gəʊ/
/tʃ/	church /tʃɜːtʃ/
/dʒ/	jumper /'dʒʌmpə/
/f/	for /fɔː/
/v/	love /lʌv/
/θ/	think /θɪŋk/
/ð/	this /ðɪs/
/s/	six /sɪks/
/z/	is /ɪz/
/ʃ/	shop /ʃɒp/
/ʒ/	leisure /'leʒə/
/h/	house /haʊs/
/m/	make /meɪk/
/n/	name /neɪm/
/ŋ/	bring /brɪŋ/
/l/	look /lʊk/
/r/	road /rəʊd/
/j/	young /jʌŋ/
/w/	wear /weə/

Stress

Dictionaries usually show stress by a mark (/'/) before the stressed syllable: teacher /'tiːtʃə/; about /ə'baʊt/; America /ə'merɪkə/.

4.1 Painting by numbers

4.2 Birthday presents

12.1 Describing people

A

B

C

D

E

Acknowledgements

The authors would like to thank the following for their contributions to *Language in Use Beginner*:

- for contributing to the recorded material: Mohammed Bakali, Richard Chan, Sean Connolly, Dawn Coutts, Natasha Doff, Hazel Jones, Henry Jones, Thomas Jones, Alessandra Salvalajo, André Zaharias, Gabriella Zaharias.
- for research into reading material: Sean Connolly.
- for providing data for the Unit 7 questionnaire: students and teachers at the Bell Language School, Anglia Polytechnic University, Newnham Language Centre and EF International School, Cambridge.
- for designing the course: James Arnold and Stephanie White (Gecko Ltd).
- for commissioning artwork: Wendy Homer (Gecko Ltd).
- for commissioning photographs: Karen Homer (Gecko Ltd).
- for the production of recorded material: Martin Williamson (Prolingua Productions) and Peter and Diana Thompson (Studio AVP).
- for picture research: Sandie Huskinson-Rolfe of PHOTOSEEKERS.
- for help in producing the Pilot edition: Victoria Adams.
- for illustrations in the Pilot edition: Tania Lewis.

The authors would also like to thank the following at Cambridge University Press:

- Colin Hayes for his continuing support and help.
- Peter Donovan for organising the project.
- Jo Barker for overseeing the design of the course.
- Linda Matthews for control of production.
- Sue Wiseman and Val Grove for general administrative help.
- all CUP staff for arranging piloting and the following for providing feedback: Stephanie Collins, Kate Cory-Wright, Lindsay Kelly.

Special thanks go to:

- James Dingle of Cambridge University Press, for his expert management of the various stages of the project, and his close involvement with the development of Beginner level.
- Meredith Levy, our editor, for her professionalism, good judgement and tireless attention to detail.

The authors and publishers would like to thank the following individuals and institutions for their help in commenting on the material and for the invaluable feedback which they provided:

Maria Edvirgem Zeny, Sociedade Brasileira de Cultura Inglesa, Curitiba, Brazil; Marketa Kozerova, The Bell School, Prague, Czech Republic; Duncan Lambe, Mr Diab and Mr Azzam, British Council Teaching Centre, Giza, Egypt; Jennifer Tavassoli, Gif sur Yvette, France; Susanna Magnani, ITC Rosa Luxemburg, Bologna, Italy; Cinzia Riguzzi and Sonia Selleri, Bologna, Italy; Nicolo Arcadipane, International House, Livorno, Italy; Sharon Hartle, Verona, Italy; Paul Lewis, Aichi Shukutoku Junior College, Nagoya, Japan; Akishi Kimura, Kato Gakuen Gyoshu Koko, Numazu, Japan; Zofia Riesinger, Prywatne LO, "University II", Chorzow, Poland; Magda Moran, English Unlimited, Gdańsk, Poland; Anna Sikorzyńska, Warsaw, Poland; Heather Meachem, Cambridge School, Lisbon, Portugal; Helen Engel, Lomonosov State University, Moscow, Russia; Brian Brennan, International House, Barcelona, Spain; Peter Myring, Merit School, Barcelona, Spain; Liz Bitterli, Kaufmannische Berufsschule, Uster, Switzerland; Rodney Moore and Terence Broomfield, Dream Development Centre, Bangkok, Thailand; Andrew Coyle, Australia Centre, Chiang Mai, Thailand; Vahide Tümleayan and Zehra Gurtin, Özel Bornova Koleji, Izmir, Turkey; Anita Akkas, Middle East Technical University, Ankara, Turkey; Pauline Desch, Brasshouse Centre, Birmingham, UK; John Kay, ITTC, Bournemouth, UK.

The authors and publishers are grateful to the following copyright owners for permission to reproduce copyright material:

Dick James Music Ltd © 1967 for the extract from 'Love is all around', written by Reg Presley, lyrics reproduced by kind permission of the publisher, lyrics reproduced for the European Union (excluding Italy, Sweden and Denmark) by kind permission of Music Sales Ltd; Josephine Jones for the poem 'Friends' on p. 33.

The authors and publishers are grateful to the following illustrators, photographers and photographic sources:

Illustrators: Gerry Ball: pp. 29 *ml*, 53 *m*; Chris Brown: pp. 9 *tr*, 44 *t*, 96, 104 *t*; Paul Davies: p. 83 *t*; Rachel Deacon: pp. 8 *t*, 8 *m*, 19 *t*, 33, 34, 48 *t*, 81 *t*; Karen Donnelly: pp. 84, 108 *b*, 115, 116, 117, 118, 119, 120, 121, 123, 124, 125; Nick Duffy: pp. 10, 20 *tr*, 26 *m*, 48 *b*, 54 *tl*, 55, 70 *b*, 76 *t*, 87 *l*, 92 *t*, 97 *b*, 102 *b*; Phil Healey: pp. 8 *b*, 17 *m*, 29 *mr*, 31 *l*, 40, 47 *m*, 49 *m*, 57, 63 *bl*, 93, 103 (F); Rosalind Hudson: pp. 11, 52 *b*, 60, 64, 95 *l*,

103 (B); Nadime James: pp. 16 *b*, 17 *t*, 25 *t*, 31 *mr*; Mark McLaughlin: pp. 30 *l*, 43, 65, 67, 86 *l*; Amanda McPhail: p. 91; David Mitcheson: p. 106 *b*; Des Nicholas: pp. 20 *m*, 25 *t*, 31 *br*, 35 *t*, 56, 71 *m*, 106 *t*, 107, 108 *t*; Mark Olyrold: p. 52 *m*; Pantelis Palios: pp. 36 *mb*, 38 *ml*, 49 *b*, 54 *ml*, 62 *t*, 79 *tl*, 99 *b*, 103 (D); Jeff Parker: pp. 39 *mr*, 42 *m*, 90 *m*; Tracy Rich: pp. 14 *bl*, 28 *t*, 45 *t*, 51 *t*, 52 *m*, 54 *br*, 58, 69, 71 *t*; Rachel Ross: p. 102 *t*; James Sneddon: pp. 11 *b*, 12 *t*, 13 *m*, 15, 18, 19 *mb*, 22, 25 *b*, 27 *t*, 28 *b*, 32, 38, 39 *t*, 39 *b*, 42 *t*, 44 *m*, 44 *b*, 46 *b*, 47 *t*, 47 *b*, 53 *b*, 63 *br*, 67 *mr*, 75, 76 *b*, 77, 79 *tr*, 82, 83 *b*, 90 *t*, 92 *m*, 95 *r*, 101 *b*, 103 (J), 105, 106 *m*, 108 *m*, 109, 115 *bl*, 116 *t*, 118 *b*, 122; Holly Swain: pp. 50, 99 *t*; Kath Walker: pp. 9 *tl*, 14 *br*, 16 *t*, 30 *r*, 41 *b*, 54 *l*, 62 *b*, 70 *m*, 78, 86 *b*, 94.

Photographic sources: Adams Picture Library: pp. 17 *bl*, 105 *tl*, *tc*; Allsport/Chris Cole: p. 9 (D), Allsport/David Rogers: p. 9 (E); Art Directors and TRIP Photo Library: pp. 29 *bl*, 103 (L), Art Directors/TRIP/T Schwarz: p. 88 *l*; Gavin Hellier/Aspect Picture Library: pp. 17 *bc*, 61 (A), Derek Bayes/Aspect: p. 104 *br*; Biofotos Associates: p. 21 *mc*; *Wheatfield with Cypresses*, 1889 (oil on canvas), by Vincent Van Gogh (1853–90), National Gallery/Bridgeman Art Library, London/New York: pp. 19 *bc*, 105 *m*; *The Thinker (Le Penseur)* (bronze), by Auguste Rodin (1840–1917), Private Collection/Bridgeman: p. 73; *Joan of Arc at the Coronation of King Charles VII 1422*, 1854, by Jean Auguste Dominique Ingres (1780–1867), Louvre, Paris/Peter Willi/Bridgeman: p. 87 *cr*; Britstock/Bernd Ducke: p. 61 (D & G); R. Ellis/Camera Press London: p. 104 *tr*, John Zimmerman/ Curtis/Camera Press: p. 72 (1.1) *br*; Canon (UK) Limited: p. 89 *m*; The J. Allan Cash Photolibrary: pp. 25, 103 (A); *Lady in Blue* by Henri Matisse, © Succession H. Matisse/DACS 1999; James Davis Travel Photography: pp. 68 *m*, 103 (I); Delas Tours, Ithaki: p. 77 *t*, *tc*; Colin Keates, Natural History Museum/Dorling Kindersley: p. 21 *tl*, *tc*, *bcl*; *Unmasking the Face*, by Paul Ekman and Wallace V. Friesen, 1975, © Paul Ekman: p. 101; ET Archive: p. 87 *cl*; Mary Evans Picture Library: p. 87 *l*; Eye Ubiquitous Picture Library/Gavin Wickham: p. 17 *br*, Eye Ubiquitous/Julia Waterlow: pp. 24 *r*, 45 *bc*; Nick Tapsell/ Ffotograff: p. 59 *tr*; Getty Images: p. 72 (1.2) *bc*; The Ronald Grant Archive: p. 72 (1.2) *tr*; Sally Greenhill: p. 105 *tcl*; Robert Harding Picture Library: pp. 59 *bl*, *br*, 80; David Hockney, *A Bigger Splash*, 1967 (acrylic on canvas, 96" × 96") © David Hockney: pp. 19 *br*, 105 *br*; Michael Holford/V & A Museum: p. 21 *br*; Nick Hadfield/The Hutchison Library: p. 104 *bc*; The Image Bank/David Vance: p. 105 *tr*; Images Colour Library: p. 13 *tl*; CFCL/Image Select: pp. 59 *tl*, 81 *tr*; Roger Scruton/Impact Photos: p. 81 *bl*; Chris Jones: p. 77 *bc*; Carolco (Courtesy Kobal): p 40 *l*, RKO (Courtesy Kobal): p. 17 *tl*, Universal (Courtesy Kobal): p. 72 *ml*; London Features International: p. 53 *tl*; 'Courtesy of McDonald's Restaurants Limited': p. 40 *r*; Bossemeyer/ Bilderberg/Network: p. 45 *br*; Tayacan/Panos Pictures: p. 24 *bl*, Gregory Wrone/Panos: p. 45 *bc*; The Photographers' Library: p. 89 *b*; Photostage/ Donald Cooper: p. 72 (1.2) *br*; Pictor International: pp. 51 *tr*, *bl*, 72 (1.1) *tr*, 104 *tl*; Pictures Colour Library/Clive Sawyer: p. 61 (B); Popperfoto/ Anthony Bolante: p. 29 *br*, Popperfoto: p. 87 *m*, *br*; PowerStock/Zefa: pp. 14 *tcr*, *tr*, Powerstock/Zefa/Charles Tyler: p. 61 (F); Redferns Music Picture Library/Mick Hutson: p. 9 *bc*, Redferns/Des Willie: p. 9 *br*, Redferns/ Tim Hall: p. 17 *tc*, Redferns/RB: p. 53 *cr*/RB; Rex Features Limited/Sipa: p. 9 (B), Rex/Tim Rooke: p. 17 *tr*, 29 *tl*, Rex/Boulat/Jobard: p. 29 *tr*, Rex/ Brian Rasic: p. 53 *bl*; Vaughan Fleming/Science Photo Library: p. 21 *ml*; Scotland in Focus/D. Torrance: p. 24 *tl*; Jules Selmes: pp. 12 *b*, 20 *tl*, 20 *tl*, 27 *m*, 35 *b*, 36 *t*, 37 *b*, 41 *t*, 45 *m*, 46 *m*, 49 *t*, 97 *m*, 98 *t*, 100, 103 (C & G); Spectrum Colour Library: p. 85 background; Sporting Pictures (UK) Limited: p. 9 (F), 85 inset, 103 (K), 104 *tc*; The Stockmarket: pp. 51 *tl*, 103 (H), TSI/Tony Latham: p. 51 *tl*, 103 Tony Stone Images/Martin Rogers: p. 21 *tr*, (H), TSI/Dale Durfee: p. 51 *bc*, TSI/David Hanover: p. 51 *br*, TSI/Glen Allison: pp. 61 (E), 103 (E), TSI/Neil Beer: p. 68 *b*, TSI/Cosmo Condina: p. 88 *r*, TSI/Richard Passmore: p. 96, TSI/Stephen Studd: p. 104 *bl*; Ann Suter: p. 77 *b*; SuperStock/Musée du Louvre, Paris: p. 72 (1.1)*tl*; Tempsport/S. Ruet/Sygma: p. 9 (A), Tempsport/T. Orbant/Sygma: p. 9 (C), Micheline Pelletier/Sygma: p. 9 *bl*; Telegraph Colour Library/Antonio Mo: pp. 14 *tcl*, TCL/Spencer Rowell: p. 32, TCL/Gavin Hellier: p. 68 *t*, TCL/Benelux Press: p. 81 *br*; Press Association/Topham: p. 72 (1.2) *tl*, Topham Picturepoint: p. 72 (1.2) *bl*; Courtesy of the Topkapi Palace Museum, Turkey: p. 21 *bl*; Janine Wiedel: p. 105 *tm*; Kyocera Yashica (UK) Limited: p. 89 *t*.

t = top   m = middle   b = bottom   r = right   l = left   c = centre

Picture Research by Sandie Huskinson-Rolfe of PHOTOSEEKERS.
Cover design by Dunne & Scully.
Design, production, colour scanning and reproduction handled by Gecko Limited, Bicester, Oxon.
Sound recordings by Martin Williamson, Prolingua Productions at Studio AVP.
Freelance editorial work by Meredith Levy.